From Elections to Democracy

Democracy is not yet fully consolidated in Central Europe. Even in the countries that were in the first round for admission to the European Union, much remains to be done. All of these countries have constitutional, electoral democracies and market economies. However, policy makers inside the government often lack accountability to the general public and to important organized groups. This study documents the weaknesses of public oversight and participation in policy making in Hungary and Poland, two of the most advanced countries in the region. It discusses five alternative routes to accountability including European Union oversight, constitutional institutions such as presidents and courts, devolution to lower-level governments, the use of neocorporate bodies, and open-ended participation rights. It urges more emphasis on the fifth option, public participation. Case studies of the environmental movement in Hungary and of student groups in Poland illustrate these general points. The book reviews the United States' experience in open-ended public participation and draws some lessons for the transition countries from the strengths and weaknesses of the American system.

Susan Rose-Ackerman is the Henry R. Luce Professor of Jurisprudence (Law and Political Science) at Yale University. She holds a Ph.D. in Economics from Yale University, has held Guggenheim and Fulbright Fellowships, and has been a Research Fellow at the World Bank, the Center for Advanced Study in the Behavioral Sciences (Stanford, CA), the International Institute for Applied Systems Analysis (Austria), and Collegium Budapest. Professor Rose-Ackerman is the author of *Corruption and Government: Causes, Consequences and Reform* (Cambridge University Press, 1999, with subsequent translations into nine languages), *Controlling Environmental Policy*, and *The Nonprofit Enterprise in Market Economies*. She is one of the editors of *Building a Trustworthy State in Post-Socialist Transition* and *Creating Social Trust in Post-Socialist Transition*. Both of these books as well as *From Elections to Democracy* are products of the project Honesty and Trust: Theory and Experience in the Light of Post-Socialist Transformation, jointly organized by the author and János Kornai at Collegium Budapest. Professor Rose-Ackerman has also published widely in law, economics, and policy journals. Her research interests include comparative regulatory law and policy, the political economy of corruption, public policy and administrative law, and law and economics.

From Elections to Democracy

Building Accountable Government in Hungary and Poland

SUSAN ROSE-ACKERMAN

Yale University

CAMBRIDGE
UNIVERSITY PRESS

CAMBRIDGE UNIVERSITY PRESS
Cambridge, New York, Melbourne, Madrid, Cape Town, Singapore, São Paulo

Cambridge University Press
40 West 20th Street, New York, NY 10011-4211, USA

www.cambridge.org
Information on this title: www.cambridge.org/9780521843836

First published 2005

Printed in the United States of America

A catalog record for this publication is available from the British Library.

Library of Congress Cataloging in Publication Data
Rose-Ackerman, Susan.
From elections to democracy : building accountable government in Hungary and Poland /
Susan Rose-Ackerman.
p. cm.
Includes bibliographical references and index.
ISBN 0-521-84383-9 (hardcover)
1. Political participation – Hungary. 2. Transparency in government – Hungary.
3. Democracy – Hungary. 4. Political participation – Poland.
5. Transparency in government – Poland. 6. Democracy – Poland. I. Title.
JN2165.R673   2005
320.9438 – dc22   2004024986

ISBN-13   978-0-521-84383-6 hardback
ISBN-10   0-521-84383-9 hardback

For János Kornai

Contents

Tables

Preface

From Elections to Democracy is part of the Collegium Budapest Project on Honesty and Trust: Theory and Experience in the Light of Post-Socialist Transformation. Research was conducted at the Center for Advanced Study in the Behavioral Sciences (CASBS), Stanford, California; Collegium Budapest; and Yale University. I am grateful to all three institutions and to their funding sources for support. In particular, the William and Flora Hewlett Foundation supported my research in two ways. First, through a grant to Collegium Budapest for the Project on Honesty and Trust co-organized by János Kornai and myself between 2000 and 2003; second, through a grant to CASBS.

I am very grateful to Madiha Afzal, Katalin Füzér, Anna Horolets, Csilla Kalocsai, Maciej Kisilowski, Lisa Marshall, Nawreen Sattar, and Aleksandra Sznajder for excellent research help; to Judit Balassa for preparing the index; to Gene Coakley of the Yale Law Library for help in locating sources; and to Cathy Orcutt for assistance in preparing the final manuscript. I was especially dependent on the skill, integrity, and good will of Kati, Anna, Csilla, Maciej, and Aleksandra, native speakers of Polish or Hungarian, who helped me with interviews and secondary sources. I am also grateful to Bruce Ackerman, Cary Coglianese, János Kornai, Bo Rothstein, András Sajó, and Kim Lane Scheppele for helpful conversations on the book's topic and for comments on the draft manuscript.

Articles based on portions of this manuscript have been published in the *Journal of East European Law* and in *Building a Trustworthy State in Post-Socialist Transition*, one of two edited volumes that resulted from the Collegium Budapest project. The present project also builds on the second volume, *Creating Social Trust in Post-Socialist Transition*, on my background articles for the project: Trust and Honesty in Post-Socialist Societies and Trust, Honesty and Corruption: Reflections on the State-Building Process (Rose-Ackerman 2001a, 2001b), and on numerous interactions in fall 2002 in Budapest with other project participants. This monograph is in some ways a sequel to *Controlling Environmental Policy: The Limits of Public Law in Germany and the United States* (Rose-Ackerman 1995), my study of administrative law and environmental policy making in Germany and the United States.

ONE

Policy-Making Accountability and Democratic Consolidation

The dawn of the twenty-first century has seen a tremendous increase in the number of "democracies," but only under a minimalist understanding of the term. On one account, democracy requires only a stable, competitive electoral system with broad suffrage, institutionalized political parties, and alternations in power.[1] I challenge this definition and argue that full democracy cannot be attained unless the policy-making process is accountable to citizens through transparent procedures that seek to incorporate public input. In a democracy, individuals and institutions must justify the exercise of power over others, and success in an election is, I argue, insufficient to make this claim.

I illustrate my argument through the study of two postsocialist countries, Hungary and Poland, that have made the transition to electoral democracy but have relatively weak policy-making accountability. The efforts at state building that followed the end of the socialist regimes in Eastern Europe focused on the establishment of free elections and on

---

[1] This view of democracy builds on Schumpeter (1942, chapter 12). It has been most forcefully expressed in recent years by Przeworski, Alvarez, Cheibub, and Limongi (2000). Przeworski et al. develop a clear set of rules that permits them to classify a country as a democracy or a dictatorship. A country is classified as a dictatorship in a particular year if at least one of the following four conditions holds: The chief executive is not elected, the legislature is not elected, there is no more than one party, or, if none of the above holds, there is no recent alternation in power [Przeworski et al. (2000: 28–29) provide a full definition of the last two conditions]. Under that view of democracy, most countries in Central Europe, Latin America, and Asia have made the transition to democracy. Using a similarly minimal view of democracy and arguing that nothing more can be expected, Mueller (1996, 2004) argues that the transition was already complete in most postcommunist countries by the mid-1990s.

assertions of individual rights against state overreaching. Many of these states, including Hungary and Poland, have made impressive progress in effecting dramatic changes in their governments, economies, and societies. They have gone a long way toward "rebuilding the ship at sea," as Jon Elster, Claus Offe, and Ulrich Preuss (1998) demonstrate in their study of the first years of the transition. But the task is not complete even among the frontrunners.

During the first decade of the transition, little emphasis was given to broader issues of popular control and government accountability outside the electoral process.[2] This relative neglect has been costly for countries like Poland and Hungary and deserves greater emphasis as the transition proceeds. The costs are not primarily economic. Rather there is an increased risk of popular disengagement from political life based on disillusionment and distrust of the state and its officials.[3]

I explore ways to strike a balance between accountability to citizens, on the one hand, and the development of public policies that are competent and fair, on the other. Of course, even autocratic regimes may take on some of the trappings of accountability outside of contested elections. Under socialism, both Hungary and Poland created institutions designed to give them legitimacy in the eyes of ordinary citizens. In a democracy, however, the government's need for popular legitimacy is much more salient. Contested elections are not sufficient but should be combined with procedures that promote accountability on a policy-by-policy basis. The state must take into account the interests and views of citizens – both broad-based attitudes and those directed toward particular policy choices.

Libertarians would limit the state to a few basic tasks, such as setting the background rules of the game and providing for security and defense. However, the minimal or "night watchman" state is not one that minimizes the unjustified exercise of power. Private individuals and organizations exercise power as well as state officials. Consider, for example,

---

[2] For example, Elster, Offe, and Preuss (1998: 110–111) mention elements of the transition from socialism that their book ignored in spite of their importance. Two of the issues they mention are the reform of the state administration and devices for interest articulation in addition to political parties. This book studies the intersection of these two factors.

[3] Elster et al. (1998). Tables 1.1 and 1.2 show that citizens mostly approve of democracy in principle but are unwilling to engage in even very modest forms of nonelectoral political activity. For other survey data see Miller, Grødeland, and Koshechkina (2001), the World Values Survey as analyzed by Howard (2003), and the reports by Richard Rose and colleagues. Some of this material is summarized by Rose-Ackerman (2001a, 2001b). Howard (2003) also includes some interviews.

the role of monopoly businesses or oppressive family patriarchs. Furthermore, collective action problems lead to the imposition of external costs and the underprovision of "public" goods. The benefits that flow to those who start out with economic and social advantages are likely to persist in the absence of state action. Minimizing the exercise of political power cannot solve the problem of power in society so long as one is concerned about excesses of both public and private power and so long as one also has substantive goals for human well-being.

If limits on the role of the state are not sufficient, then constitutional and administrative systems need to require the state to justify its actions and ought to enhance its competence. Elections limit the power of individual politicians and political parties, and map citizens' preferences and goals into public policies. But that is only one step toward the construction of an accountable and competent democracy. Like Robert Dahl (1971, 1989) and Guillermo O'Donnell (1996), I emphasize the need for additional checks on political power.[4] Part of my interest is in what O'Donnell (1994, 1999) calls "horizontal" accountability – that is, special state institutions that engage in oversight and control of operating agencies to keep them within the law.[5] He has in mind audit offices, courts,

---

[4] Dahl's concept of polyarchies includes: (1) elected officials, (2) free and fair elections, (3) inclusive suffrage, (4) the right to run for office, (5) freedom of expression, (6) alternative information sources, and (7) associational autonomy (Dahl 1971, 1989). O'Donnell (1996, 1999) proposes adding the following: (8) elected officials (and some appointed ones, such as high court judges) should not be arbitrarily terminated before the end of their constitutionally mandated terms; (9) elected officials should not be subject to severe constraints, vetoes, or exclusion from certain policy domains by other nonelected actors, especially the armed forces, and (10) there should be an uncontested territory that clearly defines the voting population.

[5] That is, "the existence of state agencies that are legally enabled and empowered, and factually willing and able, to take actions that span from routine oversight to criminal sanctions or impeachment in relation to actions or omissions by other agencies or agencies of the state that may be qualified as unlawful" (O'Donnell 1999: 38). Some who challenge the minimal view of democracy add a range of other criteria to the definition, including measures of individual freedom and rights and other institutional features of government such as independent courts. This has led to the development of one-dimensional democracy scales that aggregate a range of factors to produce a "score." See Munck and Verkuilen (2002) and the associated commentaries for an overview and critique of the major indices with citations to the literature. See also Beetham (1994) and Jaggers and Gurr (1995). Przeworski et al. (2000: 55–59) explain the relationship between their measure and the indices. Collier and Adcock (1999) seek a middle ground but limit their discussion to one-dimensional scores, whether dichotomous or continuous. Whatever value these scales have in facilitating statistical work, they omit much of the interest in the democratization debate by forcing a rich multidimensional phenomenon into a single-dimensional metric.

and ombudsmen. I build on his framework but then go on to focus more intensely on other routes to popular involvement such as decentralization, neocorporate mechanisms for social dialogue, and direct public participation.[6]

Democracy breeds partisanship, but a democratic state should treat its citizens impartially and fairly. To be sure, the potential alternation in power of different party coalitions does give incumbents a reason to avoid certain blatant forms of self-dealing. If parties and politicians expect to survive electoral defeat, they will fear that the opposition will discover their fraud and corruption. But, rotation in power is unlikely to induce incumbents to behave impartially. Winners want to help their supporters and to hurt their opponents. They want to enhance their power so that reelection is more likely. Neutrality in the interpretation and implementation of laws is not what many politicians want.

The potential for electoral defeat is a constraint on outright corruption and fraud if incumbents believe they will face investigation upon leaving office.[7] However, it also encourages partisan favoritism within the law. If the border between legal and illegal behavior is unclear and shifting over time, one politician's efforts to benefit his or her supporters may be viewed by others as a corrupt attempt to undermine state legitimacy. The reluctance of politicians to embrace reforms that would enhance the overall performance of democratic government presents a challenge for those who favor such reforms. Partisan politicians will be uninterested in or opposed to certain efforts to improve accountability (Krastev and Ganev 2004).

---

[6] On the particular case of corruption control see Rose-Ackerman (1999: 143–174). Lindseth's work on Western Europe takes a similar view. In a paper on delegation, he focuses on ways to balance "constitutional democracy with the reality of regulatory autonomy in the modern administrative state." To him, transparency and participation rights "are not simply a matter of political expediency but rather are an integral part of the constitutional settlement of administrative governance...." (Lindseth 2003: 24). My approach is also close to that advocated by Smulovitz and Peruzzotti (2000) in the Latin American context. They discuss both formal institutional routes for accountability and more informal types of pressure often exerted with the help of media coverage. On the important contribution of the media in holding government to account, see Adserá, Boix, and Payne (2003), Besley and Prat (2004), Brunnetti and Weder (2003), Djankov, McLiesh, Nenova, and Shleifer (2003), and McMillan and Zoido (2004).

[7] Kunicova and Rose-Ackerman (2005). The exception here is a very unstable system where incumbents, if overthrown, do not expect to reenter politics and may even expect to have to flee the country. In such cases, they face an end game in which they may try to steal as much as possible before leaving office. This has happened at the end of autocratic regimes throughout the world. See Rose-Ackerman (1999: 113–121).

Even if a political coalition does support the development of accountable government institutions, the issue is a complex and subtle one.
Accountability means two different things in a democracy.

First, it means that government agents, elected or appointed, are responsible to their principals through systems of monitoring and oversight.
This involves internal procedures by which elected politicians can control
the career bureaucracy (Dunn 1999). But ordinary citizens are the principals of these same elected politicians. For them to be able to monitor their
representatives, the government must operate with transparency and the
press must be free so the public can hold the government to account for
both overall policies and the day-to-day implementation of programs. If
the law requires impartiality, the citizens can, at least, observe whether
officials are following these standards. If the rules single out particular
groups for special treatment, citizens can observe the practical effects.
Under this aspect of accountability, one takes policies as given, and the
central issue is performance. Call this performance accountability.[8]

In contrast, policy-making accountability requires that the policies be
a reflection of the interests and needs of the population. Competitive
elections and a competent legislature are necessary but not sufficient. As
anyone who has studied the legislative process understands, statutes are
frequently vague and unclear and leave many difficult policy issues to the
implementation stage (Rose-Ackerman 1995; Rothstein 1998). Governments use different mechanisms to fill in these policy gaps.

In one formulation, Rothstein (1998: 108–112) mentions four major
alternatives: internal rules governing the actions of bureaucrats, delegation to professionals, corporatism, and co-determination by service users.
Under any of these options, lower-level governments may have delegated responsibilities, and independent courts can act as appellate tribunals. These are all relevant institutions, but there is an omission from
Rothstein's formulation that is fundamental to the achievement of policy-
making accountability. In an important class of cases, cabinet ministers,
assisted by career bureaucrats, issue regulations with the force of law.
These rules govern the day-to-day implementation of statutes. They are

---

[8] This is the focus of much of Rothstein's work (1998, 2004). He is especially concerned
with what he calls "the black hole of democracy" or the fact that the officials who make
individualized decisions are difficult to hold accountable. As a consequence, he argues
that universal welfare programs are more compatible with democracy than means-tested
programs. He backs up his claim with data from Sweden showing that those who participate
in means-tested programs have less trust in the state. For a skeptical view of the generality
of Rothstein's argument see Uslaner and Badescu (2004).

crucial policy documents that require consultation with organized groups and citizens with a special interest in or expert knowledge of the matter at hand. The drafting of rules should seldom use consensual processes, such as corporatism or co-determination. Interest groups should not have a veto over the final outcome. Instead, although the groups do not make policy themselves, the law should provide them with the tools to force the bureaucracy and the cabinet to take them seriously. Procedures that require government ministries to listen to such groups are not a challenge to democracy. Instead, they fill an important gap in the system of policy-making accountability.[9] Creating institutions that channel and manage public participation by individuals and groups in policy making should be high on the reform agenda of the postsocialist states and of consolidating democracies throughout the world.[10]

Debate about policy-making accountability in European parliamentary democracies swings between those who emphasize the role of the legislature in drafting statutes subject to electoral checks and those who seek to strengthen neocorporate decision-making procedures, particularly in the field of labor-management relations. I argue for a middle ground that recognizes the reality of vague and open-ended statutes and that seeks to involve citizens and organized groups in government policy-making processes while retaining the government's authority to issue general rules consistent with its statutory mandates.

In contrast to most other work on implementation, my topic here is the policy-making accountability of government as it carries out statutory mandates, not performance accountability. Corruption, self-dealing, and simple laziness and incompetence can undermine both types of accountability, and some of the institutions I discuss can help limit these problems (Rose-Ackerman 1999). However, in discussing institutions – such as the ombudsman – that aid individuals with grievances against the state, my main interest is in the role of these institutions in pushing the government toward more accountable policy making.

---

[9] In this respect my position is close to what Vogel (1980–1981) calls the "public interest movement" in the American regulatory context. Unlike that movement, my goal is a more accountable democratic state, not the achievement of particular substantive policies. As Vogel points out, advocates of greater government openness in the United States helped put in place institutional structures that are used by all those with an interest in policy, not just "public interest" advocates.

[10] For a discussion of these issues in comparative perspective see Rose-Ackerman (1995) on Germany and the United States and Bowen and Rose-Ackerman (2003) on Argentina and Brazil.

Policy-making accountability requires participation and oversight by a range of interested actors, but it also requires that the resulting policy be effective, transparent, and capable of assessment by ordinary citizens. Institutional design, then, is a tricky balancing act. How can public bodies be responsive to the concerns of citizens and yet remain insulated from improper influence? How can they perform both as competent experts and as democratically responsible policy makers?

This tension is a fundamental one in the public law of all democratic systems, but it has particular salience in the new democracies of Central and Eastern Europe. These countries inherited top-heavy bureaucracies that had lost legitimacy in the eyes of their citizens.[11] The initial temptation was to dismantle, rather than reform, these structures. But after an initial round of privatization, the state was left with the provision of public services such as defense and public safety, education, health care, and infrastructure. Furthermore, the state created new bureaucracies to regulate the newly privatized industries and to establish a legal framework for private economic and social life. Now that many of the states in Central Europe have reasonably well-established electoral systems and functioning market economies, their citizens are beginning to criticize both the poor quality of many public services and the lack of transparency in much public decision making.

I focus on Poland and Hungary, two of the most successful of the transition economies that joined the European Union in May 2004. They became socialist only after World War II and did not suffer much from the disruption of the Balkan wars.[12] According to Elster, Offe, and Preuss

---

[11] Elster et al. (1998), Howard (2003). In concluding his 1992 book on the socialist system, Kornai (1992: 580) puts it well: "the attitude of people remains ambivalent: they want to see the state intervening cleverly, but they remain suspicious of it. That suspicion is going to take a long time to dispel." Ekiert and Kubik (1999: 22) claim that the socialist regimes "were cumbersome but ineffective bureaucracies and faced crucial challenges to maintaining political stability, especially in their declining years." See Mishler and Rose (1998) for survey evidence.

[12] According to Grzymała-Busse and Luong (2002: 544), Poland and Hungary are "nearly consolidated democratic states." They also place the Czech Republic, Slovenia and the Baltic States in that category. Grzymała-Busse (2003) argues that both Hungary and Poland have been relatively successful in establishing a depoliticized bureaucracy. She attributes this result to competitive party systems that check rent-seeking. Gill (2002: 24–31), in a broad overview of the postcommunist transition, places Poland and Hungary alone in the category of countries where civil society forces emerged before the fall of the regime and were seen as appropriate negotiation partners by the incumbent leaders. The result is a stable democracy where the former Communist Party has transformed itself into a social democratic party.

(1998: 43–46, 59–60), they underwent parallel transitions – socialism eroded in the late 1980s, civil society groups gained importance at the end of the old regime, and the old elites managed to survive in the new system. Given their relative success in making the transition, it is safe to assume that other transition countries have similar or deeper problems (Gill 2002).

The European Values Study, carried out in 1999–2000, indicates that the citizens of Central Europe – Hungary and Poland, in particular – share attitudes toward democracy similar to those of their Western European neighbors. The differences are in degree, not in kind. Table 1.1 compares Eastern Europe (Russia, Belarus, Ukraine), Central Europe (the other European ex-Socialist countries), and Western Europe.[13] In general, more than two-thirds frequently follow politics in the media, with the Eastern Europeans showing the most interest, and 40% to 50% are interested in politics. The preference for a strong leader is much higher in Eastern Europe than elsewhere, but even in the rest of Europe one-fifth to one-third favor a strong leader. Disillusionment with democracy is high in Eastern Europe, but only about 13% of Central Europeans are disillusioned with democracy compared with 7.3% in Western Europe. One important contrast, however, is worth keeping in mind as my analysis proceeds. Central Europeans have much more faith in expert decision makers than residents of either of the other regions to the east and the west.

In spite of similar attitudes toward democracy in Western and Central Europe, striking differences appear for political action beyond voting.[14] Table 1.2 shows that people in Central and Eastern Europe are much less willing than Westerners to engage in protest activities, including something as innocuous as signing a petition. They also admit to less political activism in the past. Even though popular protest was one factor in bringing about regime change, especially in Poland, few people admit to past action, and most appear unwilling to engage in the specified activities

---

[13] The regional statistics are calculated by weighting individual country scores by the population of that country as a share of its region and summing the results. Appendix 2 provides more details on the survey and on the calculations. I am grateful to Madiha Afzal for performing the calculations and preparing the appendix. Dekker, Ester, and Vinken (2003: 232–233) use European Values Study country averages to show that people in ex-communist countries are just as likely to discuss politics as those in the rest of Europe.

[14] See Dekker et al. (2003: 234–237, 250–253), who use the European Values Study to reach similar conclusions. They provide summary information on a country-by-country basis for all of Europe.

Table 1.1. *Interest in Politics and Support for Democracy in Europe*

Region	Percentage Following Politics in Media: Every Day or Several Times a Week	How Interested are you in Politics? (% Answering Very Interested/Interested)	Strong Leader (% Answering Very Good/Fairly Good)	Experts Making Decisions (% Answering Very Good/Fairly Good)	Democratic Government (% Answering Very Bad/Fairly Bad)
Eastern Europe	82	40	50.8	52.5	31.4
Central Europe	73	50	33.6	81.5	12.9
Hungary	68	n.a.	22.3	86.6	16.4
Poland	75	43	20.4	85.3	12.6
Western Europe	67	43	23.4	51.1	7.3

Source: Calculated from European Values Study 1999/2000, questions 77, 51a, 62a, 62b, 62d. The question on interest in politics was not asked in Sweden, Estonia, Latvia, Slovakia, Hungary, Romania, Croatia, and Slovenia. Eastern Europe includes Russia, Belarus, and Ukraine. All regional figures weight country-specific surveys by the population of each country. Details in Appendix 2.

Table 1.2. *Individual Political Activity in Europe (Excluding Voting and Political Party Activity)*

Region	Have Done (%)	Might Do (%)	Would Never Do (%)
	Signing a petition		
Eastern Europe	12	32	56
Central Europe	24	32	43
Poland	21	28	51
Hungary	16	32	52
Western Europe	59	27	14
	Joining in boycotts		
Eastern Europe	3	22	75
Central Europe	4	25	70
Poland	4	23	73
Hungary	3	20	77
Western Europe	12	40	49
	Attending lawful demonstrations		
Eastern Europe	22	32	45
Central Europe	13	38	50
Poland	9	30	61
Hungary	5	30	65
Western Europe	30	37	33
	Joining unofficial strikes		
Eastern Europe	2	15	83
Central Europe	4	16	78
Poland	5	14	81
Hungary	1	10	89
Western Europe	7	24	69
	Occupying buildings/factories		
Eastern Europe	1	7	93
Central Europe	2	11	87
Poland	3	14	83
Hungary	1	4	95
Western Europe	5	20	75

Source: European Values Study 1999/2000, questions 51a-e. All regional figures weight country-specific surveys by the population of each country. Details in Appendix 2.

in the future. On the one hand, this bodes well for the stability of these regimes. On the other hand, the answers suggest a rather passive populace compared with their Western European counterparts.[15] This passivity also shows up in data on the share of the population that belongs to

---

[15] Körösényi (1999) coined the phrase "stabilizing apathy" to refer to this phenomenon.

or volunteers for nongovernmental organizations. Such participation is considerably lower in Central Europe than in Western Europe, with Eastern Europeans particularly unlikely to be involved (see Table 8.1 in chapter 8).

These data suggest a disjunction between broad attitudes toward democracy and politics, on the one hand, and specific actions, on the other. Of course, the range of activities in Table 1.2 is not exhaustive and ignores other ways of attempting to influence policy such as testifying before legislative bodies or consulting with policy makers. Nevertheless, even in established democracies, few individuals do these things. Representatives of organized groups will have trouble claiming that they speak for the interests of a broader community if that community is not even minimally involved.

Thus, the problem of state building in Hungary and Poland has two sides. These polities need to create accountable governments that can competently handle the tasks of the regulatory welfare state. But they also need to confront the seeming unwillingness of citizens to engage in political action. Weaknesses on both fronts mean that governing politicians in Eastern and Central Europe have often been able to run their governments in extremely partisan ways.[16] This produces a polarized electorate that expects good treatment from government only if "their" party is in power. To the extent such problems become entrenched, they present a threat to the legitimacy of the underlying democratic forms the population welcomed so warmly in 1989.

The agenda for democratic consolidation should move beyond the issues of political party development and legislative performance. Instead, one must confront the interaction between government policy making and implementation, on the one hand, and citizens' engagement with and participation in public affairs, on the other. This is not just a question of

---

[16] Howard (2003) describes the lack of organizational participation in Eastern Europe with a focus on East Germany and Russia. In the Czech Republic between 1992 and 1997, Prime Minister Václav Klaus consolidated power by failing to establish a civil service and by undermining centers of dissent such as universities, non-governmental organizations, and interest groups. He avoided dialogue with civic groups and did not foster public discussion of issues. He delayed a law on nonprofit organizations until 1995; a freedom of information act was not passed until 1998 (Vachudova 2001a: 337). Criticisms also have been leveled at left-of-center governments. See the discussion of social policy under the left governments in Poland (1993–1997) and Hungary (1994–1998) in Cook and Orenstein (1999). The Hungarian experience is distinctive in that a left government, pushed by economic and outside pressure, introduced an austerity plan with many neoliberal features.

creating a professional civil service but of recognizing that public administration is inherently political and policy oriented. Emerging democracies
must design institutions that permit participation while avoiding both
confusion and delay and capture by narrow interests.[17]

My study of Hungarian and Polish institutions seeks to inform the
search for reasonable ways to achieve improved policy-making accountability. Performance accountability is also weak in some areas, but it is
less fundamental to democratic consolidation and is, in any case, beyond
the scope of this study.

The next chapter begins with a taxonomy of options – ranging from
external checks, to state-sponsored bodies, to decentralization, to corporatist structures, and finally to open-ended public participation in policy
making. Then, a chapter sets the stage for my analysis of the current situation with a discussion of the legacy of the socialist past. The chapters that
follow assess the institutional structures that currently exist in Hungary
and Poland. My message is mixed. On the positive side, both countries
have responded constructively to reform pressures from the European

---

[17] Writing on the Polish case, Łętowski (1993: 7–8), at that time a member of the Supreme
Court and a law professor, stressed the importance of developing the "principle of mutual
confidence" between the citizenry and public authorities. According to him, confidence
"needs to be complemented by increased openness in government and administration.
Openness is understood as the obligation on the part of the administration to supply the
public with better and more complete information about the rationale, goals and methods
of administrative action." Openness and information "are means which allow the public a more effective control over public administration." Łętowski criticized the Polish
administration for often presenting plans that are characterized by "wooliness and im-
penetrability" and suspected these practices are strategic efforts to avoid accountability.
He spoke of the emergence of a "new conception of the rights of citizens" that does not
just refer to individual rights but also includes "'participatory' rights and entitlements."

Closely related to my study is a work by Stark and Bruszt (1998) that concludes: "[Gov-
ernment] executives that are held accountable to other state institutions and held in check
by organized societal actors are not necessarily weaker executives; in fact, their policies
may be more effective" (Stark and Bruszt 1998: 188). "Extended deliberations moderate and pragmatize the programs of political elites: By constraining decision makers to
take into consideration ex ante the social and political consequences of their policies, it
lengthens their time horizons, and in so doing, increases policy coherence" (Stark and
Bruszt 1998: 126–127). I share these authors' basic view that a constrained executive is
essential to the consolidation of democracy but believe they have not gone far enough.
Stark and Bruszt focus on the strength of political parties and on corporatist structures
that bring government together with labor and business groups (Stark and Bruszt 1998:
183–187). They are not much interested in civil society groups beyond labor unions and
business associations, and they do not consider individual citizen initiatives. They mention
other constraining institutions such as the Hungarian Constitutional Court and the Czech
Central Bank (Stark and Bruszt 1998: 171, 182) but do not analyze these institutions.

Union. In addition, beginning at the end of the socialist regimes, they started to establish a set of oversight institutions – ranging from constitutional courts to audit offices to ombudsmen – common in more established democracies. And they have strengthened local governments and established tripartite groups to incorporate the "social partners" – labor unions and business associations – into economic policy making. However, they seldom allow ordinary citizens and civil society groups to participate in policy making. This limitation suggests the importance of understanding how public participation processes actually operate in Hungary and Poland. The tentative steps that have been taken suggest that some people, both inside and outside government, recognize the value of increased openness and public involvement. But the existing situation has serious limitations that cannot be easily overcome through marginal adjustments. Governments have little experience in public involvement beyond the use of tripartite corporatist councils, formal advisory committees, and consultation with professional elites. Although numerous political parties compete for electoral office, non-party advocacy groups are few and generally are small and financially insecure. Worse yet, there is little tradition of private charity, and international donors are cutting back their financial support. As a consequence, civil society groups may be facing a crisis just when their involvement in policy making seems most crucial.

If Hungary and Poland seek to create systems with more active, open-ended public participation in policy making, they may be able to learn from the rule-making experience of the United States. Clearly, U.S. law and practice cannot be transferred uncritically, both because they have flaws and because new democracies, such as Hungary and Poland, do not have the institutional capacity to adopt the practices of those countries with more resources and longer democratic traditions. Nevertheless, fundamental features of U.S. administrative law – notice, openness to a wide range of opinions and expertise, transparent and well-justified decisions, and external oversight – seem basic principles that ought to guide actual public policy-making processes in democratic governments. I conclude with a discussion of these possibilities and some recommendations for reform.

TWO

Alternative Routes to Policy-Making Accountability

An idealized model of parliamentary democracy stands behind many discussions of policy-making accountability in European democracies. In that model, partisan politics is a sufficient route for citizen control of government. Citizens vote for politicians who are members of political parties. The parties are represented in the legislature in proportion to their voter support, and a party coalition forms a government that promulgates policies after consultation with the partisan groups in the legislature. This process of political-will-building expresses the preferences of the society, and an apolitical, professional bureaucracy, which is not influenced by political considerations, administers the resulting statutes. Politics and administration operate in separate spheres. The main constraint on self-seeking behavior by politicians is the threat of a loss at the polls in the next round of elections.[18]

Under this view, it is undemocratic and unfair to permit organized groups or individuals to participate in the administrative process. Participation is unnecessary because bureaucrats operate according to technical, legal, and scientific criteria that provide the "right" answers. The civil service follows clear rules that require little discretion, and officials treat everyone even-handedly. Review is available only to protect individual

---

[18] Kurczewski and Kurczewska (2001: 973) criticize what they call the "liberal theory of democracy," under which "the political participation of groups of citizens is banned except for political parties, which ought to mediate between the state and the individual citizen...." In Poland, the 2001 elections were the first in which only political parties could participate, and other steps have been taken to strengthen parties relative to other groups at the local level. The authors criticize this trend "as an attempt to limit the competition over public access to power."

rights that otherwise might be ignored by bureaucrats focused on general administrative goals.

This model is most clearly expressed in justifications for the postwar German "party-state" and in related claims that procedural guarantees in the administration of programs are unimportant. But, this model is a poor description of German reality, and it is being increasingly challenged. It coexists with a conflicting consensual or corporatist model of governance that covers many aspects of business-labor relations and has influenced the development of other cooperative forms. Because the classic German constitutional model has had an important influence on state-building in Central Europe, it is important to understand its strengths and weaknesses and to see how democracy actually operates in Germany as well as in postsocialist countries.[19] Both Hungary and Poland are parliamentary democracies, but, like Germany, they have supplemented the simple parliamentary model with institutions designed to facilitate accountability and popular control.

The simple parliamentary model falters in assuming that citizens can effectively control their government through voting alone. Of course, parties can seek to represent particular groups of voters or express certain ideologies, and voters can evaluate their performance in periodic elections. But elections are a very rough check on government performance. They occur only infrequently and bundle many issues together in a party platform that presents an aggregated set of policies that does not permit voters to express a differentiated set of viewpoints. In coalition governments, the actual policy will be the outcome of compromises across multiple platforms. In addition, statutes are likely to lack many important specifics. This is partly because the legislature is uninformed about the technical details of things such as financial market regulation and

---

[19] See Johnson (1983: 9–17, 169–175), who outlines how German views of the rule of law and the separation of administration and politics arose in the nineteenth century and continued to have salience in the twentieth century. He discusses the rise of the idea of a *Rechtstaat* "defined in terms of the supremacy of law, the subordination of the administration to law, ... and finally a continuous improvement in the system of public law to exclude from it those elements which reflect the capricious influence of political or administrative convenience" (Johnson 1983: 15). Jann (2003: 111) confirms Johnson's historical overview and brings the discussion up to date. He shows how recent contrary trends are developing that stress the role of the "third sector" and seek new forms of negotiated public-private coordination. Rose-Ackerman (1995) critiques the lack of outside participation in German environmental policy making. A review of her book by Henne (2003) reveals that the classic model of an independent administration insulated from outside influences still retains a hold in the field of German public law.

environmental protection. However, it is also because a parliamentary regime, which unifies executive and legislative power, has little interest in supporting very detailed statutes that will tie its hands. Of course, the expected alternation in power provides a check on incumbents. This is an important constraint, but its probabilistic nature and the long time delay between elections limit its effectiveness (Rose-Ackerman 1995: 7–17).

Bureaucrats and cabinet officials carry out political and policy-making tasks as they implement imprecise statutes, especially in technically complex areas. They require oversight, but the governing coalition has little political incentive to create independent mechanisms that could interfere with the partisan exercise of its power. As a result, oversight is likely to be weak or biased, especially for high-level policy making. Any independent oversight bodies and participation rights that do exist are likely to be the result of either constitutional mandates or pressure from politically powerful groups. Even if these bodies try to maintain a nonpartisan stance, incumbents may see bias lurking in any aggressive attempts at oversight. If some groups, such as labor unions, local governments, the church, and business associations, have powers that others lack, this not only may affect the substantive laws but also may lead to an unbalanced pattern of participation rights. At the same time, citizens may play little role in monitoring lower-level governments and "street-level" bureaucrats. Instead, oversight is likely to focus on internal monitoring by higher levels of government and by bureaucratic superiors. A vicious cycle may exist where lack of opportunities discourages the formation of just those types of advocacy groups needed to push for change.

Citizen participation and oversight outside of elections are necessary to achieve the policy-making accountability that democratic consolidation requires. This claim is controversial. Some argue against any public participation that goes beyond political party affiliation and voting. They worry about dilution in the power of parties if people affiliate with other groups, and they claim that interest group participation in policy making invites bias.[20] But these counterarguments depend on an exaggerated faith in the legislative process and in the professional bureaucracy. It is better to acknowledge that the legislature cannot solve all political and policy issues, to admit the value of opening up the government and the bureaucracy to oversight by outside groups, and to seek ways to counter the possible excesses and biases of such openness.

---

[20] See the literature reviewed by Jann (2003) and Johnson (1983).

One can isolate five stylized options that can contribute to policy-making accountability in parliamentary systems.[21] These are external international constraints, independent oversight bodies inside the nation state, delegation to lower-level governments, neocorporatism or delegation to consensual bodies, and public participation in government-led policy making.

International Constraints

International treaties and international aid and lending organizations impose constraints on nation states. These are not always unwelcome. In some cases, an incumbent government can benefit from tying its own hands through an international commitment that promises long-term gains and reduces the bargaining power of some domestic groups.[22] Member states of the European Union may obtain long-term trade benefits by binding themselves to refrain from imposing restrictions that otherwise might be hard to resist politically. In Hungary and Poland, the European Union is a centrally important actor with a major impact on the legislative agenda and the policy-making process. In both countries, incumbent governments used the threat of delayed European Union membership to counter political resistance to reforms. Concern about unfavorable European Commission reports helped set the legislative and policy-making agenda. In the early years of the transition, the World Bank, the International Monetary Fund, and the European Bank for Reconstruction and Development played a similar role, and they continue to have influence in the transition countries farther to the east.[23]

---

[21] In presidential systems, the separation of powers between the executive and the legislature gives the legislature an incentive to create oversight mechanisms lacking in parliamentary systems. Students of American politics analyze cases in which the legislature establishes oversight structures similar to some of those described below (McCubbins and Schwartz 1984). However, presidential systems may also create explicitly partisan oversight as in Argentina where most oversight of the executive branch is by groups under the control of political parties. See Bowen and Rose-Ackerman (2003).

[22] The classic statement of this point is by Putnam (1988).

[23] An example from Hungary is the large-scale austerity package developed by finance minister Lajos Bokros under Prime Minister Gyula Horn with International Monetary Fund support and passed by the parliament in 1995. Some aspects of that program that cut back on social benefits were struck down by the Constitutional Court (Füzér 2002: 175; Scheppele 2003: 226).

Independent Oversight

A second modification of the pure parliamentary structure relies on independent bodies that provide oversight of the core activities of government. This option recognizes that politics does not, in practice, stop with the passage of legislation but influences implementation as well. It shares with the simple model a dislike of the "infection" of public administration by politics. The goal is the same as in the simple model – insulation of the administration from politics through oversight by independent bodies. Proponents argue that insulation will not be achieved simply by creating a professional cadre of bureaucrats but that it requires the creation of new institutions isolated from partisan influence. For example, agencies may have specific oversight roles with respect to financial controls or corruption. Other options are an independent, nonpartisan judiciary and a president with monitoring rather than executive functions.

Oversight is carried out by a range of institutions in Hungary and Poland. Constitutional provisions that establish a directly elected president in Poland and constitutional courts in both countries try to ensure that the government adheres to the constitution. However, ostensibly independent domestic bodies such as the audit office, the ombudsmen, and parliamentary committees may have difficulty establishing true independence if they are appointed by and report to the legislature. Nevertheless, some of these offices and individuals play important roles in maintaining the constitutional order and constraining incumbent governments, but others are struggling to find a role in the new system. Furthermore, to the extent they succeed, they help ensure performance accountability but do little to foster policy-making accountability.

Delegation to Lower-Level Governments and Self-Governments

Policy-making responsibility can also be delegated to lower-level governments and other self-governing bodies. This option allows local political coalitions to affect policy and permits a multiplicity of rules tailored to local conditions and political influences. The national government sets out broad framework statutes with lower-level governments developing their own policy responses. Both Germany and the European Union frequently operate in this way.

But there are problems with this approach. Local officials may have personal and political incentives that conflict with the goals of the central government. Local control can ensure that decisions satisfy local voters who participate through electoral bodies and direct participation. However, footloose firms can avoid national regulations administered by local bodies by going to the weakest link. Furthermore, local governments may not have the expertise to resolve complex problems and may be dominated by narrow groups of citizens. Decentralization may reduce overall accountability if the lines of authority are unclear so that citizens and businesses have difficulties knowing where to turn.

The term "self-government" is also used in both Poland and Hungary to refer to legally mandated associations of groups such as students, the professions, and Hungarian minority communities.[24] These statutory associations, with governing bodies elected by their members, receive funds from the government and often play a role in the institutions of social dialogue described in the next section. They frequently control access to the professions they regulate. They are public in the sense of having official status to take decisions on behalf of their constituent groups and to represent their interests in government policy debates. However, if they fail to represent the broad interests of their constituents or are taken over by one faction, excluded groups may challenge their authority. These types of self-governments face the same problems of accountability and competence as local and regional governments.

The proper degree of decentralization is a subject of debate in both Hungary and Poland. Neither country is a federal state, but both have independently elected local governments and a range of self-governments created by statute to govern other areas of public life. Both have experimented with alternative organizational frameworks that illustrate the costs and benefits of devolution and fragmentation of power.

Neocorporatism and Social Dialogue

Fourth, social dialogue denies the primacy of the government and the bureaucracy in policy making. Instead, it envisages a negotiation process in which the affected groups send representatives to hammer out a compromise subject to statutory constraints. This method limits participation to specific groups identified in statutes or by the government. Sometimes these include only self-governing groups with official status, such as the

---

[24] Kisilowski (2004) reports that Poland has 19 such statutory associations governing groups such as lawyers, judges, physicians, and university students. Hungary has comparable bodies as well as self-governments for minority, especially Roma, communities (Soós and Kálmán 2002: 77–78).

professional, student, and minority self-governments mentioned previously. The state's power to exclude other groups and individuals from the policy-making process can have an important impact on the outcome even if the actual decision is taken by agreement of those around the table. In the extreme, this alternative replaces the legislative process; organized interests meet and set the rules. Generally, however, the government has a seat at the table. Thus, a tripartite commission of labor, business, and government may determine employment policy. The body becomes an alternative legislative forum but one that operates by consensus and with members selected on the basis of group membership, not broad-based voting. There is often only a limited role for judicial or legislative review of decisions that have been agreed upon by a consensus of those at the table. Only violations of constitutional rights may prompt a legal challenge.

Following Western European models, both Poland and Hungary have established tripartite institutions and have created analogous institutions in other policy areas. In practice, however, these institutions are not very powerful partly because of the weakness of organized labor and other organized groups and partly because of a failure to agree on policies that can be presented to parliament as a fait accompli (Ost 2000).

Public Participation in Policy-Making Processes

The fifth option recognizes that the implementation of complex statutes raises political issues, but it accepts these concerns as a valid extension of democratic ideals. The basic problem of administrative law is then to incorporate these political concerns without giving up the benefits of delegation by a democratically elected legislature. In other words, the open public participation option recognizes that participation can introduce bias arising from the poor information, narrow focus, or short-run orientation of special interests. However, it emphasizes the countervailing value of incorporating broad-based public input.

The institutional implications of this view are not straightforward, but they have been most fully worked out in the administrative law system in the United States. American bureaucracy operates under delegated authority to promulgate rules with the force of law. But agencies generally must carry out these tasks under procedural constraints. They must publicize their rule-making efforts, be open to information and testimony from outsiders, and justify their decisions in writing. The courts review rules for conformity with statute and check that the procedural requirements have been followed. Thus, the bureaucracy manages the process and issues rules in the name of the national government but must follow a process that is open to broad outside participation.[25]

In Poland and Hungary, most formal participation takes the form of advisory committees and tripartite bodies with group representation. The groups represented on the committees generally are fixed by law or by practice, with the groups appointing their own representatives. There is often a clear distinction between professional groups – such as associations of doctors and lawyers – and other interest and lobby groups that promote causes such as environmental protection and women's rights.

Even when more open-ended participation does occur, it has little impact in areas in which civil society groups are weak. The role of nonprofit organizations as advocates and gadflies varies by policy area. This is partly because of the weakness of some groups and partly because of the limited opportunities for participation. Some examples exist of constructive interactions between government agencies and organized groups that influenced policy outcomes, but consultation is largely a government-led process. There are only limited options to appeal to the courts, so civil society groups seldom can demand the right to be heard. Access to the constitutional courts is possible on some matters in both countries but has played little role in improving public participation. In short, the weakness of other forms of accountability means that public participation ought to play an important role. However, in practice, such participation is weak and is biased in favor of those with membership on advisory committees and those with inside connections.

Conclusions

Under the simple, parliamentary model, the route for citizen influence is only through political parties in the legislature. However, in practice, the cabinet and the ministries make policy under statutory mandates and, hence, organized groups and citizens are likely to want to influence these decisions. A major issue of institutional design is how to channel and manage that participation in a way that enhances policy-making accountability without undermining government effectiveness. The options sketched above do this in different ways. The first two use international pressure and independent government bodies, respectively, to limit the role of private

---

[25] For a comparison of the U.S. rule-making system with the German case see Rose-Ackerman (1995).

groups, reduce bias, and provide internal checks. In the third, political parties are important but only through their state and local branches.

The participatory options seek to incorporate organized groups and citizens directly into the national policy-making process. The social dialogue model does this through officially recognized groups that are members of a statutorily mandated council. The state specifies which groups are allowed to sit at the table but then delegates some decision-making authority to the council. Under the public participation model, the state organizes a more open-ended process to gather public input, interest group views, and expert opinions. Public officials, however, have ultimate decision-making authority. In between is a model of "civil dialogue" that combines the creation of a permanent body of stakeholders with a public agency that has decision-making power. This intermediate case is especially common in Hungary and Poland. I will argue, however, that it has considerable weaknesses compared with more open-ended participatory procedures.

All options, but especially those that depend on public participation, function better if private groups exist that are organized around concern for particular policy issues. The members of such groups may share certain partisan allegiances, but the groups are not arms of the political parties. The success of participatory processes thus depends on the strength and coverage of groups willing to be part of the policy-making process and on their access to a free press that engages in investigative reporting. There may be a positive feedback loop here. If organized groups have a function, then individual citizens and businesses have an incentive to organize if the cost is low. Some states may try to limit their role in policy making and, at the same time, make it difficult for them to organize. Others give these groups a role, keep the cost of establishing nongovernmental organizations low, and facilitate fund raising.

I consider these accountability options in the following pages. I devote a chapter to each of the first three and then concentrate on the range of possibilities for public and group participation. My analysis of the situation in Hungary and Poland is based on open-ended interviews, conducted in the fall and winter of 2002–2003 and in the winter of 2003–2004 in Hungary and Poland. I also rely on several types of literature to provide a fuller picture of the operation of the government.[26] To make

---

[26] A list of those interviewed is in Appendix 1. The interviews were informal, open-ended discussions generally lasting 1 to 2 hours. In some cases, I was accompanied by a native speaker to help with translation, and, in some cases, the primary subject of the interview invited an assistant to sit in as well. Several interviews were conducted by Katalin Füzér

my picture concrete I report two sets of interviews with the leaders of environmental groups in Hungary and of student and youth groups in Poland. My research provides a series of snapshots of the law, of public attitudes, and of organized civil society, but none of these should be taken as representing a stable outcome. The countries of Central Europe are in the process of experimenting with alternative institutional structures, and one can expect more shifts over time. Nevertheless, it is possible to make some connections between these diverse strands of scholarship and to point to successes and pressure points in the transition process.

Open public participation in government-led policy-making processes is an essential part of the democratic project. This type of accountability needs to be strengthened in both Hungary and Poland. There are inherent limitations to internationally imposed constraints, to oversight by public institutions, to decentralization, and to social dialogue in ensuring policy accountability. Although all these methods could be strengthened, those interested in the consolidation of democracy should place particular emphasis on citizen participation in government policy making that goes beyond efforts to include organized economic interests such as business and labor unions.

in Hungarian and by Maciej Kisilowski or his associate in Polish under my guidance, and these are noted in the text. I informed subjects of my research interests ahead of time and made clear the topics I wanted to cover. The public officials were those in key positions in the government or who had held such positions in the past. In Hungary, I interviewed the executive director or the president of many of the major environmental groups. The list of top groups was compiled from Pickvance (1998) for older groups and from the overlapping lists supplied by Sándor Fülöp of the Environmental Management and Law Association and by Professor Péter Mészáros of Green Future. In Poland, several interviews were conducted by Maciej Kisilowski with past and present leaders of the most important student and youth organizations. In the interview list and in the text and footnotes, all interviewees are listed with the position they held at the time of the interview as well as relevant past positions.

THREE

Legacy of the Past

Poles and Hungarians, like other Central Europeans, have generally favorable views of democracy. Their support is below the level in Western Europe but is comparable to that of Central Europe as a whole (see Table 1.1). Nevertheless, although more satisfied than their neighbors to the east, respondents express quite high levels of distrust of government institutions. Only 43% of Poles and 31% of Hungarians are satisfied or very satisfied with democracy in their own country, compared with 57% of Western Europeans and 10% of Eastern Europeans (Russia, Belarus, and Ukraine). Less than half the population has confidence in parliament, the civil service, or the justice system (Table 3.1). These numbers, however, are not markedly different from the responses for Western Europe and in one case – Hungarian views of the civil service – exceed Western European levels.

The most dramatic contrasts between Western Europe and Central Europe show up in people's willingness to engage in political action and to participate in voluntary or charitable activities. Both types of reported behavior are much lower in the former socialist countries such as Poland and Hungary (see Tables 1.2 and 8.1). Some special features of the Central European transition contribute to these differences. A historical legacy of governments that lacked popular legitimacy persists into the present and influences people's willingness to participate in political activities. The process of moving from one system to another has created uncertainty about the rules and the chains of authority, and some officials simply take advantage of their power to further their own interests and demand

Table 3.1. *Generalized Trust and Confidence in Democratic Institutions*

Region	Trust	Democracy	How Much Confidence in (Great Deal + Quite a Lot) (%)										
			Parliament	Civil Service	Justice System	Armed Forces	Education System	Social Security System	Health Care System	Police	European Union	Trade Unions	Press
Eastern Europe	25.6	10.2	22.6	38.0	36.2	68.2	72.3	46.5	55.2	31.0	31.2	32.7	34.6
Central Europe	18.6	32.9	27.1	31.7	37.7	62.8	72.9	35.9	51.6	47.2	43.2	29.3	41.6
Poland	18.4	43.1	33.9	32.5	43.1	69.2	80.8	39.3	56.9	56.4	42.9	34.0	48.4
Hungary	22.4	31.4	32.5	49.3	44.2	45.5	63.3	41.1	40.8	43.5	58.0	23.0	30.0
Western Europe	33.9	57.0	39.4	40.9	47.4	58.2	66.9	49.5	60.6	66.6	44.5	33.9	34.9

Note: Column 1 (Trust) is the percentage saying most people can be trusted. Column 2 (Democracy) is the percentage answering either very satisfied or rather satisfied to the question: "Are you satisfied with democracy?"

Source: EVS 1999/2000, questions 8, 58, 59. See Appendix 2 for details.

payoffs and favors.[27] Survey research has attempted to sort out the relative importance of history and the transition process. Although the past – both centuries of history and the recent experience of socialism – is important, people's attitudes are not just historically determined. They are also a response to citizens' everyday experience of state performance.[28]

The past exerts an influence in a number of ways. Three are particularly relevant to issues of public participation and engagement with the state. First, the recent history of socialism helps to explain the largely peaceful nature of the transition. Democratic consolidation has proved vexing and complex, but popular demonstrations have been largely peaceful, and no country in Central Europe outside the Balkans has faced large-scale violence and civil war. Second, the socialist system relied on certain institutions that still have salience today, and some reforms were put in place in the regimes' waning days that have survived into the present. Third, civic associations and professional groups were not entirely absent under socialism, and some carried out state-guided functions. People's experience with these groups has colored their view of voluntary associations in the present, especially because some groups founded under the past regime have survived and prospered in the transition.

This history creates difficulties for government oversight and public participation in policy-making processes. Both oversight institutions and organized private groups are sometimes looked on with suspicion. Yet, both are necessary as the democratic transition proceeds. Reformers need to confront the special hurdles these organizations face in the postsocialist countries. Oversight institutions must be of undoubted integrity and independence, and domestic civil society needs strengthening in the face of structural weaknesses.

Peaceful Protest

The transitions in Hungary and Poland, as in most of the former socialist countries, were peaceful. Poland had a period of martial law in the 1980s,

---

[27] Elster et al. (1998: 3–34). For a discussion of the Polish case in the early years of the transition that raises all these issues, see Łętowski (1993: 1–7). Psychological studies of public attitudes in Eastern and Western Europe carried out in 1989 and 1996–1997 found that differences in personal attitudes persisted over time. The study compared Hungary, Poland, and Slovakia with a group of Western European countries. The people from Eastern Europe were committed more to conservative and hierarchical values and less to values of egalitarianism and autonomy than their counterparts elsewhere and there was little change between surveys (Schwartz, Bardi, and Bianchi 2000).

[28] See the survey evidence of Miller et al. (2001). Howard (2003) demonstrates that the shared history of socialism has led to an unwillingness of people to join organized groups.

but there was no use of military force in either country (Elster et al. 1998: 6–11). Key leaders supported a gradual and peaceful transition. There are several reasons for this.

First, the older generation had lived through two world wars. In Hungary, the Soviet crackdown in 1956 left many with no stomach for violent confrontation. Second, a large proportion of the population was associated with the old regime: many had been Communist Party members and most had worked for state institutions. A complete overthrow of the old elite was not feasible or widely supported. Third, the old elite gained by obtaining some of the privatized state property. This gave them a stake in the system and made them uninterested in a return to state ownership. They were essentially bought off and did not seek to subvert the democratization process (Greskovits 1998: 84). Fourth, in both countries a portion of the old nomenclatura reorganized itself into an effective social democratic political party. These parties have won elections with platforms supporting continued market and democratic reforms. As Gill (2002) and Grzymała-Busse (2002) demonstrate, this last tendency was not general. Only in Hungary and Poland did this happen in the immediate aftermath of regime change.

Reflecting the peaceful, negotiated character of the change, the second Polish ombudsman, Tadeusz Zieliński, stated in 1992 that the systemic changes taking place in Poland should be nonrevolutionary in legal character to avoid violating human rights. This meant, in practice, that some of those with rights acquired under the socialist government retained them in the new system. For example, a 1992 judgment of the Polish Constitutional Tribunal held that the state could not deprive people of vested rights – pensions in this case – granted under the communist government.[29] Similarly, the first ombudsman, Ewa Łętowska, successfully convinced government officials that the International Covenant on Civil and Political Rights applied in Poland and prevented the state from firing teachers simply on the basis of Communist Party membership without any procedural protections (Klich 1996: 44–45).

In addition to the co-optation of the old elite, ordinary people did not support violent protest. As Table 1.2 shows, most people in Central Europe would never join an unlawful strike or occupy a building. Although citizens express widespread discontent both with the market

---

[29] Klich (1996: 42). The case is Judgment of February 11, 1992, K 14/91, excerpted in Poland, Constitutional Tribunal (1999: 57–71).

and with the state, their protests are seldom violent.[30] Greskovits stresses the way the communist legacy contributed to this result. He points to the relatively equal distribution of income, the small number of marginalized poor, and the absence of recent violent coups and riots. The new democracies have trod cautiously in trying to keep much of the existing social welfare state in place, and people have both public and private reserves to get through hard times (Greskovits 1998: 85). As a result, the quality of some services deteriorated; others, such as health care, experienced de facto privatization through pervasive corruption. However, people are still coping on a day-to-day basis. Societies have become more unequal since the transition, but a safety net – however limited – remains, based on public programs and ties of family and friendship.

Institutional Legacies

Three institutional legacies are important for understanding the present situation. First, under socialism, Hungary and Poland were governed largely by government decrees and resolutions, not statutes (Nunberg and Barbone 1999: 10; Nunberg 1999: 98–99). Second, the planning process required strong internal controls. Third, the socialist regimes instituted some reforms before the end of their time in power, and these persist into the present.

First, consider law making. In Hungary, the Council of Ministers had broad discretion to enact decrees with legal force when the parliament was not in session, and parliaments were essentially rubber stamps. Even with a weak legislature, the government often did not bother to obtain legislative support for its actions. The legislature met for only two periods of 2 or 3 days each year. In most years, the parliament enacted only

---

[30] See Table 3.1 and Csepeli, Örkény, Székelyi, and Barna (2004); Ekiert and Kubik (1999); and Mishler and Rose (1997, 1998). This pattern may be changing, at least in Poland. In November and December 2003, there were several aggressive strikes and protests organized by the Solidarity trade union, some of which turned violent. However, only a small proportion of the population was involved in each one. There was a demonstration against the closing of coal mines that ended in a battle with the police. Nurses occupied various buildings in a labor dispute; farmers and nurses blockaded highways; and workers occupied factory buildings that were set to close down. In November, railroad workers threatened a general strike. Although a national rail strike was averted by government concessions, other informal work stoppages and protests occurred on the railroads in December. Workers also protested at enterprises that were about to shutdown. Examples are from Anna Horolets; Aleksandra Sznajder provided documentation from press reports in an e-mail of July 19, 2004.

a handful of laws, mostly concerning budgetary matters. In one case, an impatient government issued decrees with legal force while the parliament was adjourned for lunch break.[31]

In Poland, the situation was similar. The socialist constitution permitted the Polish Council of State to issue decrees with the same status as statutes. However, these decrees required approval by the Sejm (Parliament) at its next session. Although this might not seem much of a constraint given the dominance of the Communist Party in the Sejm, the Council of Ministers and individual ministers avoided this route and instead issued "independent resolutions," which were not formal decrees and so did not need Sejm approval. They were called "mimeograph" laws to distinguish them from formally published statutes. The Council of State used its power to issue decrees rarely. One example occurred in 1981 when it declared martial law – because it wanted the increased legitimacy that Sejm approval might supply.

This history made reformers in both countries skeptical of granting legal force to unilateral government decrees or resolutions. Although delegation to the government could not be avoided in practice, reformers sought to constrain its scope and to strengthen parliament. As a result, reformers neglected the need to hold the government to account for its remaining acts of discretion. The primary aim was to limit the government's decree power rather than to manage that power in the public interest.

The second socialist legacy is the elaborate planning process, involving extensive paperwork and an overall structure of control. The planning exercise was internal to the state; it was not meant to generate participation and challenge from the citizenry.[32] On this view, bureaucratic rules

---

[31] Interview with Prof. Dr. Géza Kilényi, D.Sc., Pázmány Péter Catholic University, Budapest, former justice of the Constitutional Court, December 18, 2002, Budapest.

[32] As Kornai wrote in describing the socialist system (1992: 47): "The bureaucracy is not subordinate to any stable legal system.... [T]here are a vast number of state regulations that do not receive the rank of law even formally: they remain as government or ministerial orders, or, most common of all, simply the personal ruling of a particular member of the bureaucracy. For the bureaucracy itself decides the kind of legal shape it wishes to give its various rulings,... [T]he bureaucracy is not subordinate to the legal system. The line of effect is precisely the opposite direction: the formal system of law is subordinate to the current endeavors of the bureaucracy." Even during the reform period in countries such as Hungary and Poland, Kornai argues that there was no separation of powers. "Government is basically applied by decree even if measures may qualify formally as laws passed by parliament.... Some decrees and internal regulations contradict the legislation passed by parliament. There are still numerous secret decrees and instructions" (Kornai 1992: 411). Furthermore, the classic socialist system "never felt embarrassed about its secretiveness," and this reflex persisted into the reform period (Kornai 1992: 425–426).

serve as internal guides for officials only. Traces of this view remain in the existing systems of administrative law and limit the external force of some provisions of the administrative codes.

A final legacy dates from the last decade of the socialist regimes. In both countries, political leaders sought to deal with growing discontent by introducing new institutions designed to increase governmental accountability without dismantling the one-party state (Elster et al. 1998: 12–13; Klich 1996: 38). Thus, Poland established the Office of Ombudsman in 1987, strengthened the independence of the Supreme Chamber of Control (an institution that dates from 1919), and created an Administrative Court in 1980 and a Constitutional Tribunal in 1986.[33] Agnieszka Klich (1996: 37) claims that the ombudsman and the Constitutional Tribunal were window dressing to make the regime appear progressive in Western eyes but without giving them real influence. The first ombudsman said the political establishment hoped her office "would prove to be a submissive, easy-to-manipulate entity." She suggested that it was probably no accident "a woman with no political affiliations and no prior involvement in any public activity was appointed...." Her independence and activism were "an unpleasant surprise for the regime" (Łętowska 1996: 3). However, when she began to criticize the new democratically elected government, she was also criticized as a holdover from the past (Łętowska 1996: 6). In her defense, she argued that the new government administration proved unable to implement the "rule of law, a concept that was absolutely foreign to the communist power system." In an article published in 1996, she claimed that the administration did not yet understand the idea of parliamentary supremacy, the need for proper procedures, and the prohibition of arbitrariness and secrecy (Łętowska 1996: 10).

In 1987, Hungary promulgated a Law on Normative Acts that mandated consultation with organized groups for draft laws and decrees (XI/1987). This process was on the books in 1988 when Parliament passed a series of important reform statutes. In the area of labor-management relations, the Hungarian government set up a tripartite committee of labor,

---

[33] See Łętowska (1996: 3). A commemorative volume published on the twentieth anniversary of the Administrative Court describes it as being rushed into existence "by awesome murmurs coming from various environments." The court was advertised "as a satisfaction of social postulates" (Poland, Naczelny Sąd Administracyny [Supreme Administrative Court] 2000: 188).

management, and government in 1988 that has continued in one form or another to the present.[34]

Thus, forms of accountability and oversight that did not involve competitive elections were relatively common at the end of the socialist period in Poland and Hungary. Perhaps for that reason, they are sometimes looked on, even today, as of secondary importance or even as cynical attempts to provide the form, but not the substance, of accountability. Given this legacy, efforts to create genuine accountability outside the electoral process have not been a major focus of democratic reformers.

Civic Associations Under Socialism

In both Poland and Hungary, foundations were disbanded in the early years of the socialist regimes; in Hungary, associations were banned as well (Kurczewski and Kurczewska 2001: 944; Kuti 1993: 4; Leś, Nałęcz, and Wygnański 2000). What remained were "social organizations" that served both as mass organizations and as authorities. Overall, there was a heavy emphasis on sport, culture, and recreation. Some labor unions administered welfare funds, and membership in a professional association could be equivalent to a permit to engage in that profession (Kornai 1992: 39–40; Salamon et al. 1999: 283–370). An umbrella student organization represented university students and administered clubs, dormitories, and cafeterias as well as some scholarship funds.[35] According to Ekiert and Kubik (1999: 100), in the early years of the communist governments, membership in some organizations was mandatory so that "more people belonged to various formal organizations and movements (trade unions, youth and professional associations, etc.) than under any other type of regime." They were often a source of benefits and services not available elsewhere. Even when there was no formal membership requirement, as with the university student organization in Poland, the benefits they controlled were so valuable that most students joined.[36]

---

[34] Hungary established a system of tripartite governance (government, labor, management) in December 1988 under the last socialist government (Héthy 1995; interview with László Herczog, Deputy Secretary of State in Charge of Employment Policy, Ministry of Economic Affairs, January 9, 2003, Budapest).

[35] Interview with Waldemar Zbytek, Chairman of the Association of Polish Students (ZSP), the successor to the socialist student organization, conducted in Warsaw in December 29, 2003, by Maciej Kisilowski.

[36] Interview with Zbytek.

In Hungary, more than 95% of registered organizations focused on sports, recreation, hobbies, and firefighting (Vajda 1995–1996: 83; Jenkins 1999: 182). The state-financed social organizations, such as the Red Cross, the Adult Education Society, the Peace Council, and the Patriotic Front, worked closely with the Communist Party (Kuti 1993: 4–5). In Poland, there were groups of housekeepers, volunteer fire brigades, and various organizations of youth and students. They "were political at the top and non-political at the bottom" (Buchowski 1996: 84). Fire brigades, still common in rural villages, were not just charged with firefighting but were, and continue to be, multifunctional volunteer and social organizations for young men (Kurczewski and Kurczewska 2001: 965–966). As in Hungary, groups such as the Polish Red Cross, the Society for Polish-Soviet Friendship, the Polish Anglers Association, and Polish Scouts were complements to the socialist state, not independent voices. Political authorities controlled staffing and the distribution of funds (Leś et al. 2000). Some, such as the Anglers and one Scouting organization, date from before the introduction of socialism, remained in existence under socialism, and have maintained a strong membership base today. Others have survived by taking new names and missions and using property bequeathed to them by the new state.[37]

In Poland, the one partial exception to state control was the Roman Catholic Church. The complexity of church-state relations in that period is illustrated by state policy during the height of state socialism. In 1950 the state dispossessed the Church of most of its assets, but at the same time created a special budgetary fund from which it supported clergy and various church activities.[38] Although partly supported by state funds, the Catholic Church retained some limited independence during this period, and became a focal point for dissent in the 1980s.[39]

---

[37] See Kurczewski and Kurczewska (2001: 948). Since 1989, there have been two scouting groups, one more connected with the state and the other associated with Catholicism and the promotion of patriotic values. During the 1970s and 1980s, one group of scouts was allied with Solidarity and was involved in some underground activities. Thus, scouting echoes some of the divisions in the student groups discussed in Chapter 10. I am grateful to Anna Horolets for this information.

[38] See Ustawa z dnia 20 marca 1950 r. o przejęciu przez Państwo dóbr martwej ręki, poręczeniu proboszczom posiadania gospodarstw rolnych i utworzeniu Funduszu Kościelnego [Statute of March 20, 1950 on nationalization of mortmain estates, on guaranteeing rectors possession of farms and on creating the Church Fund], Dz. U. 1950, No. 9, Item 87. The Church Fund, which still exisits, now supports the activities of other churches besides Roman Catholic ones.

[39] See Leś et al. (2000: 11); e-mail from Aleksandra Sznajder, July 19, 2004.

Many informal groups existed, based on kinship and shared interests, and the role of the family as a bulwark against totalitarianism has survived the end of the socialist regime (Buchowski 1996: 84; Howard 2003; Kornai 1992: 455–459). Local community cooperation based on close-knit networks of individuals was important in coping with the difficult political and economic situation (Buchowski 1996: 85; Kurczewski and Kurczewska 2001). Most of these groups, however, were "escapist, inward-looking micro-groups of individuals trusting each other, helping each other in coping with everyday problems and creating some space for intellectual survival...." (Elster et al. 1998: 13). To the extent that the loyalties and connections that were developed in these groups continue to be important, they could be either the core of more politically effective organizations or a barrier to the creation of democratically accountable state institutions.

Socialist governments actively discouraged the creation of independent groups that had public policy agendas. In Hungary, a 1970 decree required that even preparations to establish a voluntary association should be reported to the authorities (Kuti 1993: 5). Nevertheless, officially recognized pressure groups did exist in areas such as agriculture, nature protection, mining, and culture. They engaged in activities that would be described as lobbying in the American context – that is, using personal connections to push their concerns and engaging in political pressure of various kinds (Kornai 1992: 45). Some of these groups still exist, but their role as checks on the bureaucracy is likely to be limited and unbalanced.

In the latter years of the socialist regimes, older organizations took on stronger roles as pressure groups, and many new associations were founded "spontaneously through initiative from below" (Kornai 1992: 418–421). Some independent organizations existed (Ekiert and Kubik 1999: 101; Marschall 1990; Sztompka 1999: 151–160). In Poland, the Solidarity labor union, although it was illegal for most of the 1980s, played a key role in the transition and was a popular social movement. Hungary had no single organization of such overarching importance (Elster et al. 1998: 14).

The legal situation changed before the change in regime. The liberalizing regimes permitted the foundation of voluntary groups, often with external financing, and they became a catalyst for citizens' discontent (Harper 1999: 62–93; Kuti 1993: 5; Pickvance 1998: 75–76). In 1984, Poland reversed a ban on private foundations that dated from 1952 and in 1989 revised the laws on associations and on the relationship between church

and state (Leś et al. 2000: 12). These laws, which many viewed as inadequate, controlled the operation of the nonprofit sector until 2003 when
they were supplemented by a new statute on public benefit organizations and volunteerism. After the change in regime, some foundations
were formed just to manage the "social facilities" that had been part of
state enterprises (Kurczewski and Kurczewska 2001: 944–946, 953–954;
Leś et al. 2000: 12). Hungary permitted nonprofit organizations to register and operate openly in the 1980s. In Hungary, in the mid-1990s the
successors to organizations that existed before the change in regime were
generally stronger than newer organizations (Vajda 1995–1996: 84).

Thus, with the fall of the socialist regimes, some nongovernmental organizations already existed, although some were deeply connected with
the previous regime. Others, in contrast, were in the forefront of protests
against the socialist government and played a key role in the Roundtable
negotiations (Ekiert and Kubik 1999: 101). This mixed legacy has made
nonprofit associations problematic as representatives of citizen initiatives.
Those whose roots lie in groups that were the willing captives of the
old regime may have difficulty in the present when they claim to be independent voices. They walk a tightrope between their former roles as
state-sponsored entities and present efforts to be seen as independent organizations. In contrast, newer groups with undoubted reform credentials
sometimes have had trouble making the transition from mass movements
organizing protests against a repressive regime to institutionalized organizations operating in a democratic state.[40]

Another complication is the relationship between nongovernmental
groups and political parties during the transition. Some civil society
groups, founded at the end of the socialist period, helped negotiate the
transition, and their members formed the core of some political parties
that currently play an important role.[41] All the original groups faced the
difficult question of whether to become active in electoral politics, and

---

[40] Examples of both types of groups are included in my interviews of activists in environmental groups in Hungary and in student and youth groups in Poland.

[41] According to Kuti (1993: 5): "In the 1980s, many of the newly emerging nonprofit organizations [in Hungary] were substitutes for political parties. The highly political nature
of these nonprofit organizations was obvious to the State and the population alike. For
instance, one of the most important charities, the Fund for Poverty Relief, was the cradle
for the Liberal Party. . . ." In Poland leaders of student organizations were part of the original roundtable discussion, but, unlike in Hungary, they did not found a political party
of their own [interview with Witold Repetowicz, former vice-chairman of the national
board of the Independent Students' Association (1993–1994, 1998), former chairman
(1994–1995), conducted by Maciej Kisilowski, December 30, 2003, in Warsaw].

the legacy of their choices still affects the standing of independent groups. With the transition to electoral democracy secure, the possible tradeoff between the strength of party organizations and the vitality of civil society is part of an ongoing debate about the relationship between state and society (Arato 2000: 425–426). Thus, some groups may not be accepted as independent voices because of past associations with the old regime, whereas others have difficulty establishing an independent stance because of present connections with organized parties.

Organizational membership is markedly lower in Central and Eastern Europe than in older democracies and in postauthoritarian states. In statistical tests at the country and the individual level, prior experience of a communist government was significantly and negatively related to group membership.[42] Marc Morjé Howard (2003: 92–145) studied the low and falling membership in groups through surveys and interviews in East Germany and Russia. These reveal that mistrust of communist era "voluntary" organizations has a negative impact on willingness to join any kind of organization in the recent transition period. Disappointment with the transition process also contributed to the failure to join groups. This is a pessimistic conclusion because it implies that dissatisfaction with the status quo has led to passivity, not political involvement. However, some of the people he interviewed were former activists at the end of the communist period, and many of them remained active. A link to involvement either in communist era official groups or in dissident groups seemed to be associated with current voluntary sector activity. Some of the people currently active in environmental groups in Hungary and student and youth groups in Poland fit this profile. Many other citizens, however, are disengaged and are concentrating on family and private life.

Conclusions

As we begin to look at alternative routes to public accountability in Hungary and Poland, it is well to remember that many of the institutions and their functions are new or newly reconstituted. Their ultimate success or failure may be related to their history. Citizens may view government legitimacy through the lens of the simple democratic model, with its focus on parliamentary legislation, elections, and political parties. They may be critical both of the exercise of policy-making responsibility by cabinet

---

[42] See Howard (2003: 62–70, 85–90). He used data from the World Values Survey 1995–1997.

ministries and of efforts by civil society groups to influence policy. If that is so, then it may be difficult to begin a dialogue over alternative routes to state accountability that involves both government institutions and private sector organizations.

Although the legacy of the past may fade with time, it is also possible for a downward spiral to develop in which a dysfunctional state of affairs leads not to pressure for change but to an even worse situation in the next period. This study argues that history is not destiny but that the past needs to be self-consciously taken into account in designing reforms that consolidate democracy. An optimistic functionalist perspective seems naïve. Public skepticism about both democracy and civil society can combine to stall the transition. This would be an unfortunate result because a modern democracy needs responsible delegation to government ministries watched over by institutions of accountability and by private organizations.

FOUR

External Accountability and the European Union

A country with weak and untried institutions may rely on multinational institutions to help insulate parts of its legal system from the opportunistic behavior of insiders. This can help consolidate democracy if the external conditions improve the position of otherwise excluded groups or strengthen domestic democratic structures. However, deference to external pressure is a controversial strategy because it seems a challenge to local sovereignty and popular control. There is something paradoxical about a democratically elected government succumbing to outsiders' demands as a means to increase its democratic legitimacy. This can create special difficulties in Central Europe where the external pressure is exerted by the European Union (EU), a body that is an evolving democracy much like the countries of Central Europe.

Citizens in Central and Eastern Europe (CEE) often view their governments as ineffective and biased. Politicians have trouble convincing voters that nominally independent oversight or regulatory agencies will operate in a nonpartisan manner. Thus, there seems to be room for external constraints to help consolidate democracy. Reformers justify submitting to external constraints not simply as an unfortunate necessity but as a welcome limit on parochial, self-serving behavior. This is, however, a risky position to adopt because "the popularity of government . . . might be (negatively) affected if competence that the society had long hoped to achieve is freely delegated internationally" (Salzberger and Voight 2002).

A country's politicians may comply with external rules if the benefits of delegation exceed the costs. However, compliance does not necessarily

further the consolidation of democracy.[43] A strategy of relying on standards promulgated from outside will succeed in furthering that goal only if three conditions hold.

First, the external requirements must help rather than hinder democratic consolidation and must be seen to do so by citizens (the content condition). External requirements are of two types. They can either determine the substance of legal rules or mandate particular procedures inside the state. Thus, it is important to determine whether the substantive rules are consistent with the public interest and to ask whether the required procedures further democratic values. Second, the international body must have the authority and the will to influence the behavior of domestic governments (the political-will-and-authority condition). International mandates will have little bite if they are merely hortatory. Third, the supranational institution must be legitimate in the eyes of citizens to avoid undermining the acceptability of otherwise valuable policies (the legitimacy condition).

The international body most relevant to the countries of Central Europe is the EU. Fulfilling the conditions for membership has imposed many limits on domestic policy making (Vachudova 2001a, 2001b). Countries in CEE, which are eager to be part of Europe both politically and economically, are bearing domestic costs to obtain the greater benefit of joining the EU. Even if the conditions imposed do nothing to enhance domestic government performance, they may be accepted, however reluctantly, simply because they are a condition for membership.[44]

---

[43] Pevehouse (2002) analyzes a sample of democracies from 1950 to 1992. He finds that simply being a member of several democratic regional organizations does not help consolidate democracy but that joining democratic regional organizations is associated with increased longevity for new democracies. This is an encouraging result for the accession countries such as Hungary and Poland. Even though the EU is frequently criticized for having a "democracy deficit," it is much more democratic than many other regional international organizations included in Pevehouse's study.

[44] Schimmelfenig, Engert, and Knobel (2003) study compliance with EU mandates in Slovakia, Turkey, and Latvia. In Slovakia, under the Mečiar government domestic politics trumped EU demands, but underlying support for EU membership contributed to his eventual electoral defeat. In Latvia, EU pressure to ease the requirements for Russians to become Latvian citizens helped shape the law. Note, however, this is not a case of EU conditions overcoming the power of narrow organized groups but one in which the EU defended a minority against majoritarian preferences. In Turkey, EU pressures led to significant responses but only in areas where domestic political costs were not too high. Moravcsik (1998) argues that EU membership permits member states to implement unfavorable but necessary policies. It strengthens governments at the expense of particular groups. The impact of EU membership on democratic accountability in member states, however, depends on whom the member states are representing. Korkut (2002) points

This chapter proceeds as follows. The first section outlines the complex nature of the EU and its relationship to domestic law in the accession countries. The next section briefly considers the content of EU requirements with respect to both substance and process. It asks if they can help to consolidate democracy in Central Europe in spite of the fact that they are imposed from outside as part of the accession process (the content condition). This is not the place for an exhaustive analysis of the multitude of conditions imposed by the EU. However, I suggest that some requirements are problematic; the EU laws that new members must accept cannot all be justified as efficient, fair, and democratically efficacious.

The EU's ability to impose rules was at its height in the years before accession and fell off when the countries became full members on May 1, 2004. With accession, laws may be promulgated in Brussels that the new member states will find unacceptable. This will create problems because the leverage of the EU is now much reduced. There are two potential difficulties – one linked to the political-will-and-authority condition and the other to the legitimacy condition.

The political-will-and-authority condition does not always hold. EU policy vacillates between a desire to goad members and potential members into action and a commitment to decentralization and devolution. This sends a mixed signal to new members. The third section of this chapter discusses the impact of this ambiguity on new member states.

Finally, the EU's legitimacy is problematic. As the fourth section argues, the democracy deficit in the EU's legislative and regulatory processes limits its claims to authority over member states. If the EU's processes lack legitimacy, this may make it difficult for its initiatives to gain acceptance now that the accession countries have become full members of the EU. The EU's struggles to reinvent itself may limit the political legitimacy of its constraints on accession states even though these states have formally accepted these constraints as conditions of membership.

In practice, the EU sets the legal framework with its regulations and directives but relies on member states to pass conforming legislation (in the case of directives) and to implement all EU rules. The trajectory of the EU debate over governance is toward more, not less, devolution to the member states. The EU is even going so far as to mandate devolution of political authority within member states to regional entities. The

out that some interest groups may be strengthened by EU membership because they can form cross-national alliances and exert influence at the level of the EU.

greater the level of delegation, the less leverage EU institutions can exert.
They must rely on the competence and trustworthiness of member state
officials (Bignami 2003). However, the relative weakness of government
capacity in the accession countries is one reason why their citizens supported membership in the EU in the first place. The devolutionary trend
creates a paradox. As the EU tries to push new member states to adopt
Western European legal models, it is also leaving more regulatory and
policy tasks to the national governments and urging them to devolve authority downward to even weaker government bodies below the national
level.

Treaty or Constitution?

What exactly does it mean for a country to join the EU? Is it like acceding
to a treaty or is it like becoming part of a new state? Is the EU responsible directly to individual people as citizens of "Europe" or only to its
"peoples" as they are represented through member states?[45] I do not propose to enter this foundational debate except to note that, in practice, the
EU is a composite and is likely to remain so even if a new constitution
for Europe is put in place.[46] Whether or not there is a European demos, the EU can, in practice, legislate in ways meant to bind the member
states. Equally important is the relative weakness of the EU's enforcement mechanisms. Short of the drastic step of expelling a member, it must
rely on member states to comply on their own and, in extreme cases, to
sanction reluctant members.

The European Parliament is directly elected and has gained more
powers over time, but the Commission and the Council retain dominant
roles. The former is the executive arm of the EU with agenda-setting and
policy-making responsibilities; the latter consists of representatives of all
members, although the actual attendees shift with the issue under discussion and the voting rule varies by issue. With 10 new members, including
Hungary and Poland, decision making will become more cumbersome
even though some issues are delegated to smaller bodies or are decided

---

[45] See Lindseth (2001), Sandholtz and Stone Sweet (1998), Stone Sweet (2003), and Weiler
(1995). Weiler argues that there is no European *demos* – that is, Europeans do not
understand themselves as a historically cohesive self-governing, political unit.

[46] Lindseth (2001, 2002) persuasively defends this view. The draft of the treaty establishing
the European Constitution was agreed to on June 18, 2004, and signed in the fall of 2004.
The process of member state ratification will take several years. The draft is available at
the web site of the European Council: http://ue.eu.int/cms3_fo/index.htm.

by qualified majority rule. The Treaty of Nice (2001) attempted to deal with many of these issues before the new members joined. The allocation of voting rights in the Council and the definition of qualified majority voting were designed to maintain the dominant role of the existing 15 members. Furthermore, the treaty permits some members to integrate faster along some dimensions without the approval of the rest. Thus, the most powerful existing members have dealt with the expansion of the EU not by streamlining and simplifying decision-making procedures but by maintaining their hold on power inside the EU and by permitting the more advanced countries to move ahead faster.[47]

The force of EU directives and regulations in member states depends, in part, on citizens' acceptance of the supranational authority of the EU. In both Hungary and Poland, referenda in 2003 supported EU accession. However, that does not necessarily imply acceptance of all the individual requirements of membership. At present, there are numerous complaints about the details of the laws being imposed on new members.

In the future, a deeper problem may arise. If the new members believe they have been treated unfairly in the allocation of political power in the Council, and if the result is an ongoing problem of complying with laws that are tilted against their interests, then the EU will not be able to command legitimacy in Central Europe. Its role as a guarantor of the democratic transition will be tarnished, and it may be seen more as an overbearing external, almost colonial, power than as a participant in a collaborative trans-European project (Böröcz and Kovács 2001). Of course, a small state, like Hungary, will always be at a disadvantage in a qualified majority system unless it can position itself as a swing vote willing to take the best bargain. However, the basic point is that the voting rules have been set up so that the accession states in Central Europe cannot form a blocking coalition. Thus, the rest of the EU could impose policies on them (Heinemann 2002). This is true, in general, in spite of the controversy over allegations that the Treaty of Nice gives Poland and Spain too many votes in the Council.

The problems with meshing EU and domestic law are likely to center on the practical and administrative constraints that flow from a scarcity

---

[47] Heinemann (2002) makes these points. A qualified majority is at least 74% of the votes but must also include a majority of the states. In addition, a council member may request that the majority represent at least 62% of the total population. The 12 accession countries (including Bulgaria and Romania) studied by Heinemann represent 22% of the total population.

of resources both in the EU and inside Hungary and Poland and from administrative incompatibilities.[48] Difficulties will also arise if the new members feel like second class members of the EU, operating in a political environment that keeps them in a weak position.

Content: The EU's Impact on Democratic Consolidation

The EU conditions for membership include both a democratic constitutional structure and many detailed substantive rules and regulations. Obvious tensions exist between the EU's procedural strictures and the large body of substantive law that members must accept and implement. If these legal rules were not a condition of EU membership, a well-functioning member-state democracy would not necessarily want to approve all the EU's substantive policy directives.

---

[48] A necessary condition for the successful incorporation of that law is the formal legality of EU law in the new member states. Early on, the European Court of Justice found that community law has precedence over domestic law [Case 26/62, Van Gend en Loos v. Nederlandse Administratie der Belastinger: (1963) ECR 1, (1963) CMR 105]. At the same time, domestic courts and legal scholars must be willing to accept the incorporation of EU requirements into domestic law. As a formal legal matter, both Poland and Hungary permit such legal norms to bind their citizens under some conditions. Compared with others in the region, both countries have high levels of de jure and de facto international delegation (Ludwikowski 1998: 33). Although both countries' constitutions retain some ultimate oversight rights, these seem unlikely, in practice, to impose constraints. The Polish Constitution permits the transfer of selected sovereign rights to international organizations. Ratification of such international agreements is either by a statute passed by a two-thirds vote in the Sejm and the Senate (with at least half the members present in each house), or by referendum. Other important international agreements are ratified by the president who must obtain the prior approval of the parliament in the form of a statute. The last group of least significant agreements may be ratified by the president without statutory approval, although he or she must notify the Sejm before ratification. See Konstytucja Rzeczypospolitej Polskiej z dnia 2 kwietnia 1997 r. [Constitution of the Republic of Poland of April 2, 1997], *Dziennik Ustaw Rzeczypospolitej Polskiej* [Dz. U.] [*Journal of Laws of the Republic of Poland*] 1997, No. 78, Item 483, articles 89 and 90 [hereafter Polish Constitution, English text at http://www.kprm.gov.pl/english/97.htm]. A ratified agreement is part of the domestic law and can be applied directly unless the agreement itself requires the enactment of a statute before it becomes applicable. In Hungary, the president and the government can conclude international treaties, but, as in Poland, the parliament must ratify "those of importance." The Hungarian Constitution (article 7) provides that the legal system "shall harmonize the country's domestic law with obligations assumed under international law." This is not quite the same thing as giving priority to international law, but it can have that implication in many cases (Salzberger and Voight 2002). The Constitutional Court has the right to review the consistency of international treaties with the constitution (Law on the Constitutional Tribunal, XXXII/89, article 1; Ludwikowski 1998: 53).

The extent of this problem is difficult to judge because it is hard to measure the marginal impact of the EU either on government structures and procedures or on substantive law. At the level of democratic consolidation, potential EU membership appears to have strengthened the hands of democrats in marginal cases such as Slovakia. However, the countries of CEE most likely would have adopted democratic constitutions and created market economies even if the EU did not exist. If the EU does not provide the hoped for benefits, however, the backlash may strengthen political groups with narrow, nationalist goals.

In 1993, the EU set out the basic structural conditions for membership in the Copenhagen Criteria. They require a "stability of institutions guaranteeing democracy, the rule of law, human rights, and respect for and protection of minorities." Over time the EU has refined and expanded the criteria to include other factors such as the control of corruption. They are used not only to rule on membership applications but also to determine the level of financial assistance to applicant countries (Pridham 2002: 957). These criteria are sometimes criticized as imposing higher standards on accession countries than on existing members, but in the case of Hungary and Poland gaps in formal compliance have not delayed membership.[49] In both countries, democratic constitutional structures seem to be firmly in place so that the main contested issues involve factors such as minority rights and anticorruption policies. Beginning with its 1997 reports, the Commission stated that both Hungary and Poland present the characteristics of a democracy with stable institutions that guarantee the rule of law, respect for human rights, and the protection of minorities (Commission of the European Communities 2002a: 18; Commission of the European Communities 2002b: 19).

The Copenhagen Criteria were just the beginning for the accession countries. The criteria merely specify the necessary governmental structure. The EU also has a large body of law, called the *acquis communautaire*, that sets the legal framework for member states. The *acquis* covers both substantive policies and institutional structures. It has had a major impact on the parliamentary and rule-making agenda in both Hungary and Poland. The candidate countries were in a race to get their laws in conformity and so be in the first group granted membership (Salzberger and Voight 2002). That race has now been run with both Hungary and Poland entering the EU on May 1, 2004, with laws and government institutions

---

[49] See Commission of the European Communities (2003a, 2003b).

that largely satisfy the European Commission.[50] In its 2003 annual reports on Hungary and Poland, the Commission is relatively upbeat, although it stresses the importance of putting formal rules into practice and points to the deficiencies that remain (Commission of the European Communities 2003a, 2003b).

Since 1998, the Commission has been screening the legislation of accession countries to see if it complies with the *acquis* (Carius, von Homeyer, and Bär 2000: 155). The results have been impressive – a large number of statutes have been passed in response to EU requirements (Commission of the European Communities 2003a, 2003b). They range from economic and social regulatory policy, to social service spending, to internal government organization.[51]

For example, in the environmental area formal compliance with EU law by the accession countries was high even as early as the mid-1990s (Knill and Lenschow 2000). Interviews in Poland, Hungary, and the Czech Republic during that period indicated that the EU accession criteria were much on the mind of environmental ministry officials. Their main concern seemed to be "the need to fulfill the obligations imposed by the *acquis*" and not the domestic environmental benefits of the legislation (Hines 2000: 300).

In 2002, the Commission provisionally closed negotiations with Hungary over the environmental portion of the *acquis*, but the 2003 report points to a number of deficiencies, particularly with respect to new directives, industrial pollution, and nature protection (Commission of the European Communities 2002a: 108; Commission of the European Communities 2003a: 43–45). The Commission is beginning to emphasize implementation and to require procedural reforms that enhance participation rights and increase information provision (Carius et al. 2000: 143).

A similar situation prevails in Poland. The Commission finds substantial compliance with environmental requirements but points to some areas of concern (Commission of the European Communities 2003b). In 1994, the government adopted a resolution requiring that draft laws and ordinances be checked for conformity with EU environmental law.[52]

---

[50] See Cameron (2002) and Commission of the European Communities (2003a, 2003b).

[51] The Czech Republic provides a particularly clear example of the way such pressure works. The European Commission criticized the Czech's slow progress in judicial reform in its 1999 report. This induced the government to act to avoid slowing down the accession process (Pridham 2002: 960–961).

[52] Uchwała Nr 16 Rady Ministrów z dnia 29 marca 1994 r. w sprawie dodatkowych wymogów postępowania z rządowymi projektami normatywnych aktów prawnych ze względu na

However, Poland is behind Hungary in overall compliance. It has been granted compliance delays in eight areas and needs to adopt much implementing legislation and strengthen its administrative capacity to implement the law (Commission of the European Communities 2002b: 109; Commission of the European Communities 2003b). Poland retained its Soviet era law for many years in spite of EU pressure and adopted some laws in spite of their incompatibility with the *acquis* when political support was high enough (Żylicz and Holzinger 2000: 217–218). Several commentators conclude that EU standards will not be met in the near future.[53]

Even when the formal laws comply with the *acquis*, lack of administrative capacity and lack of resources will limit these countries' ability to implement EU rules (Jovanović 2000; Vachudova 2000). The problems they face are based not simply on the fragility and weakness of government institutions but also on a lack of resources and the correspondingly difficult tradeoffs their relatively low incomes produce. In 2001, each of the Central European candidate countries had a per capita gross domestic product (GDP) far below the EU average. Only Slovenia's GDP per capita was close to that of Greece, the poorest member state. Hungary at $12,340 and Poland at $9,450 were 51% and 40% of the EU average (UNDP data; Commission of the European Communities 2002a: 38; Commission of the European Communities 2002b: 35; see also Jovanović 2000: 4). The leverage of the EU on the new members has been a powerful incentive for law reform, but its impact is limited by basic economic and political constraints and by the limited financial help available from the EU.[54]

konieczność spełniania kryteriów zgodności z prawem Unii Europejskiej [Resolution No. 16 of the Council of Ministers of March 29, 1994, on additional requirements in proceeding with the governmental projects of normative acts because of the need to fulfill the criteria of compatibility with the law of the European Union], *Monitor Polski* [M.P.] [*The Polish Monitor*] 1994, No. 23, Item 188. At present, the issue is regulated by Uchwała nr 49 Rady Ministrów z dnia 19 marca 2002 r. regulamin pracy Rady Ministrów [Resolution No. 49 of the Council of Ministers of March 19, 2002. The rules of proceedings of the Council of Ministers], M.P. 2002, No. 13, Item 221 with amendments.

[53] Knill and Lenschow (2000) cite one study that predicts that Poland will take 15–20 years to comply with EU standards. Other work they cite finds this unrealistic and estimates that it would take 5% of gross domestic product to reach that goal, three to four times the current level.

[54] The EU provided preaccession assistance through several programs, most importantly PHARE (the acronym stands for Poland and Hungary: Aid for Economic Restructuring, but the program applied to all preaccession countries). But the financial aid did not match the substantial payments from the EU structural funds that were made to the southern countries when they joined the EU. Such support is not available to the current

The marginal impact of the EU appears to have been especially strong at the level of the policy initiatives required by the *acquis*. Here, a candidate country may create laws using its own democratic forms only because it seeks EU membership and not because the new laws respond to domestic political realities. However, the actual extent to which this has happened is unknown. For example, both Hungary and Poland probably would have passed environmental statutes during the transition process even if the EU did not exist, and advisors from the United States had an important influence on the statutory drafting process. In Hungary, environmental concerns were part of the early Roundtable discussions that led to the change in regime and were one of the issues that mobilized public opposition. Furthermore, just because opponents of a measure argue that the government is buckling to pressure from Brussels does not mean the law is ill advised or lacks popular support. Nevertheless, in some cases the rules required by Brussels do seem to have had an impact. Unfortunately, some of them impose unrealistic burdens on the financially strapped new members, and they are not always well designed to solve domestic policy problems.[55] Even if some individual directives and regulations seem onerous, however, the choice of staying outside the EU was not a realistic option. As a concession, the EU frequently has accepted formal compliance rather than active implementation as satisfying the conditions for membership.

A basic tension exists between the EU's efforts to promote democracy inside member states and its desire to obtain compliance with its own substantive rules and ways of operation. David Cameron (2002) puts it well: "It does not exaggerate greatly to say that, upon accession, the new members will be recreated as states, committed to processes of policy making and policy outcomes that in many instances bear little or no relation to their domestic policy making processes and prior policy decisions but reflect, instead, the politics, policy-making processes, and policy choices of the EU and its earlier member states." Nevertheless, such tensions are not apparent in the Commission's documents, which point to delays but no fundamental disagreements (Commission of the European Communities 2003a, 2003b). Within the new member states some politicians, bureaucrats, and interest groups embrace EU requirements to further their own

batch of new members (Bailey and de Propris 2004, Carius et al. 2000: 145, 155). See Schimmelfennig et al. (2003) for case studies.

[55] Some examples come from the environmental area. See Caddy (2000), Carius et al. (2000:167–175), and Żylicz and Holzinger (2000).

goals over and above accession per se, while others conform reluctantly and seek to delay effective implementation.

Political Will and Authority: Subsidiarity and Delegation

The principle of subsidiarity, incorporated in the Treaty of Amsterdam, requires that EU policies be carried out by the lowest level of government or institution consistent with avoiding spillovers.[56] There is a presumption in favor of member state or even local and regional government implementation. The presumption can be overcome by a showing that such bodies are not competent or will not take all the relevant interests into account. If applied consistently, the subsidiarity principle means that, when the EU acts, it does so only after having concluded that other governments or institutions would do an inadequate job. It also implies that, even when the EU legislates, it will leave many implementation decisions to member states. EU legislation does not generally differentiate between states on the basis of their capacity.

The subsidiarity principle, meant to give the EU added legitimacy, can undermine its authority and its will to serve as a goad to reform in the accession states. In states with weak legislative and government institutions, open-ended delegation to member states may simply mean that certain directives are poorly implemented. To the extent that this becomes a problem, the weak response of some member states in turn will undermine the force of EU law as members see others abusing the discretion built into the system.[57] Compliance with EU law could unravel with even states that complied in the past refusing to comply because of the lack of cooperation by others.[58] This contrasts with the virtuous cycle

---

[56] Protocol on the Application of the Principles of Subsidiarity and Proportionality, 1997 OJ (C 340) 105. The treaty puts the burden on the EU to justify the need for legislation under these principles (Føllesdal 2000; Lindseth 2001: 162).

[57] Bignami (2003) claims that "existing regulators do not have faith in the capacity of East European regulators to administer the *acquis communautaire.*" The relatively weak judicial systems in the accession countries may make the threat of legally imposed damages of less concern in the accession states. However, the accession treaties "authorize member states to take measures . . . in response to any shortcoming in the implementation of the *acquis*" during the first 3 years after admission (Bignami 2003).

[58] Carius et al. (2000: 149) worry "that a merely partial implementation and/or enforcement of Community legislation in the accession countries could have the knock-on effect of further reducing the willingness of current member states to effectively implement European environmental law." According to Bignami (2003): "The shift from strategies of power to strategies for cooperation will not be easy." She also worries about a "defect-defect" equilibrium.

that many hope for in the new members and claim to see in the history of the EU up to the present (Pridham 2002; Stone Sweet 2003).

Some commentators urge even more delegation to member states (Commission of the European Communities 2001c), and the EU encourages delegation within member states to regions and local governments. If this trend continues, the expectation that EU membership will constrain domestic politicians will not be fulfilled. Instead, issues decided at the EU level will simply be put back on the agenda of member states or even of subnational governments. Budget-strapped states may give these tasks low priority, and, if the EU becomes more decentralized, Brussels will have little leverage. For example, consider the Czech Republic, a small state the size of a region in some of the larger members. Having separated from Slovakia in 1992, its leaders worry that too much devolution to regions will encourage Moravian nationalism and will lead to inefficient service delivery (Marek and Baun 2002). This seems to be a paradoxical case in which the EU's commitment to subsidiarity leads it to centralize to itself the question of how much devolution should occur within the new members.

The tension in EU policy between centralized control and subsidiarity is highlighted in a study of EU agricultural and rural development policy (Nemes 2003). According to this study, the EU is losing an opportunity to induce central governments to decentralize decision making and is concentrating on keeping program administration simple and centralized. Ensuring financial and bureaucratic accountability to Brussels is trumping a more nuanced view of how agricultural and rural policy actually might benefit struggling farmers and impoverished rural families. The SIPARD[59] program is decentralized but only to the level of CEE central governments. The program keeps "extremely tight control on lower (regional, local) levels," depriving them of any independent power (Nemes 2003: 6). This makes it easier to avoid the misuse of funds, but it also limits experimentation. As one Hungarian official stated in an interview, "[The EU] did not want offices with people working in them. They intended to eliminate human decisions in the process; [they] wanted to have a huge living computer, made up of people, buildings, and machines." This quote and the frustration it evinces highlight the tension inherent in the accession process for member states with relatively weak institutions. In this case, EU policy was tailored to fit these weaknesses but in the process did

---

[59] SIPARD stands for Pre-accession Special Instrument for Agriculture and Rural Development.

nothing to improve domestic democratic accountability and produced programs that were easy to monitor but apparently were not effective responses to local problems.

Under the political-will-and-authority conditions, the EU's relationship with the states in CEE suffers from two contrasting problems. First, to the extent it pushes for decentralization, it undermines its own leverage as a spur to reform. Second, when it insists on centralized national control in EU program administration, it tends to impose rigid requirements that are just the reverse of its own stated commitment to experimentation and locally tailored solutions.

Legitimacy: The Democratic Deficit of the EU

In the new member states, the EU acts as an independent check on self-seeking domestic politicians by spurring the passage of legislation required of members. However, the willingness of democratic states to comply with EU law will depend, in part, on the legitimacy and accountability of the EU's processes.[60] At the EU level, the problem of balancing narrow versus general interests reappears. A debate about EU governance is going on at the same time as the EU is requiring the accession states to bring their laws into compliance with its requirements. The less legitimacy EU law has within the EU, the more difficult it will be to convince the citizens of accession states to accept its strictures. The legitimacy of the EU "depends on national institutions for its democratic linkage to the peoples of Europe . . . [However, it] seeks to constrain . . . the propensity of nation states to parochialism and self-interest. . . ." (Lindseth 2001: 148).

In the run up to accession, the applicant countries had no choice but to pass laws implementing EU law. The EU had considerable leverage because it could negotiate more or less favorable terms with applicant countries and fail to admit a country. This had nothing to do with the formal character of EU law but depended only on the bargaining power of the EU over applicant states that feared being left out. However, going forward, the leverage of Brussels is much reduced. Citizens can be expected to resist directives and regulations that their politicians oppose. This can be a serious problem, because the enforcement capacity of the EU is weak against member state resistance. For all the talk about meddling Eurocrats, the bureaucracy of the EU is small and not very

---

[60] See Joerges (2001), Joerges and Dehousse (2002), and the papers in Eriksen and Fossum (2000).

powerful on its own, and the compliance budget of the Commission is very limited.[61] The extension of qualified majority voting in the Council to more issues may set the stage for enforcement problems down the line, especially because the new members are unable to form a blocking coalition on their own for issues decided by a qualified majority (Heinemann 2002). Even if the legislative mandate of the parliament is increased, it is not obvious that this will enhance the acceptability of EU legislation in countries with small populations. People may believe in majority rule within their own country but not be willing to accept it at the level of the EU. However, alternative more consensual processes invite deadlock.

The Commission makes many important decisions in the drafting and implementation of EU law. On the one hand, some criticize the Commission for being an insular bureaucracy. On the other hand, to the extent it does consult with outsiders, others criticize it for being the captive of interest groups and member state officials. The commission's relatively low budget and staffing levels, along with member state pressure, have led it to offload tasks to committees of member state experts and bureaucrats (the so-called "comitology" system). The process was developed to bring member state officials and interest group representatives into Commission policy making while still retaining the Commission as agenda setter and manager of the process. Whether this represents a welcome openness to the concerns of the public and the member states or capture by organized groups with narrow agendas is at the heart of the debate over the Commission's processes.[62]

In addition to the organized comitology processes, other more informal lobbying occurs. Michael Gorges (1996: 39–43) calls this U.S.-style

---

[61] As Heinemann (2002: 23) points out, if 12 countries join (including Bulgaria and Romania) the number of countries will increase by 80%, the population by 28%, and the budget, fixed at 1.27% of EU GDP, by 4.5%. This will put considerable pressure on the capacity of the EU to engage in oversight, especially because even this small budget is spent mostly on agricultural benefits and structural funds.

[62] See Frost (2003: 94), Gorges (1996: 23–30), Joerges and Neyer (1997), and Lindseth (2001: 149). The system grew up informally but was formalized by the EC Treaty (article 202). Under a 1999 council decision, the committees' norms are subject to oversight by the Council of Ministers (Council Decision 1999/468/EC, replacing 1987/373/EEC). In particular areas, interstate negotiations frequently occur. For example, in the area of broadcast regulation, "a committee of national broadcast regulators regularly confers and hammers out the differences that surface in the application of Directive 89/552/EEC (May 1995, as amended by Directive 97/36/EC)" (Bignami 2003). The committee is chaired by the Commission, but its representative has no vote.

lobbying and argues that the Commission, with its small staff, dislikes such lobbying, preferring to deal with already organized peak associations of interests. This preference disadvantages those interests that are not well represented by such associations. EU enlargement may exacerbate this preference; as more groups seek access, the Commission may push for more consolidation (Gorges 1996: 196).

I discuss the official preference for organized consultation more fully when I confront the details of the Hungarian and Polish cases in later chapters. It is a feature not just of Commission officials but of European public officials in general. Part of the explanation for this preference may simply be a desire to conserve time and energy. A more principled claim is that organized groups better represent affected interests than less established groups and individuals. Hence, some presume that procedures requiring opposed groups to confront each other face to face are the best way for officials to weigh conflicting concerns. Later, I argue against a strong form of this presumption.

In spite of Commission resistance, some large enterprises attempt to influence rule making on their own or in concert with other large firms, because they believe the official business associations do not represent their interests well. According to Gorges, such efforts to influence Commission bureaucrats are more legitimate in the EU than in the U.S. Congress, because EU officials are not elected and thus have no need to attract campaign funds (Gorges 1996). He argued that the lack of democratic pressures enhances the legitimacy of Commission decisions. Nevertheless, he is concerned about officials leaving their posts for positions in the industries they regulate.

The Commission (Commission of the European Communities 2001c) dealt with these questions in a White Paper on Governance that has generated a good deal of reflection over the accountability of the EU and its relationship to EU citizens and organized groups.[63] The debate over competence and accountability has become particularly sharp in recent years with the downfall of the Commission headed by Jaques Santer in 1999 amid allegations of impropriety and with the EU's uncertain response to issues relating to food safety (Buonanno, Zablotney, and Keefer 2001). On one side are those who urge the creation of more independent, expert regulatory agencies in areas such as transport, food safety, and telecommunications. They point to the current system's lack of transparency and

---

[63] See, for example, Armstrong (2002) and the papers prepared for Joerges, Mény, and Weiler (2001).

accountability and to the way it confuses scientific expertise and member
state politics (Majone 2001).

Others, in contrast, criticize the Commission's lack of rules to guide
participation and urge greater political accountability rather than more
deference to experts (Joerges and Vos 1999; Kohler-Koch 2001). Recent
improvements in the openness and transparency of EU procedures, however, will have little impact on democratic legitimacy unless they include
increased routes for public participation in policy formation (Frost 2003:
89, 98–99, 101). At present, no participation rights exist in the formulation
either of statutes or of Commission rules, and some commentators argue
that closed processes are needed to permit successful interstate bargaining. Some view greater democratic accountability as harmful. Yet, unless
citizens of member states, including the newest members, believe the EU
is exercising legitimate power, it will have difficulty getting support for reforms within member states, especially those that demand greater democratic accountability. Although supporting greater openness and transparency, Peter Lindseth (2001, 2002) argues that, as a practical matter,
nation states retain democratic legitimacy in people's minds that the EU
lacks. More participatory administrative procedures cannot substitute for
the fact that the EU basically depends on member states. Lindseth argued that a major reason to promote greater transparency in EU decision
making is to facilitate legislative oversight of the government inside member states. All commentators agree, however, that the current system is
flawed.[64]

The issue of democratic legitimacy is particularly relevant in the labor-
management area because the treaty permits an alternative process for
making binding rules. The EU can establish directives in labor law through
a process that involves the Commission and the social partners (representing management and labor) that negotiate the language of directives.
The Council, voting by qualified majority, must then approve the directive. The parliament plays no role.[65] This process and other Commission
efforts to include the social partners have been buttressed by a group
of scholars who urge more experimentation both in the EU and in its

---

[64] The creation of an agency for food safety illustrates the nature of the discussion. The new
agency, whose weak mandate is limited to providing advice and information, satisfied
none of the critics (Buonanno et al. 2001).

[65] Bernard (2000); Gorges (1996: 152–162). The Treaty on European Union negotiated at
Maastricht includes a Protocol on Social Policy that includes the details of the process in
the Social Chapter.

member states.[66] Although the process has not been used much (Mosher and Trubeck 2003), it challenges the view of the EU as a democratic polity. In spite of the need for both Commission and Council involvement, such directives are more like a contract between labor and management than a statute. They raise obvious problems about the representative nature of the participants. An EU court upheld a directive issued through this process, but at the same time flagged the issue of representation as one it would consider in deciding future cases.[67] In particular, coalitions of unions represent labor; yet, the share of the workforce that is a member of a union varies widely across the member states from very high levels in most of Scandinavia to a low of 10% in France. Furthermore, labor unions do not always agree on the value of participation or on how to structure their participation (Gorges 1996: 76, 100, 103).

The debate over the democratic legitimacy of the EU mirrors debates at the national level that are being played out in the new democracies of CEE. One can view both the EU and the countries of CEE as consolidating democracies where many basic structures are new and untried and subject to debate. The more problematic are the EU's processes; the less moral authority it has as a goal to reform in the new member states (Cameron 2002). During the accession process, the Commission was able to get what it wanted in terms of formal law because it had a bargaining advantage over the new entrants. However, over time this advantage will be lost, and the EU will need to convince the citizens of the new member states that its rules have been produced by a process that deserves respect. Then, even if some disagree with the substance of particular rules, they will go along with their domestic enforcement. Only then can the EU spur internal reform. At present, it can make no strong claims to greater public accountability than domestic legislatures even in the newly democratic states.

---

[66] See, for example, Mosher and Trubeck's (2003) assessment of the European Employment Strategy and Dorf and Sabel (1998).

[67] EC Treaty articles 136–145 (old numbers 117–122). The decision by the Court of First Instance in 1998 upheld the legality of a particular directive but held that, because the parliament was not involved in promulgating the directive, the Commission and the Council must verify that the signatories are truly representative. Bercusson (1999) critiqued the decision, arguing that a process based on social dialogue should be viewed not as a legislative process but as analogous to a collective bargaining agreement. The case is T-135/96, Union Européenne de l'Artisanat et des Petites et Moyennes Entreprises v. Council of the European Union (1998) ECR II-2335.

Conclusions

Politicians in CEE cannot simply defer to EU requirements as a substitute for designing home-grown reforms. Internal struggles at the EU are likely to interact with domestic politics within the new member states to limit the role of the EU as an external guarantor of reform. Part of the problem goes to the content of the rules, which are not above criticism as responses to policy problems. My emphasis, however, is on the EU's conflicting emphases on devolution and centralized control and on its limited democratic legitimacy. Neither the political-will-and-authority condition nor the legitimacy condition is consistently met in the legal requirements the EU imposes on new member states.

The more the EU supports decentralization and adaptation to local conditions, the less it can act as a spur to member states to improve their own policy-making processes. Furthermore, some evidence suggests that when it does exercise centralized control – for example, over the spending of subsidies – the EU acts in a heavy-handed and rigid way that stifles innovation. Thus, the EU exercises too little leverage in some cases and imposes too many constraints in others.

The EU, because of its lack of democratic legitimacy, may be undermining some of the popular support for EU membership. Its role in increasing the democratic accountability of new member states, such as Poland and Hungary, is limited because it cannot rely on its own democratic credentials as a justification for member state compliance.

If Hungary and Poland delegate most policy making to the EU, they will fail to create enduring democratic structures at home. If they adopt the EU's recommendations for public participation and openness at home, they will miss a chance to think through these issues themselves. The remaining chapters describe and evaluate the choices Hungary and Poland have made as part of their efforts to consolidate democracy. Because the EU's criteria for ensuring government accountability are not above criticism, I take an independent look at the choices being made by Hungary and Poland and assess them on their own merits and not just as a response to pressure from the EU.

FIVE

Oversight

Hungary and Poland have a full complement of public institutions that oversee government behavior. None of these is unique to the countries of Central and Eastern Europe (CEE), and the offices are frequently part of regional and global associations that set standards of behavior. Some are playing distinctive roles in the transition process and have had a pivotal impact on democratic consolidation. This chapter reviews Hungarian and Polish experience with these institutions. It argues that, valuable as these institutions are in upholding the rule of law, they are not sufficient to ensure policy-making accountability. Their role is mostly to enhance performance accountability. In other words, they help keep the government operating within the law – both statutes and the constitution – but they are not well designed to monitor policy making.

I consider six key institutions: the presidency, the constitutional court,[68] administrative and ordinary courts, the ombudsman, the procuracy, and the supreme audit office. They are interconnected so that the clout of one may be weakened because it needs to work through another. These offices have a range of direct and indirect links to the general public. In some cases, citizens can petition them directly; in other cases, popular control is indirect through parliamentary oversight. They vary in their independence from the legislature and the government and in their authority to make decisions that bind the government.

---

[68] Hungary has a Constitutional Court, and Poland has a Constitutional Tribunal. These are merely differences in terminology. In both cases, they are specialized courts dealing only with constitutional matters.

Table 5.1 summarizes the legal status and role of these institutions and summarizes the selection processes and terms of office of their chief officials. The table highlights each institution's degree of independence from the government and its interrelationships with other offices. The table begins with legislative bodies, not because I study them directly, but because they play important roles in appointments and consultation. Whenever one body has a formal link with another, the name of the second institution is highlighted in bold. One can see in Table 5.1 that most of the top officials have terms of office and appointment processes that give them some independence. Most institutions have constitutional status so that a parliamentary majority cannot eliminate them if they become inconvenient; the terms of their top officials are usually longer than a parliamentary session so they generally serve during at least two governments.

The legal status of these institutions is only the first step toward understanding their role. In addition to cataloguing their legal position in the system of government, I conducted open-ended interviews in the fall of 2002 with present and former ombudsmen, constitutional court justices, heads of the supreme audit offices, an official in the office of the Hungarian President, and the President of the Polish Administrative Court. I supplemented the interviews with additional legal and scholarly documents.

The Presidency

The Polish President is directly elected, which gives him some degree of popular legitimacy. In Hungary, Parliament chooses the president, who has few powers. In both countries the presidents play an oversight role. They can refer doubtful statutes to the nation's constitutional court for a ruling before signing them into law.[69]

Poland

The Polish presidency arose from a compromise between the communists and Solidarity in 1989 that initially left the presidency in the hands of the

---

[69] Ludwikowski (1998: 42–47) provides a table that summarizes the powers of the president in the constitutions of most of the countries of CEE. See also the collection of essays on postcommunist presidents by Taras (1997), including the essays on Poland by Jasiewicz (1997) and on Hungary by O'Neil (1997).

Table 5.1. *Institutions for Accountability: Poland and Hungary*

Institution	Poland	Hungary
Parliament (Sejm in Poland)	Yes (constitutional status) Direct election, 4-year term	Yes (constitutional status) Direct election, 4-year term
Senate	Yes (constitutional status) Direct election, 4-year term (simultaneous with Sejm)	No
President Selection method	Yes (constitutional status) Direct election with runoff of top two if no one obtains more than 50% of vote	Yes (constitutional status) Secret ballot in **Parliament**, winner must get 2/3 support in either of first two rounds or win in a runoff of top two after second ballot
Term	5 years, one reelection	5 years, one reelection
Executive powers	Some in foreign and military affairs with concurrence of ministers; other mostly ceremonial tasks	Mainly ceremonial
Legislative powers	Veto power with 3/5 vote in **Sejm** to override	Veto power with 2/3 vote in **Parliament** to override. Can refer laws back to **Parliament** for reconsideration
Referrals to Constitutional Court and other institutions	Can ask **Constitutional Tribunal** to rule on constitutionality of a statute before it goes into effect. Can request **Supreme Chamber of Control** to carry out an audit	Can ask **Constitutional Court** to rule on constitutionality of a statute before it goes into effect
Appointment authority	Appoints prime minister subject to **Sejm** approval, presidents and vice presidents of **Constitutional Tribunal** and **Supreme Administrative Court** (both from justices' list), a part of the Broadcasting Council, and of the Council for Monetary Policy, etc.	Appoints president and vice president of National Bank, etc., but subject to prime minister's counter signature

(*continued*)

Table 5.1 *(continued)*

Institution	Poland	Hungary
Constitutional Tribunal/Court	Yes (constitutional status)	Yes (constitutional status)
Selection method of Justices	Nominated by any 50 members of the **Sejm** or by the **Sejm** Presidium. Selected by a majority vote of **Sejm**	Nominated by **parliamentary** committee with all parties represented. Selected by 2/3 vote of all members of **Parliament**
Number, term	15, 9 years (no renewal)	11, 9 years (one renewal)
Access	Limited list including the **president**, the **ombudsman,** president of the **Supreme Administrative Court, the general prosecutor,** the president of the **Supreme Chamber of Control**. Limited possibilities for individuals to claim a violation of their constitutional rights	Most types of review can be sought by anyone. Only **president** can seek review of statutes before they are signed
Role	Review government actions (statutes, regulations, etc.) for conformity with the constitution and with other acts that are higher in the constitutional hierarchy	Review government actions and inactions (statutes, decrees, enforcement actions, etc.) for conformity with the constitution
Administrative Court	Yes (constitutional status)	No
Selection of President	By **President** of the Republic of candidate proposed by judges of Supreme Administrative Court, 6-year term	
Organization	Since January 2004: 14 regional courts with appeal to Supreme Administrative Court	
Role	Review administrative adjudications for conformity with law. Review of local government enactments for conformity with the constitution and statutes	

Institution	Poland	Hungary
Ombudsman	Yes (Commissioner for Citizen's Rights. Several specialized ombudsmen established by statute. Table entries are for Commissioner for Citizen's Rights)	Yes (two with constitutional status; two specialized ones without. Material below refers to all four.)
Selection method	Majority vote of **Sejm** with approval by **Senate** (no involvement of president)	Nominated by **president** and appointed with 2/3 vote of all members of **Parliament** on a recommendation of the **president**
Term	5 years with one renewal	6 years with one renewal
Report to	**Sejm** and **Senate** with annual report	**Parliament** with annual report
Access	Anyone	Anyone
Functions	Investigate complaints of violations of rights and initiate investigations. Resolve cases by negotiation with government agencies or go to court. Can bring cases to the **Constitutional Tribunal**	Investigate complaints in their respective jurisdictions and initiate investigations. Resolve cases by negotiation with government agencies or can refer cases to the **prosecutor** or issue public reports
General Prosecutor	Yes (no constitutional status)	Yes (constitutional status)
Location of procuracy	Under Ministry of Justice	Independent
Selection method	Minister of Justice is the general prosecutor	Nominated by **president** with approval by **Parliament** with a simple majority of those present.
Term	Discretion of prime minister	6 years
Report to	Prime minister	**Parliament**
Function of procuracy	Prosecuting violations of the law, mostly criminal but also general oversight of legality	Ensure protection of rights and maintain constitutional order. Prosecute violations of the law, mostly criminal but also general authority to uphold the law.
President of the Supreme Chamber of Control State Audit Office	Yes (constitutional status)	Yes (constitutional status)

(continued)

Table 5.1 *(continued)*

Institution	Poland	Hungary
Selection method	Majority of **Sejm** with consent of **Senate**	Nominated by parliamentary committee, approved by 2/3 of the members of **Parliament**
Term	6 years, one renewal	12 years, one renewal
Report to	**Sejm**	**Parliament**
Function of Supreme Chamber of Control State Audit Office	Independent audit of government, budget review, topical investigations, advice to **Sejm**	Independent audit of government, budget review, topical investigations, advice to **Parliament**

Note: Interactions between the institutions included in the table are represented in bold. The table reflects the legal situation in mid-2004. This table summarizes the basic features of these institutions as they are relevant to the issue of government oversight. It does not include all the details of the constitutional texts and the laws establishing these bodies. Readers are referred to the Constitution of the Republic of Hungary (Hungary 1998) and the Constitution of the Republic of Poland (Poland 1997) as well as to the statutes that implement each of these institutions.

communists. A September 1990 constitutional amendment introduced direct election, and the election of Lech Wałęsa to the presidency in 1990 undermined the Roundtable compromise and produced pressures to limit the power of the office.[70] As a result, the Constitutional Act of 1992 reduced the president's power, but he was still authorized to veto statutes.[71] A two-thirds vote in the lower house of Parliament (Sejm) was necessary to override a veto. The Constitution of 1997 reduced the supermajority to three-fifths and included other limitations that give preference to the parliamentary system. Nevertheless, the potential for oversight remains.[72]

Features of the office give it some independence from the rest of the state. Direct election is the most obvious guarantee. Furthermore, the

---

[70] For background material see Arato (2000: 156, 204–205, 213–215, 224); Jasiewicz (1997); and Ludwikowski (1998: 35–38).

[71] See Ustawa konstytucyjna z dnia 17 października 1992 r. o wzajemnych stosunkach między władzą ustawodawczą i wykonawczą Rzeczypospolitej Polskiej oraz o samorządzie terytorialnym [Constitutional Act of October 17, 1992, on mutual relations between the legislative and the executive of the Republic of Poland and on territorial self-government], Dz. U. 1992, No. 84, Item 426 with amendments, article 18, section 3.

[72] At least half the deputies must be present for the vote to override the veto.

president holds office for 5 years, with one reelection possible. The term of the Sejm is 4 years so elections usually are not simultaneous. If no candidate wins a majority in the first round of voting, there is a runoff between the top two candidates (Polish Constitution articles 126–129). This ensures an incumbent with a popular mandate and may produce a winner backed by a political coalition different than that of the prime minister and the cabinet.

A president who opposes a particular statute has an alternative to a veto. He can appeal to the Constitutional Tribunal for a ruling on the constitutionality of a proposed statute. If the tribunal upholds it, the president must sign it.[73] Thus, the president has a special role in maintaining the constitution that is legitimized by his independent accountability to citizens through the electoral process. The president can be a conduit for raising constitutional objections that neither the government nor the Sejm is eager to bring to light (Salzberger and Voight 2002). For example, in 2002 the president asked the tribunal to review the constitutionality of a tax amnesty law, an issue the government would have preferred to keep out of the court.[74]

The president's role as an independent actor inside the state extends beyond the area of constitutional law. He has appointment authority with respect to judges and members of several national councils, including the National Council of Radio Broadcasting and Television. He can request the Supreme Chamber of Control to carry out an audit. (The entire list is available in Polish Constitution article 144, section 3.) In all cases, his role is indirect. He can either refer an issue to another body, such as the Constitutional Tribunal or the Supreme Chamber of Control, or appoint members of a body meant to be independent of the rest of the government.

---

[73] Polish Constitution article 122, section 5. The president thus has three distinct choices: sign the bill into law, veto it, or refer it to the tribunal. If the Sejm overrides the veto, the president cannot refer the bill to the Constitutional Tribunal. The president can also issue regulations if legally authorized by statute. However, most of his "official acts," including such regulations, must be countersigned by the prime minister or another minister who applies to the president (Garlicki 2002: 276). Statutes can give the president independent power to issue internal rules, which, however, are not part of "universally binding law." Thus, these powers do not seem to give the president appreciable independent authority (Polish Constitution article 144, section 3, point 29 and article 93; Galligan and Smilov 1999, 212–214).

[74] The decision, discussed below, is Judgment of November 20, 2002, K. 41/2002, Orzecznictwo Trybunału Konstytucyjnego Zbiór Urzędowy [OTK ZU] [The Official Collection of the Jurisprudence of the Constitutional Tribunal] 2002/6A, Item 83.

Although the Polish presidency arose during the negotiated transition as a way of satisfying the incumbent regime, its role has evolved since 1989. The president is mainly an independent monitor of other state actors. His or her legitimacy as a check on the rest of the state derives, in part, from direct election and from the 5-year term of office, both of which ensure some independence from the parliament and the governing coalition.

Hungary

In the transition to democracy, the old regime, which had a popular candidate in mind, wanted a strong, directly elected president. Some at the Roundtable talks, held after the Polish pattern, supported an implicit deal under which this candidate would become president with limited powers. Part of the deal was a direct election for president, which would take place before the new parliament was elected. However, the issue was not solved at the bargaining table, with some opposition groups opposing this part of the agreement. These groups organized a nonbinding referendum in the fall of 1989 that produced a narrow vote against a directly elected president. Instead, the constitutional text provides that Parliament elects the president by secret ballot for a 5-year term with one reelection. As in Poland, this is 1 year longer than the parliamentary electoral cycle. During the first two rounds of voting, a candidate wins if he or she obtains at least two-thirds of the votes of all members of Parliament. After that, the top two candidates enter a runoff (Hungarian Constitution articles 29–32). Although a candidate who is acceptable across the political spectrum can win on the first or second round, a majority government, which is determined to push its own candidate, ultimately can prevail. Using this selection method, the result turned out just the opposite of that anticipated by those seeking a directly elected president. Árpád Göncz, a member of one of the dissenting groups, was elected president by the new parliament in May 1990.[75]

Some early decisions of the Constitutional Court limited the president's authority,[76] but the office, nevertheless, retains one key responsibility. The president must sign all laws except those he considers constitutionally doubtful. The constitution instructs the president to refer those

[75] See Arato (2000: 78), Elster (1997), and O'Neil (1997). For more details on the roundtable negotiations see Bozóki (2002) and Tökés (1996).
[76] Sólyom (2000: 45–48); see, for example, Decision 48/1991 (IX.26), excerpted by Sólyom and Brunner (2000: 159–170).

statutes to the Constitutional Court for a ruling. Ordinary citizens have broad access to the court to challenge existing statutes, but only the president can keep a law from going into effect through a challenge before the law is signed. Through this route, the court has struck down several important legislative acts, and the legislature had to rewrite them (Brunner 2000: 79; Ludwikowski 1998: 42–43, 52; Hungarian Constitution article 26, section 4). Alternatively, the president can refer a doubtful statute back to parliament with a list of reasons for reconsideration (Hungarian Constitution article 26, sections 2, 3). If it passes again by a majority vote, the president must sign it unless he has constitutional objections.

In practice, presidents have been reluctant to make referrals to the Constitutional Court. President Göncz made eight referrals, seven between 1990 and 1994. The second President, Ferenc Mádl, has submitted seven statutes since taking office in August 2000. The court found constitutional failings in all the referrals, although not always the same ones identified by the president.[77] The 100% success rate, of course, suggests the two presidents' cautious attitudes.[78]

Conclusions

The presidency in both countries arose from negotiations over the transition. The presidents have essential, but relatively limited, oversight roles. In particular, they are the primary route to constitutional court review for statutes before they take effect. This role is especially important in Poland, where overall access to the court is more limited than it is in Hungary. Presidents also appoint or nominate other officers who need to be independent of the rest of the state. They can force the legislature to reconsider legislation but cannot prevent a highly popular initiative from going into effect. The main difference, from the point of view of oversight, is the greater popular legitimacy of Polish presidents stemming from their direct election. The presidents' ability to trigger constitutional court review, however, is only as important as that court's competence and legitimacy.

---

[77] The information is from a November 29, 2002, interview with Botond Bitsky, Head, Constitutional and Legal Department in the Office of the President, and from a July 26, 2004, e-mail to Katalin Füzer from Bitsky.

[78] The Hungarian President has a short list of additional responsibilities and appointment powers. The only one that seems important, however, is the right to appoint and dismiss the Chairman and Vice-Chairman of the National Bank (Hungarian Constitution article 30).

Constitutional Tribunals

Both Poland and Hungary have special tribunals that rule on the constitutionality of government actions and legislation. These tribunals are among the most active and independent in the region (Ludwikowski 1998: 51–63; Salzberger and Voight 2002; Schwartz 1999; Sólyom and Brunner 2000). They can review the constitutionality of statutes before they go into effect (abstract norm review) and judge constitutional issues that arise in the implementation of laws and regulations over time.

Poland

The communist government established a Constitutional Tribunal in 1986 in response to pressure from Solidarity and other groups. It was part of the effort by that government to enhance its legitimacy in the face of growing criticism. It was retained in the transition to democracy and subsequently obtained increased independence.

The 15 justices are elected to 9-year terms by a simple majority of the Sejm. The President of the Republic appoints the President and Vice President of the Constitutional Tribunal from a list proposed by the justices (Ludwikowski 1998: 52; Polish Constitution article 194). At first, the tribunal's decisions could be overruled by a two-thirds vote in Parliament, then under the control of the communists. The tribunal invoked provisions of the 1952 Constitution as well as unwritten *Rechtsstaat* principles to constrain the government. In a series of cases, it established basic restraints on the issuance of government decrees that paralleled those common in established democracies (Schwartz 1999: 201). For example, it ruled that agencies require explicit statutory authorization to issue decrees, cannot delegate authority to other bodies unless permitted by statute, and have to conform to all statutes (Brzeziński and Garlicki 1995: 13). Only in 1989 did the tribunal begin to review statutes; of the 60 statutes it reviewed between 1989 and 1994, it found 40 unconstitutional (Schwartz 1999: 201–202).

Review of the constitutionality of statutes is solely a matter for the Constitutional Tribunal, and under the 1997 Constitution its rulings are now final with no possibility of a legislative override. The tribunal provides oversight of the government. In dealing with the legacy of the socialist past, it has been especially sensitive to the problem of government overreaching. However, it cannot review the constitutionality of government regulations before they go into effect.

Only a limited number of institutions, including the President and the Ombudsman, can bring cases to the tribunal, but any court can request the tribunal to review the constitutionality of a law involved in an ongoing case (Polish Constitution articles 191 and 193). Citizens whose constitutional rights have been violated in very concrete ways, and who have exhausted their appeals in other courts, can also appeal to the Constitutional Tribunal (article 79). This is a more restrictive condition than in the Hungarian case discussed later, but it does open the door to cases involving individual rights. In recent years, individuals have filed about 200 cases per year under article 79, but the tribunal accepted only about 25 per year.[79]

In a 2002 case brought by the president, the tribunal held that the details of a law designed to manage a tax amnesty program were unconstitutional. The tribunal held that the imprecision and ambiguity of one part of the statute conflicted with article 2 of the constitution, which states that Poland is a democratic state ruled by law. The amnesty provisions violated sections requiring equality before the law and establishing a common duty to pay taxes (articles 32 and 84). Furthermore, the required property declarations impinge on the right to privacy (article 47) and do not satisfy the principle of proportionality.[80] Justice Mirosław Wyrzykowski, interviewed on December 5, 2002, emphasized the importance of the decision as an example of the tribunal providing an independent check on the government.

In another case involving a contested policy area, the tribunal in January 2004 voided a statute that created the National Health Fund, a special agency designed to administer a large public program to provide free health care to all citizens. However, the tribunal gave the Sejm until the end of 2004 to amend the law.[81] The statute's ambiguous language and its lack of control over public funds violated article 2 according to the justices. Article 68 of the constitution states that "everyone shall have the right to have his health protected" and that "equal access to health care services, financed from public funds, shall be ensured by public authorities to citizens, irrespective of their material situation." The tribunal judged

---

[79] See Polish Constitution articles 79, 188–191; Ludwikowski (1998: 61–62); Salzberger and Voight (2002); and Schwartz (1999: 202). Ewa Łętowska, a justice on the tribunal, reported that under article 79 the annual number of cases filed was 124 as of September 2003, 195 in 2002, 181 in 2001, and 200 in 2000. However, the tribunal reviews only 25–27 of these cases each year (e-mail from Łętowska, September 17, 2003).

[80] Judgment of November 20, 2002, K. 41/2002, OTK ZU 2002/6A, Item 83. The tribunal derived the principle of proportionality from Polish Constitution article 2. Maciej Kisilowski prepared the translation and summary of the case.

[81] Compare with Rose-Ackerman (1992: 70–78), who argues that in the United States the federal courts should strike down underfunded programs but give congress 2 to 3 years to amend the statute or appropriate funds.

the challenged law to be unconstitutional because it was an ineffective response to the constitutional requirement.[82]

These cases suggest that the tribunal is playing a proactive role in reviewing statutes. However, the importance of these rulings for the future depends on whether those entitled to bring cases – for example, the president and the ombudsman – act aggressively. The impact of these decisions also depends on how expansively the tribunal interprets the provision permitting individuals to bring suits if their rights or freedoms have been violated (article 79).

Hungary

In Hungary, the Constitutional Court was established in 1989, and the 11 justices took office in January 1990, 5 months before the first multiparty election for the legislature. Thus, it was a creation of the transition process and preceded electoral democracy. The Roundtable negotiators apparently agreed on a court because no group could be sure of consistently winning the elections and thus wanted some check on the behavior of incumbents (Boulanger 2002; Scheppele 1999, 2001). This also may explain the constitutional status of the president, the ombudsmen, and the audit office. Christian Boulanger's (2002) research shows that none of the negotiators knew much about the operation of constitutional courts. The institution was added to the amended constitution late in the Roundtable process on the basis of a proposal from the justice ministry. According to Géza Kilényi, a former justice of the Constitutional Court, the justice minister suggested establishing a Constitutional Court as early as 1987.[83] In other words, the last communist government, perhaps looking to the Polish model, considered establishing a court as a way to shore up its failing legitimacy. This made the opposition suspicious, fearing the court would be packed with old cadres. However, the drafters eventually accepted the idea and gave the court extensive competence including broad rights of citizen access (Hungarian Constitution article 32/A).

As in Poland, the appointment process provides some independence from day-to-day politics. A committee of the National Assembly consisting of one member of each group of parties represented in the assembly

---

[82] Judgment of January 7, 2004, K. 14/2003, OTK ZU 2004/1A, Item 1. Maciej Kisilowski translated and summarized the case. One of the justices dissented.

[83] Interview with Prof. Dr. Géza Kilényi, D.Sc., Professor, Pázmány Péter Catholic University, Budapest, former member of the Constitutional Court, December 18, 2002, Budapest. Katalin Füzér translated.

nominates justices for 9-year terms. They are elected by a two-thirds vote of the members of Parliament, a process that usually requires some input from opposition legislators. They can be reappointed for one term (Hungarian Constitution article 32/A; Salzberger and Voight 2002).

The constitutional provisions establishing the court are spelled out in the Law on the Constitutional Court (Act XXXII of 1989 as amended; Galligan, Langan, and Nicandrou 1998: 593, 609–616). The act gives the court competence to review the constitutionality of a broad range of government actions and inactions including government decrees. A constitutional case is the only way to challenge decrees, which are otherwise viewed as discretionary acts of the administration (Galligan et al. 1998: 429).

The court was very active in the early years of the new regime.[84] It began striking down laws even before the first democratic legislature had begun to sit. The court issued 1,326 judgments between 1990 and 1995 (Scheppele 2003). The court sees itself as the ultimate interpreter of the constitution. This led it to hold portions of many statutes unconstitutional, especially in the early years of the new regime. In all, 905 cases involved the review of national statutes and binding government regulations and decrees. In these cases, the court made 273 findings of unconstitutionality. As the transition began, it also ordered Parliament to pass laws in a number of areas required by the constitution (Scheppele 2003: 224).

Although the constitution can be amended by a two-thirds majority and the act governing the court by two-thirds of those members present (Hungarian Constitution article 24, section 3; article 32, section 6), no change in either law was made even when the governing coalition had sufficient votes. (The socialist/liberals governed with a 72% majority after coming to power in 1994.) Furthermore, most of the court's rulings were accepted even when they were very controversial (Boulanger 2002; Scheppele 1999, 2001, 2003).

Why were the courts' judgments accepted and usually complied with? One possibility is that the court resolved disputes about the constitutional framework that otherwise might have produced constitutional crises. The Hungarian Constitution is vague on many issues relating to the separation of powers, and the court has been especially important in resolving such disputes (Boulanger 2002). For example, the court's decision that the president was relatively weak compared with Parliament resolved an

---

[84] See Arato (2000: 202–203), Boulanger (2002), Ludwikowski (1998: 68), and Sólyom and Brunner (2000).

ambiguity in the text. In general, it has sided with the prime minister against assertions of power by the president (Schwartz 1999: 203–204; Brunner 2000: 79). However, this may have occurred simply because at times the prime minister and leading members of the court were political allies.

In the first years of the transition, the court frequently referred to principles of natural law that were not included in the constitutional text (Sólyom and Brunner 2000). This approach was heavily criticized, but by using abstract principles to decide cases, the court claimed to be above politics (Boulanger 2002). Such reasoning gave its decisions legitimacy in the eyes of elites for whom legality counted as a legitimating principle.[85]

Of particular interest are the constitutional provisions determining who may initiate which kinds of actions in the Hungarian Constitutional Court. Only political actors can seek review of bills before they are signed into law by the president, seek a judgment on the conformity of a treaty with domestic law, or ask for a constitutional interpretation (Brunner 2000: 78–79, 87–88; Hungarian Constitution articles 33–36, 51). At the opposite extreme, "anyone" can ask the court to rule on the constitutionality of "legal rules as well as other legal means of state control," adjudicate alleged violations of constitutional rights, and seek the elimination of an unconstitutional situation "manifesting itself in omission" (Hungarian Constitution article 1; article 21, section 2; articles 37–43; 48; 49; Brunner 2000: 79–86; Galligan et al. 1998: 609–610; Schwartz 1999: 203). Thus, in contrast to the U.S. model, the court is encouraged to resolve constitutional issues, not avoid them (Schwartz 1999: 198). These provisions give citizens and organized groups widespread access to the court to test the constitutionality of government actions without establishing a violation of their personal rights. For example, a group of law professors initiated an early case that struck down capital punishment (Schwartz 1999: 198). Other issues reached the court through petitions filed by friends and relatives of court staffers (Scheppele 1999, 2001). More recently, petitioners unsuccessfully asked the court to find that parliament had violated the constitution by failing to pass an antidiscrimination law [Decision 45/2000(XII.8) AB; Constitution Watch: Hungary 2001a: 21–22]. The widespread right to petition the court gave it enhanced

---

[85] A leading politician told Scheppele (2003) "we are a country of lawyers" in explaining to her why he would not oppose a court ruling that had just struck down his favorite new law. However, Andrew Arato (1994: 271–273) and András Sajó (1996: 31–41), a leading Hungarian constitutional law scholar, are critical of some of the court's decisions.

democratic legitimacy at a time when the rest of the state was struggling to become established (Scheppele 1999, 2001). Although most early petitions were from individuals, by the end of the 1990s petitions from organized groups were more common; these groups saw the court as an alternative way to promote their agendas.[86]

The large number of complaints led the court to impose some controls and to recommend legal changes. It may insist that plaintiffs exhaust appeals within the administration and in the civil courts before turning to the Constitutional Court. The court also may simply leave cases undecided. The U.S. Supreme Court rejects a large number of appeals by declining to review decisions of lower courts in spite of a request by one of the parties. In such cases, the decision of the lower court holds. Any part of the Supreme Court's docket not decided by the end of a court term must be reargued the next term. This practice gives the justices a strong incentive to resolve contested issues before they leave for the summer break. No such rules apply in Hungary. The court accepts all cases, and many remain on the docket for years.[87] Even during the period of high activity in the early transition years, the court avoided some types of constitutional issues. In particular, unless specific individual rights were at stake, it did not intervene to constrain government or parliamentary policy-making processes in the name of broader democratic values.[88]

For a variety of reasons, the court experienced an almost complete change in personnel in 1998 and 1999. Neither the left-leaning Prime Minister Gyula Horn, who left office in July 1998, nor the right-leaning Viktor Orbán, who took over in July 1998, was eager to reappoint Chief Justice László Sólyom and his allies, whose terms expired in November 1998. The justices were of two minds about reappointment, with some believing that a single, albeit somewhat longer, term would be optimal. The new chief justice, János Németh, is a legal positivist who rejects the use of natural law to decide cases. Some criticize the court's opinions as "ad-hoc, under-theorized, and result-oriented" (Boulanger 2002). Others, however, do not believe there has been a dramatic shift; by the end of Chief Justice Sólyom's term, the court no longer struck down many

---

[86] Personal correspondence from Kim Scheppele, September 3, 2003.

[87] See Boulanger (2002, note 12): "The 'action popularis' was basically a petition system which left the justices with broad discretion as to what they wanted to decide." Scheppele (2003, note 32) reports that the court would put petitions that it did not want to reach "at the bottom of a pile in someone's office, not formally rejecting it, but not exactly getting around to it either." Scheppele's observation is based on a period of time she spent at the court in the mid-1990s.

[88] This issue is discussed in Chapter 7.

statutes on constitutional grounds. One reason the change in personnel
was possible, however, was that the opposition still remembered its defeats at the hands of the court. Even if the court was no longer as activist
as in its early years, Parliament had no desire to prolong the justices in
power and appointed a new court (Scheppele 2001). Nevertheless, however one judges the decisions of the current court, it remains an important
institutional check that played a strong, if controversial, role in the early
years of the transition.

Conclusions

In both Poland and Hungary, the constitutional tribunals are a source
of independent review of some aspects of government activity. However,
three factors limit their role in providing government oversight. First, they
consider only violations of constitutional provisions and rights. Thus, they
are unlikely to claim wide jurisdiction over the administrative and policy-
making process. Second, in Poland access to the tribunal is quite limited.
In Hungary, access to the court is broad, but the court's refusal to decide
many petitions submitted to it means it can avoid controversial issues.
Third, the method of appointment may give the justices partisan agendas
of their own, especially in Poland, where election by a majority of the
Sejm can produce justices with the support only of the governing coalition. In Hungary, justices require broader support, but this can produce
deadlock and appointment of relatively weak candidates (Schwartz 1999:
199). Nevertheless, the constitutional courts have been essential to the
process of democratic consolidation and continue to be a source of external oversight. However, one should not expect them to be the primary
monitors of government policy-making activity.

Administrative and Ordinary Courts

Given the limited jurisdiction of constitutional courts, other courts provide day-to-day oversight of state actions. There are two models: one
represented by the United States and one by Germany. In the United
States, most courts have general jurisdiction and review administrative
law cases along with the rest of their case load. In Germany, a system
of administrative courts reviews only public law disputes. It is independent of the government and subject only to Constitutional Court checks
(Rose-Ackerman 1995: 12–13, 138–139). Poland has an administrative
court system that echoes the German model. In Hungary, legal challenges

to administrative actions are heard by the ordinary courts unless they raise constitutional issues.

Poland

Poland has had a Supreme Administrative Court since 1980.[89] It reviews individual administrative agency actions for conformity with law.[90] It interprets vague concepts in statutes and regulations and oversees the exercise of discretion. The court can invalidate an administrative action but only on the basis of its illegality (Wierzbowski 2003: 299–300). It does not issue injunctions or resolve substantive issues beyond a finding of illegality. For example, one can bring a case arguing that agency inaction violates the law. Even if the Administrative Court agrees with this claim, the agency still might withhold action.[91] Of course, sometimes a finding of illegality implies that some other action would satisfy legal requirements, but the court does not order that next step.

Those who have a legal interest can bring a case as well as prosecutors, the Ombudsman, and (on a limited basis) social organizations.[92] The court is open to hear citizens' complaints, but its constitutional mandate is only to resolve individual complaints of mistreatment and violations of rights by any level of government. It can also review legal regulations issued by local governments but has no such mandate with respect to national government decrees (Galligan and Smilov 1999: 214–219; Galligan et al. 1998:

---

[89] Much of the material in this section is based on an interview by the author with Roman Hauser, President of the Supreme Administrative Court (1992–2004), on December 4, 2002, Warsaw. Anna Horolets helped with translation. The court was created in 1980 and operates under a 1995 law that was amended in 2002 (Galligan and Smilov 1999: 214–217; Galligan et al. 1998: 89–90).

[90] Ustawa z dnia 25 lipca 2002 r. Prawo o ustroju sądów administracyjnych [Statute of July 25, 2002, The Law of the System of Administrative Courts], Dz. U. 2002, No. 153, Item 1269, article 1, section 1.

[91] The new statute of August 30, 2002, Prawo o postępowaniu przed sądami administracyjnymi [The Law of Proceedings before Administrative Courts], Dz. U. 2002, No. 153, Item 1270, with amendments, provides, however, that the court can give the agency a deadline for taking action (article 149), although there are no sanctions similar to those for contempt of court in U.S. law. An individual can call on the government body only to fulfill the judgment and then again complain to the court. The court can then impose a monetary penalty on the agency or even decide the case when the circumstances are "not in question" (article 154). The individual can also seek civil damages in ordinary court. These procedures are lengthy and seem not to be particularly effective.

[92] Prawo o postępowaniu przed sądami administracyjnymi [The Law of Proceedings before Administrative Courts], Dz. U. 2002, No. 153, Item 1270, article 50.

89–91). Thus, for the national government, the court is mostly concerned with performance accountability and not policy-making accountability.

Until a January 2004 reform, the court suffered from several weaknesses according to Roman Hauser, the President of the Court until 2004. It had only limited independence because the Minister of Justice oversaw the administration of the court and approved its annual budget requests. Although government agencies looked to the court for guidance in interpreting statutes, the court's structure made it impossible to resolve conflicts within the court. It consisted of a single layer of 300 judges sitting in panels of three (or seven on appeal). Hauser reported in a December 4, 2002, interview that he organized informal consultations, but there were no formal means of resolving conflicts or of obtaining a ruling with clear national impact. Constitutional questions can be referred to the Constitutional Tribunal, but they cover only a small number of issues. Substantial delays plague its work.[93] Its case load is large. In 1999, it received 55,000 complaints – one-third related to taxation. The next most numerous groups concerned customs, construction, and land development.[94]

The 2004 reforms created a second tier of 14 courts at the regional level and give oversight responsibility to the President of the Supreme Administrative Court. He oversees the budget, its execution, and personnel issues. Reform supporters expect delays to be cut and that about 10% of the total caseload will be appealed to the Supreme Administrative Court, thus permitting unified administrative law jurisprudence.[95] In short, the Administrative Court system can now play a more effective role in government oversight over and above resolving particular disputes. It remains to be seen whether and how well it will carry out this responsibility.

---

[93] The Court's Annual Report documents the growing backlog. Incoming complaints increased from 55,000 to almost 76,000 between 1999 and 2001, and the backlog increased from 53,500 to 70,000 (Poland, Naczelny Sąd Administracyny [Supreme Administrative Court] 2002: tables 1, 18).

[94] In 1999, the number of complaints from foreigners rose as did the number concerning veterans' benefits, social aid, and regulations of self-governing bodies. Danuta Frey, "Zdążyć z reformą" ["On time with reform"] *Rzeczpospolita*, March 24, 2000.

[95] Roman Hauser, "Sądownictwo administracyjne według projektu prezydenta" ["Administrative courts according to President's bill"], *Rzeczpospolita*, January 7, 2002. Ustawa z dnia 25 lipca 2002 r. Prawo o ustroju sądów administracyjnych [Statute of July 25, 2002, The Law of the System of Administrative Courts], Dz. U. 2002, No. 153, Item 1269, article 12 provides that "Ultimate supervision over the administrative activities of the administrative courts shall be exercised by the President of the Administrative Court." Article 14 gives him the right to present the projected budget of the court to the Sejm and he has "the power of the Minister of Finance" in the execution of the budget (translations by Maciej Kisilowski).

It seems likely that most of the disputes will continue to concern the accountability and legality of government performance and not the operation of policy-making processes.

Hungary

Hungary has no administrative courts, but, since 1991, individuals can appeal to ordinary courts for claimed violations of the law. The courts will not review decisions that fall within an agency's scope of discretion (Galligan and Smilov 1999: 118). According to former Constitutional Court Justice Kilényi, interviewed in December 2002, the ordinary courts do a poor job of dealing with public law issues, and reform is needed.[96] The head of a county administrative office, an official charged with overseeing the legality of local government actions, echoed this view. He complained that courts do not function well because they are overloaded and are not knowledgeable about public law. He gave the example of a case that has been in court for 3 years with no hope of a quick resolution.[97] Hungary, however, had a very active Constitutional Court in the early transition years, so this may have compensated for the lack of an administrative court system. However, the Constitutional Court is not as active in this area at present and in any case can review only constitutional issues. Thus, judicial review of administrative decisions seems weak and ineffective. Furthermore, as in Poland, to the extent that review occurs at all, the focus is on government performance in individual cases and not on policy-making accountability.

Conclusion

In both countries, courts can resolve administrative law issues that do not reach constitutional status. The extent to which these courts provide independent oversight depends on the method of selecting and promoting judges, on the budget of the judiciary, on the courts' jurisdiction and rules of standing, on the way lawyers are compensated for bringing cases, and on the benefits to plaintiffs from winning cases. In practice, the option of bringing a lawsuit appears to be a rather weak constraint on most administrative actions because the process is costly with long delays. This seems a particular problem in Hungary. In interviews with nonprofit activists in

---

[96] Interview with Kilényi.
[97] Interview with Ferenc Bércesi, head of the Administrative Office of Baranya County, December 3, 2002, Pécs. Conducted in Hungarian by Katalin Füzér. Obviously, Bércesi's remarks are somewhat self-serving, but his reports of delays are confirmed by other observers.

Hungary, many claimed to avoid court challenges because of the delay involved and a perception that the judges usually were not competent to deal with the public law issues that arise in a modern democracy. Thus, increased judicial review of administrative actions is not a viable option unless there are reforms in the operation of the judicial system. Poland has a separate administrative court system, but it has been plagued by delays, a narrow scope of review, and a dysfunctional organizational structure. January 2004 reforms should reduce these problems, resulting in a more effective administrative court system. However, the system remains focused on individual disputes between citizens and the state and not on resolving challenges to the democratic character of public decision making.

Ombudsmen

Although uncommon in the United States, ombudsmen and similar offices are a growing presence in the rest of the democratic world.[98] Through the International Ombudsman Institute and developments at the EU level and in the Council of Europe, national ombudsmen are part of an international community.[99] Ombudsman offices in CEE are now linked to the EU office through referrals from the European Ombudsman (European Ombudsman 2003: 228–229). According to the International Ombudsman Institute,

The role of the ombudsman is to protect the people against violation of rights, abuse of powers, error, negligence, unfair decisions and maladministration in order to improve public administration and make the government's actions more open and the government and its servants more accountable to members of the public.... A crucial foundation stone of the ombudsman office is the independence of the office from the executive/administrative branch of government.[100]

---

[98] Originating in Scandinavia, ombudsmen spread first to a number of commonwealth countries and then to the EU members and to many developing and transition countries under a variety of different names. The EU established an ombudsman's office in 1995 (see http://www.euro-ombudsman.eu.int/home/en/default.htm).

[99] In the period before joining the EU, the Council of Europe was an important forum for the discussion of common European issues because its membership includes countries in the East and the West. In September 1985, the Committee of Ministers of the Council of Europe recommended that member states consider appointing an ombudsman with the power to determine whether national laws meet international human rights norms [Recommendation No. R (85) 13, Zieliński 1994: 121]. Furthermore, the Council Secretariat monitors decisions of the European Court of Human Rights and the European Commission of Human Rights and informs member state ombudsmen (Zieliński 1994: 122).

[100] http://www.law.ualberta.ca/centres/ioi/eng/eng_home.html.

Thus, an ombudsman seems an archetypal example of performance accountability at work. In practice, ombudsmen are both a means for individuals to complain about their treatment by the state and a locus of broader reform proposals. Individual ombudsmen often have policy agendas they wish to further through investigations and the preparation of reports.

Individuals bring complaints to the ombudsman, who intercedes with the bureaucracy to solve problems on a voluntary basis. An ombudsman generally cannot make binding decisions but must negotiate with the bureaucracy. Ombudsmen also can be a route to judicial review of administrative decisions, but they frequently are a substitute for individual appeals to the courts. Given the limitations of direct appeals to the courts in CEE, ombudsmen provide a way to seek redress for alleged mistreatment by the government. However, their role as an interceder for individuals is not always consistent with their broader reform agendas. Resolving individual complaints can dampen support for systemic reform, and, in any case, resolving individual problems takes time and resources.

The Polish Ombudsman, established in 1987, is the oldest one in CEE and, with help from the United Nations Development Program, has taken a lead role in helping other countries in the region develop similar offices.[101] The growing professionalism and cross-border contacts of ombudsmen's offices in CEE help individual incumbents to resist local opposition to their gadfly role. Although the details of the office vary, the ombudsmen in both Hungary and Poland look to international models both as an inspiration for their offices and as a guide to interpreting their mandates to protect individual freedoms and rights in the face of public authority (Zieliński 1994: 126). My interviews with ombudsmen in Hungary and Poland indicate that the offices are quite strong in spite of the inherent limitations of such offices. In societies where people are not used to lodging complaints against authorities, their ability to initiate inquiries is important. They also can appeal directly to the courts or refer issues to the procuracy for criminal prosecution. Both have played important roles in challenging the constitutionality of government actions in court. However, in spite of their broad mandates, they spend most of their time and

---

[101] As part of that effort, the Polish Ombudsman published a compilation of laws in 1998 that covered 13 in Western Europe and 14 in CEE (Poland, Commissioner for Civil Rights Protection 1998; Zieliński 1994: 125). The clear implication of this publication is that ombudsmen are part of a pan-European institutional pattern.

budget on individual complaints. They do not have much time to spend on issues related to policy-making accountability.

Poland

The Commissioner for Citizens' Rights (Ombudsman) can act on his or her own initiative or respond to claims from individuals, citizen organizations, or local governments.[102] Four ombudsmen filled the office between 1988 and 2003.[103] The ombudsman is not an administrative officer and reports only to the Sejm and the Senate through an annual message. Appointment is by a majority vote of the Sejm with Senate approval for a 5-year period with one renewal permitted; the incumbent can be removed only for health reasons or violation of the oath.[104] Thus, an individual ombudsman is likely to serve during the tenure of at least two governments. However, an incumbent government is likely to be able to get its candidate approved because it needs only a simple majority in the Sejm. The popularly elected president is not involved in the selection process. The independence of the ombudsman thus depends not on any requirement for partisan balance but on the integrity of the individual incumbents.

Andrzej Zoll, the Commissioner for Citizens' Rights, interviewed on December 3, 2002, pointed to the need to balance the ombudsman's particular concern for the rights and liberties of citizens with his general mandate to report on the observance of the law in the country. In addition to individual cases, the ombudsman can direct general petitions to administrative bodies concerning citizens' rights. Unlike a court, the commissioner can initiate his or her own investigations and does so on a regular basis. Balancing this wide-ranging power of investigation is the fact that the commissioner cannot initiate enforcement or remedial actions. Nevertheless, he or she can "demand" that a civil case be initiated or that the prosecutor begin a proceeding and can appeal government

---

[102] Polish Constitution articles 208–212 and Ustawa z dnia 15 lipca 1987 r. o Rzeczniku Praw Obywatelskich [Statute of July 15, 1987, on the Commissioner for Citizens' Rights, consol. text Dz. U. 2001, No. 14, Item 147]. The original ombudsman was appointed early in the transition period in 1988 before full democracy was established and played an important symbolic role. See the English language summary of the Ombudsman's report to the Sejm and Senate for 2001 (Zoll 2002) as well as Arcimowicz (2001), Galligan et al. (1998: 91–92), Galligan and Smilov (1999: 220–221), Klich (1996), Łętowska (1996), and Świątkiewicz (2001).

[103] Klich (1996: 38) and author's interview with Ombudsman Andrzej Zoll, December 3, 2002, Warsaw.

[104] In the 1997 Constitution (article 209) the term was increased from 4 to 5 years, presumably to increase the independence of the ombudsman.

decisions to the administrative court.[105] The commissioner can issue reports to the public and the media, try to persuade public agencies to change their behavior, bring cases before the Constitutional Tribunal, and advise the Sejm on law reform or ask it to order the Supreme Chamber of Control to perform an audit.[106] Only the president can seek review of a statute by the tribunal before it goes into effect. However, the ombudsman can comment on a proposed law's constitutionality. In a recent case, Zoll reported that he urged the president to bring a challenge to a law, which ultimately was successful. Sometimes, however, he refrains from commenting at that stage to reserve his right to challenge a law after it has gone into effect.

Because the election of the ombudsman requires only a majority vote in the Sejm and because the government and the Sejm are under unitary political control, there is a danger that the ombudsman will be less independent than the constitution requires. But, in practice, the incumbents have managed to maintain independent reputations. The first ombudsman, appointed at the end of the socialist regime, ran into criticism from the members of Solidarity sitting in parliament who saw both her and her office as holdovers from the past, but she maintained her position, and the office, which had considerable popular support, remained. The independence of the ombudsman from politics became an issue during the term of the second ombudsman, Tadeusz Zieliński, when he became a candidate for president. The main result of this controversy was that the Sejm did not reappoint him. The office retained strong support in the media and among the public (Arcimowicz 2001).

The ombudsman must balance individual complaints with more systematic efforts to push government to reform. The office is inundated with petitions from individuals claiming a government official has treated them badly. The complaints center on individual grievances, and much of what the office does is refer complainants to other bodies for resolution. In 2001, the ombudsman received more than 55,000 letters, up 16% from the year before. According to Ombudsman Zoll, this caseload reflects weaknesses in the system of social aid for the poor and the excessive number of legal provisions that are constantly changing and are unclear even to public officials. Zoll points to the "immensity" of laws that

[105] See Ustawa z dnia 15 lipca 1987 r. o Rzeczniku Praw Obywatelskich [Statute of July 15, 1987, on the Commissioner for Citizens' Rights], consol. text Dz. U. 2001, No. 14, Item 147, article 14.

[106] For an overview of the work of the ombudsman see Zoll (2002).

serve only to further official incompetence and carelessness and to breed corruption. However, the ombudsman has difficulty resolving individual cases in favor of the complaining citizen. In 2001, of more than 15,000 cases that were finally resolved, 26% resulted in a settlement in favor of the complainant. The rest were dismissed because the complaints could not be substantiated or for other reasons such as the lapse of time between the filing of the complaint and the date of the alleged offense. Most cases involved social assistance, penal law, housing, property, labor, taxation, and consumers' rights. Zoll argues that one reason for the difficulty of resolving complaints satisfactorily is the weakness of the underlying laws, which are filled with an "avalanche of amendments" and are often poorly drafted. Thus, the complaints may have merit, but they cannot be solved on an individual level; they require amendments to statutes and decrees (Zoll 2002: 2–4 and statistical appendix).

Furthermore, the first ombudsman, Ewa Łętowska (1996: 4), claimed that citizens have an exaggerated view of the powers of the ombudsman. Many petitions are private grievances that cannot be resolved by that office. Some people refuse to accept defeat in one forum and appeal to the ombudsman, sometimes through a member of the Sejm (Zoll 2002: 11). In the early days of the office the media expected the ombudsman to be Robin Hood and were disappointed that it could not, for example, allocate housing or distribute social services (Łętowska 1996: 5). Citizens had little understanding of the principle of the separation of powers. The communist elite interpreted the 120,000 letters received in the first term of the office as evidence for the value of the office. In contrast, Łętowska (1996:6) argued that they show "the frustration and paternalistic demoralization of society, the result of shattered hopes, and a misunderstanding of the Commissioner's role."

Because responding to complaints is a central aspect of the ombudsman's mandate, it consumes much staff time and budget. However, a focus on individual complaints will not generate many structural reforms. Thus, from the beginning, the ombudsman has pushed for more systematic reforms, arguing that settling individual cases is not sufficient when the underlying problems are structural and require legal reforms (Łętowska 1996:7). Ombudsman Zieliński (1994: 41) criticized the processes by which laws and normative acts were promulgated. For example, he criticized the fact that customs regulations and tax and tariff exemptions were sometimes issued as internal bulletins or decisions not open to the public. The first two ombudsmen brought several complaints to the Constitutional Tribunal relating to such issues and won a number of important victories.

They also brought cases dealing with social rights and housing (Zieliński 1994: 41–44). Several ombudsmen have been concerned with prison conditions and with social and economic issues (Klich 1996: 50–54). Zoll has carried out a number of high-profile investigations in areas such as the rights of patients and the rights of crime victims. The office prepares reports and tries to "inspire citizens' organizations" to follow through to push for change (Zoll 2002: 9–10). It also works with citizens' organizations to help develop civic consciousness in the population and promotes government compliance with the Freedom of Information Act passed in 2001.[107] It tries to counteract what the ombudsman sees as feelings of "social helplessness." Thus, the office is trying to leverage its scarce staff time by becoming a catalyst for civil society initiatives (Zoll 2002: 2–4).

The ombudsman faces a tradeoff between the protection of individual citizens against individual bureaucratic decisions and the promotion of democratic consolidation through broader policy reform. In spite of the press of individual grievances, the ombudsman has succeeded in overturning several problematic central government rules and local laws and has been an important source of appeals to the Constitutional Tribunal for rulings on the constitutionality of general provisions in statutes or their administration.[108] In 2001, the ombudsman made 21 petitions to the tribunal alleging the incompatibility of legal provisions with parent legislation. He also petitioned the Supreme Court twice and appealed to the Administrative Court nine times (Zoll 2002).[109]

At the level of underlying values, Zoll referred to the ombudsman's role in furthering "a community of values, which have deep roots in the achievements of European civilization" (Zoll 2002: 11). He, at least, sees

---

[107] The official title of the Polish Freedom of Information Act is Ustawa z dnia 6 września 2001 o dostępie do informacji publicznej [Statute of September 6, 2001, on the access to public information], Dz. U. 2001, No. 112, Item 1198 with amendments.

[108] Interview with Zoll, Zieliński (1994), Galligan and Smilov (1999: 241–242), and an interview with departing Ombudsman Danuta Frey, "Staralem się przestrzegać apolityczności" ["I tried to remain apolitical"], *Rzeczpospolita*, May 9, 2000.

[109] In 2001, the Constitutional Tribunal ruled that a section of the law on rent was unconstitutional in a case initiated by the ombudsman (Constitution Watch: Poland 2001b: 35). The ombudsman successfully appealed to the Constitutional Tribunal about the unconstitutionality of part of the 1997 statute on real estate dealing with the payment of compensation to those relocated by World War II. Cases brought in late 2002 involved the government's right to abolish a local government, the government's suspension of civil service laws, and complaints about inadequate compensation for property taken by the USSR. The ombudsman also brought three gender discrimination challenges before the tribunal in 2000 that succeeded in ending unequal mandatory retirement ages for men and women (Constitution Watch: Poland 2001a: 32).

no deep cultural conflicts in the transplantation of the institution of the ombudsman to Poland. The main difference between the ombudsman in Poland and the office in a country such as Norway is the magnitude of the tasks that it faces in light of the relative newness of the transition to democracy. The evidence suggests that it is an important and popular office and that it has become a focal point for discontent with administration of the law and with substantive rules and regulations. It cannot, however, responsibly perform all the roles that have been put on its plate. Although increased resources would help, the structural problems are deeper and cannot be resolved through strengthening the office. Democratic consolidation requires other routes to public accountability beyond the case-oriented approach that remains the core of the ombudsman's mission.

Hungary

Hungary has four ombudsmen, called Parliamentary Commissioners, two who were established by constitutional amendment in 1993 (Hungarian Constitution article 32/B).[110] The established commissioners focus on civil rights, the rights of national and ethnic minorities, and data protection and freedom of information, respectively. There is also an ombudsman for education.[111] The president nominates the commissioners, and the parliament selects them with a two-thirds vote of the members for 6-year terms with one renewal possible. The governing statutes must obtain a two-thirds vote of those present for passage. The ombudsmen report annually to parliament.[112] Thus, the appointments process provides for more partisan balance than in Poland, but, as a result, the process can be contested and prolonged. For example, although the ombudsmen's offices were established in 1993, it was only in 1995 that candidates were found who could obtain the requisite two-thirds support. The procedure is complicated by the fact that the vote is a secret ballot, and a candidate who loses in one round cannot be renominated.

László Majtényi, the first Ombudsman for Data Protection and Freedom of Information, explained in a 2002 interview how he ran into trouble for challenging some decisions of the government.[113] He had "fierce disputes" with the Minister of Finance over the powers of the taxation

---

[110] Some of the material in this section is derived from a published interview with Katalin Gönczöl, the Civil Rights Ombudsman, by Kosztolányi (2001).

[111] See Commission of the European Communities (2001a: 15).

[112] The reports are available in English on the ombudsmen's web site: http://www.ombudsman.hu.

[113] Interview with author, October 14, 2002, Budapest.

authority, with the Ministry of the Interior over closed-loop camera surveillance, and with the secret services over illegal surveillance (Majtényi 2001b: 340). In May 2001, "influential members of three parties tried to abolish his office" (Majtényi 2001a: 174), and, when his term expired in June, Parliament did not reappoint him. That summer the president nominated new commissioners for civil rights and for ethnic and national minorities, and Parliament approved them, but the position of Data Protection Ombudsman remained vacant until the end of 2001 when parliament confirmed a person acceptable to both the government and the opposition. The new ombudsman has been less confrontational.[114]

In March 2001, the Constitutional Court found that some aspects of the statute governing the Parliamentary Commissioner for Civil Rights were unconstitutional [Decision 7/2001 (III.14)]. It judged that the portions that gave the ombudsman jurisdiction over governmental branches, juridical agencies (except for the courts), and other extrajudicial conflict-resolution bodies were not sufficiently clear. A fundamental problem was that the phrase "governmental branches" might be taken to include parliament, which would be against the separation of powers, but other phrases were judged too vague as well. This decision leaves the ombudsman with jurisdiction over administrative agencies, the armed forces and the police, intelligence agencies, and local governments (Constitution Watch: Hungary 2001b: 21–22).

Everyone has the right to approach the ombudsmen for help in the situations permitted by the implementing statutes. The ombudsmen have broad investigative authority and can "turn to anyone to ask for information and data, may pursue on-the-spot inspections, without having to give prior warning and examine documents."[115] They can begin legal proceedings, but they cannot impose penalties. They can, however, initiate "general or specific measures" to remedy violations of rights.

Because they depend on other parts of government to respond to their recommendations, they frequently use the press as a means of publicizing the problems they find within the public administration. They also use the results of investigative reporting by the press and civic society agitation to alert them to issues that should be put on their agendas. According to the former President of the Constitutional Court, the most important weapon of the Commissioner for Data Protection and Freedom of Information is

---

[114] Constitution Watch: Hungary 2001b: 22; http://www.ombudsman.hu. The work of this ombudsman with respect to freedom of information will be discussed later.

[115] Kosztolányi's interview with Gönczöl (2001).

publicity. Publicizing the commissioner's recommendation in a particular case can have an effect beyond that of protecting a particular individual. The commissioner's annual reports summarize all important cases and can act as a kind of "law report" even if they have no formal legal status (Sólyom 2001: 248).

Most of the ombudsmen's activities involve routine attempts to resolve individual complaints that are "rooted in the case at hand" (Sólyom 2001: 246). This leads to a large caseload. The Ombudsman for Civil and Political Rights reported that complaints were up 12% in 2000 over the previous year, with most lodged by nonprofit organizations and private persons. The biggest increases concerned the rule of law and legal safety (599 compared with 379), property rights (216 compared with 128), the right to the best possible physical and mental health (153 compared with 96), the right to a healthy environment, and the right to life and human dignity. The growth suggests an increased willingness and ability of the public to use the ombudsman's services. The Ombudsman for National and Ethnic Minorities had a caseload of 459 in 2000 up from 435 in 1999. About 65% concerned the Roma minority.[116]

If an ombudsman concludes that the problem is not the behavior of an official but lies in the underlying statute, he or she can recommend that legislation be revised, especially for laws that remain in force from the prior regime or for new laws that have been hurriedly drafted. The Commissioner for Civil Rights reported in mid-2001 that she had suggested the modification of 250 laws. Under the implementing statute, the Commissioner for Data Protection and Freedom of Information can review draft laws and propose new laws and amendments (Dix 2001: 335). The ombudsmen can give their opinions directly without the intermediation of the Constitutional Court (Sólyom 2001: 244–245).[117]

The ombudsmen can carry out their own investigations on issues of public importance. The Ombudsman for Civil Rights did this with respect to residential homes and institutions for the elderly, the destitute, and the disabled. Nevertheless, her office initiates only 5% of her caseload, and

---

[116] Commission of the European Communities (2001a: 15, 19, 22), http://www.ombudsman. hu.

[117] According to Sólyom (2001: 245), the General Ombudsman is in the small group of entities that can request a ruling on the constitutionality of a law before it has been promulgated. This competency is not, however, directly listed in the text of the constitution. He infers it from the general mandate in article 32/B(1) and cites a 1997 case in which the court, where he served as chief justice, permitted such a suit [Decision 52/1997 (X.14) AB, ABH 331].

they mostly involve efforts to further the interests of vulnerable populations with little ability to complain on their own. The Hungarian ombudsmen face the same tensions as the Polish ombudsman in balancing the resolution of individual complaints with broader policy initiatives.

Ombudsmen can make referrals to the Constitutional Court in the process of attempting to resolve citizens' complaints about their treatment under existing law. For example, in 2000 two ombudsmen asked the court to determine whether the constitutional right to social security included a right to housing [Decision 42/2000 (XI.8)]. The court was unwilling to assert that such a right existed (Constitution Watch: Hungary 2001a: 21). In another case, the Ombudsman for National and Ethnic Minorities won compensation for four Romani men who had been mistreated by the police and in a local court (Commission of the European Communities 2001a: 20). However, in contrast to Poland, direct access to the Constitutional Court to challenge existing statutes is open to all citizens. Thus, this aspect of the ombudsmen's role is less central than in Poland.

Conclusions

Ombudsmen in Poland and Hungary provide important routes for citizens to complain about their treatment by the regime in power. The international network of ombudsmen helps the incumbents to maintain their independence in spite of an appointments process that is embedded in politics. Nevertheless, ombudsmen are not capable of playing a primary role in ensuring policy-making accountability. They focus on the voluntary resolution of individual complaints against the government. This gives them a large caseload that emphasizes the fair administration of existing laws and rules – that is, performance accountability. Although the most active ombudsmen have initiated policy debates in areas of concern, that part of their mandate inevitably must take a back seat to the press of individual complaints. This means they mostly react to problems in the implementation of existing programs rather than trying to shape policy or commenting on proposed laws and rules. Of course, if an ombudsman sees a recurring problem in the complaints that are filed, he or she might suggest reforms. However, the bulk of the work will be reactive and individualized, not proactive and focused on larger policy issues.

The Procuracy (Public Prosecutor)

The prosecutor is partly a holdover from the socialist past and partly a reformed cadre of prosecutors. In the Soviet Union, the Communist

Party used the procuracy – a Prussian invention – to impose its will on the country. It was exported to the satellite states in Central Europe, including Hungary and Poland, after World War II. Although the institution's central role is the prosecution of crimes, including the prosecution of high-level officials, it also has a mandate to provide general supervision of legality. However, this is not an important aspect of its workload in either country.

Poland

Poland established a prosecutor's office in 1950 following the Soviet model (Świątkiewicz 2001: 29). Under the 1997 Constitution, the Polish procuracy lost constitutional status.[118] In the mid-1980s, it was reorganized as an agency supervised by the Minister of Justice who acts as the General Prosecutor.[119] The prosecutor retains general oversight functions such as "contesting before the courts unlawful administrative decisions; giving opinions on legislative drafts; requesting the change or annulment of unlawful resolutions of municipal governments or of unlawful ordinances of local branches of central administrative agencies...." (Czeszejko-Sochacki 1999: 91–95).[120] In spite of this seemingly broad authority, however, the prosecutor is mainly concerned with criminal cases, not oversight of the administration at any level of government.

Under the law enacted in 1985, which with numerous amendments is still in force, the Minister of Justice has almost unlimited power over the procuracy. He sets the agenda and can issue internal rules and guidelines.[121] Individual prosecutors are granted some independence by statute. Although they are subject to rules and orders issued by their superiors, they can object to any particular order and ask to be removed from a case

---

[118] The procuracy had constitutional status under the communist constitution and retained that status until 1997. See Konstytucja Polskiej Rzeczypospolitej Ludowej uchwalona przez Sejm Ustawodawczy w dniu 22 lipca 1952 r. [Constitution of the People's Republic of Poland enacted by Sejm on July 22, 1952], consol. text Dz. U. 1976, No. 7, Item 36 with amendment.

[119] See Ustawa z dnia 20 czerwca 1985 o prokuraturze [Statute of June 20, 1985 on procuracy], consol. text Dz. U. 2002, No. 21, Item 206, with amendments [hereafter Procuracy Act]. Article 1, section 2, of the Procuracy Act provides that the general prosecutor is the "chief organ of the procuracy" and that the Minister of Justice serves as the general prosecutor. Translation of this and subsequent provisions of the statute by Maciej Kisilowski.

[120] It can also file a motion with the administrative court seeking to have a local ordinance declared invalid (Procuracy Act article 5).

[121] Procuracy Act article 10.

where it applies.[122] This provision gives individuals the ability to avoid cases they believe are misguided but retains the ultimate authority of the Minister of Justice because he or she can simply reassign the case. Thus, because the Minister of Justice is a member of the cabinet, it seems unlikely that the procuracy could be an energetic monitor of central government actions even if it wanted to redirect its focus away from the enforcement of the criminal law. In particular, oversight of local and regional government is not a major concern of the procuracy unless there are alleged criminal law violations.

The lack of independence of the Polish prosecutor and its weak role in overseeing government actions give added importance to the ombudsman. European law distinguishes objective and subjective law. The prosecutor focuses on objective compliance with the law (that is, not considering the subject). In contrast, the ombudsman is specifically charged with "social justice from the point of view of the subject" (Świątkiewicz 2001: 29–30).

Hungary

In Hungary, under the first communist constitution of 1949, all powers to supervise legality were vested in a chief prosecutor elected by parliament and (since 1953) reporting to parliament, not the Minister of Justice. A 1972 law defined the tasks and competence of the prosecutor. These provisions remain in the current version of the constitution (Hungarian Constitution articles 51–53), and the procuracy's authority extends to offenses committed by high-level politicians. The procuracy also has the authority to supervise the legality of state and local governments (Law V/1972 as amended; law LXXX/1994; information on the procuracy is at http://www.mklu.hu). The president nominates the general prosecutor who then must be approved for a 6-year term by a majority of the members of parliament present at the session (Hungarian Constitution article 52, section 1; law LXXX/1994 article 14, section 2). Note that this method of selection requires less input from the opposition than the selection of Constitutional Court justices, the ombudsmen, or the President of the Audit Office. All of them must obtain a two-thirds vote of all members of parliament, not just those present at a particular session. The general prosecutor "shall answer to the Parliament and shall provide a report on his activities" (Hungarian Constitution article 52, section 2). In practice,

---

[122] Procuracy Act article 8.

the general prosecutor is mostly concerned with criminal law violations, but the constitution also gives him the responsibility to help ensure that everyone complies with the law (Hungarian Constitution article 51, section 3).

The constitutional position of the general prosecutor is much debated. He has played an independent role in highly political cases that involve allegations of wrongdoing by public figures and well-connected individuals. In one important scandal, the Tocsik Affair, the procuracy appears to have been important in keeping the case alive in 1997 until the change of government in 1998.[123] The regime that left power in 2002 tried to bring the prosecutor under the Minister of Justice but Parliament, where a two-thirds majority is required to make any change, rebuffed the effort.[124] In 2003–2004 the general prosecutor, appointed under the previous government, was at the center of a controversy for his failure to prosecute former officials of that government for wrongdoing. Supporters of the current government allege bias. Members of Parliament addressed questions to the prosecutor seeking explanations, and the prosecutor asked the Constitutional Court to rule on his rights and obligations. The decision of the Constitutional Court [3/2004 (II.17)] interpreted article 27 of the Constitution, which permits members of parliament to direct questions to other constitutionally established bodies, including the general prosecutor. The case raises the important issue of the relative independence of these bodies. Although it deals specifically with the general prosecutor, its reasoning seems to apply more broadly.

The decision held that members of Parliament can ask questions concerning anything under the jurisdiction of the general prosecutor, including questions about concrete cases. However, the general prosecutor can refuse to respond to certain inquiries if they violate his constitutional position. The general prosecutor is "an independent constitutional organ" and is not accountable to Parliament for concrete decisions in individual cases. The procuracy is not subordinate to Parliament and hence cannot be ordered by it to make or modify a decision in a concrete case.

---

[123] The details of the case are too complex and muddy to present here. For a sample of the extensive press reporting on the affair see "Court Acquits Lawyer Mart Tocsik at First Instance," *Hungarian News Agency (MITI)*, LEXIS, February 8, 1999; "Hungarian Supreme Court Tries Decade's Corruption Case," *BBC Worldwide Monitoring*, LEXIS, March 28, 2000; "Supreme Court Quashes Verdict in 1990s Privatization Scandal," *British Broadcasting Corporation*, LEXIS, April 14, 2000; "Hungary: Court Rules in 'Decade's Corruption Scandal," *BBC Worldwide Monitoring*, LEXIS, July 6, 2001; "Hungary: Solicitor Sentenced to Prison in High-Fee Mediation Case," *BBC Monitoring International Reports*, March 18, 2001.

[124] *Heti Világgazdaság*, June 22, 2002.

Nevertheless, the general prosecutor has public law responsibilities toward Parliament, including a duty to report and to appear before and answer questions of parliamentary committees. The court also held that the general prosecutor cannot be removed simply because the incumbent government has lost political trust in the incumbent.

This decision confirms the prosecutor's independence from the government in power. However, in spite of this affirmation of his position, the general prosecutor is not primarily engaged in oversight, and he concentrates on criminal violations of the law. The procuracy may file protests with administrative bodies, but only rarely can these be appealed to the courts. The prosecutor can also issue interventions and warnings, but these also seem weak tools without court intervention. Its role in bringing constitutional challenges is no greater than that of ordinary citizens, and in the implementation of the law in individual cases its jurisdiction overlaps with the ombudsmen. Thus, in practice, the general prosecutor's constitutional mandate to ensure that everyone complies with the law is not an important aspect of his work.[125] The institution is an ineffective means of overseeing the public administration (Szikinger 1999: 89–90).

Conclusions

The procuracy, a holdover from the communist past, plays an important role as a criminal prosecutor – including cases involving high-level officials. However, it is an unimportant check on bureaucratic and governmental competence in the ordinary run of cases. The ombudsmen are more important in resolving allegations of official unfairness, even though their role is mainly advisory. The procuracy is unsuited for providing general oversight of the administration under present day conditions. There is no interest in Poland and Hungary in reviving its role under socialism. In Hungary, it is one of several institutions with some independence from the governing coalition, but it seems poorly equiped to monitor government policy making.

Audit Offices

Both Poland and Hungary have external audit offices reporting to the parliament.[126] Such offices, on the order of the U.S. Government Accountability Office (GAO), are a ubiquitous feature of modern government

---

[125] Interview with Professor Antal Ádám, School of Law, University of Pécs, October 12, 2002, Pécs, conducted in Hungarian by Katalin Füzér.

[126] On Poland see http://www.nik.gov.pl; on Hungary consult, http://www.ekormanyzat.hu.

even in nondemocratic states. In many countries, they developed from purely financial control offices to organizations that evaluate the quality and efficiency of service delivery. They generally report to the legislature, sometimes to a committee chaired by an opposition politician.[127]

An international professional body, the International Organization of Supreme Audit Institutions, has 170 members. It was founded 50 years ago with 34 members (http://www.intosai.org). The audit offices in Poland and Hungary are members of this group, and the president of the Hungarian office was the Chair of the Governing Board of the international association in 2003. The Polish and Hungarian offices appear to have frequent high-level contacts with each other and to be on friendly terms.[128] These cross-national contacts can help the offices maintain independence and help them to argue for stronger control mechanisms as part of these countries' efforts to meet the standards of more established democracies and of the EU accession process. The discussion below is based, in part, on the author's December 5, 2002, interviews with Mirosław Sekuła, President, Supreme Chamber of Control in Poland, and Jacek Kolasiński, Vice-Director of the President's office, and on her January 9, 2003, interview with Árpád Kovács, President of the Hungarian State Audit Office.

Poland

In Poland, the Supreme Chamber of Control [SCC, Najwyższa Izba Kontroli (NIK) is the Polish name] dates from 1919, but its independence has varied over time. During much of the socialist period it was either replaced by a Ministry of State Control or lacked independence.

---

[127] The U.S. General Accounting Office, founded in 1921, reports to Congress. In 2004, its name was changed to the Government Accountability Office. See http:// www.gao.gov. See Supreme Audit Institutions (2001) for an overview of Audit Offices in CEE as well as case studies of this relationship in some industrialized countries. Westminster parliamentary systems commonly have a public accounts committee in the parliament chaired by a member of an opposition party and charged with oversight of public finances. An audit office, if one exists, reports to this committee. Westminster systems typically produce only two strong parties so the party chairing the public accounts committee is predetermined. This might be more controversial in a multiparty system using proportional representation.

[128] See Kovács and Lévai (2001). Officials at the Polish Supreme Chamber of Control put me in touch with their Hungarian counterparts. Árpád Kovács, President, Hungarian State Audit Office, spent half a year as an observer at the U.S. General Accounting Office in 1989. He is a civil engineer who worked on financial control of transport inside the Ministry of Postal Affairs and Transport of the socialist regime. Interview with Árpád Kovács, President, State Audit Office, January 9, 2003, Budapest.

However, in 1980 an act reestablished the SCC as an independent body reporting to the Sejm. In 1994, the Sejm passed legislation governing the SCC in the newly democratic state, and the body was incorporated into the 1997 constitution (Polish Constitution articles 202–207).[129]

The SCC reports to the Sejm, which also can order the SCC to perform audits of particular programs or agencies. Thus, a key issue is the independence of the Sejm from the government. Under socialism, the Sejm had little independence, but the issue remains even under the current democratic regime because the government is formed from a coalition of parliamentary parties. A decision of the Constitutional Tribunal describes the chamber as "suspended" between the Sejm and the government.[130]

The President of the Chamber serves a renewable, 6-year term and must be approved by a majority of the Sejm and not be rejected by the Senate (Polish Constitution article 205; Supreme Chamber of Control Act (SCCA) articles 13, 14, 16). The 6-year term means that most presidents serve during at least two governments. Other attempts to ensure independence are restrictions on outside employment and prohibitions on political party membership (Polish Constitution article 205, sections 2, 3; SCCA article 19). In an interview Miroslaw Sekuła, the President of the SCC, stressed both the SCC's professional independence and its strong relationship with the Sejm.[131] Nevertheless, like the Polish ombudsman, the selection process does not guarantee independence.

The incumbent in 2002 stressed his independence and probity, but critics in the government that came to power in 2001 believe he is biased because the previous government appointed him, and he has prepared several reports critical of government activities. Reflecting this controversy, an article published in 2004 in *Polityka*, a well-known weekly, criticized the SCC. The author agreed that careful oversight requires the office to be independent of the government. However, the author claims the SCC has recently become overly partisan and has gotten involved in the general

---

[129] The Chamber is specified in article 202, section 1 of the Polish Constitution as "the chief organ of state audit." It operates under Ustawa z dnia 23 grudnia 1994 r. o Najwyższej Izbie Kontroli [Statute of December 23, 1994, on the Supreme Chamber of Control], consol. text. Dz. U. 2001 No. 85, Item 937, with amendments (hereafter SCCA).

[130] Judgment of December 1, 1998, K. 21/98, OTK ZU 1998/7, Item 116, which also summarized the chamber's constitutional position. The term is from an article by Lech Garlicki (2002), a member of the tribunal at that time. The decision is excerpted in Poland, Constitutional Tribunal (1999: 269–276).

[131] Interview conducted by the author in Warsaw, December 5, 2002. An interview the same day with Jacek Kolasiński, at that time the Vice-director of the President's Office responsible for international relations, stressed the same themes.

political turmoil. The SCC responded by claiming to be professional and apolitical. Its spokesman argued that the SCC's leadership has a variety of party backgrounds and that staff hiring is competitive. The statement deplores the fact the "for a long time now, it has been a Polish specialty to ascribe political motives to nearly every activity of all institutions and to almost all statements. . . ." It goes on to claim that politicians are trying "to play out their own interests by manipulating the results of controls, searching in them for support of their claims."[132]

The chamber has considerable freedom to set its agenda consistent with its constitutional mandate. In addition to the Sejm, the President of the Republic and the Prime Minister can request audits, but they seldom do so.[133] The chamber can initiate audits and, according to the president, determines its own priorities within its broad jurisdiction (SCCA articles 2–6, Poland, Supreme Chamber of Control 2001b, 2002). The SCC supervises both the central government and lower level governments. Its jurisdiction extends to any body that uses funds from the central budget or the budget of a local government including businesses and other organizations under government contract or using government property (SCCA article 2). In general, it uses the criteria of "legality, thrift, efficacy and integrity."[134] It can request the Constitutional Tribunal to rule on the constitutionality of laws and regulations (SCCA article 11).

The Supreme Chamber of Control provides an annual review of the budget and also has a broader mandate to investigate systemic problems and recommend solutions to the Sejm, but its role is purely advisory. In 2001, it participated in the drafting of statutes including 106 meetings of parliamentary committees. It submitted 183 reports on audit findings and 136 legislative proposals. It also issued a comprehensive two-volume

---

[132] Janina Paradowska. "NIK się wikła" ["NIK gets embroiled"]. *Polityka.* February 11, 2004. The response of the SCC is: Małgorzata Pomianowska, Press Secretary of SCC, "Znowu musimy udowadniać, że nie jesteśmy wielbłądem" ("We have to prove again that we are not a camel"), http://www.nik.gov.pl/o_nik/rzecznik/sprostowania/artykul_polit_7.pdf. These articles were read and summarized for me by Aleksandra Sznajder. An example of the controversy is the SCC's criticism of the renegotiation of a gas agreement with Russia. See "Sabat, nie raport" ("Witches' sabbath, not a report."), *Gazeta Wyborcza,* May 7, 2004.

[133] The Sejm made seven requests in 2000, and the president and prime minister made none. Thus, the chamber is mostly left to set its own priorities (Poland, Supreme Chamber of Control 2001b: 11).

[134] However, the SCC does not audit local governments for "efficacy," and only audits the books of those doing business with the state for "legality and integrity" (SCCA article 5).

study on the risks of corruption that recommended ways to reorganize government service delivery, tax collection, and regulatory and law enforcement to reduce corrupt incentives (Poland, Supreme Chamber of Control 2002: 5, 16–17). Other recommendations require the Sejm to redraft many other substantive and general laws on public administration, and the new laws would need to be vigorously enforced. The low staffing levels for most Sejm committees limit the impact of the SCC over the legislative process. This fact makes the Sejm dependent on government expertise and on the parties in control (Poland, Supreme Chamber of Control 2001b: 54–55, 67).

Following a peer review in 2000–2001, the EU found the Chamber "trustworthy and professional" (Commission of the European Communities 2001b: 99).[135] The report pointed out where the chamber fell short of international audit standards – a critique that led to internal changes. In reporting on the planned reforms, the President of the Chamber stressed his organization's international contacts with associations of Chief Audit Offices and with counterparts in the EU accession countries. He stated that the SCC "continues its efforts to harmonize its audit methodologies with the international standards" including EU requirements (Poland, Supreme Chamber of Control 2002: 18, also 20–21). The SCC sees itself as part of an international community of audit agencies, participates in international meetings, and embraces international standards as a goal.

The main weakness of the chamber stems from its very independence. It has few tools of its own to force bodies to open their books and to ensure changes in government practices. Sometimes those subject to audit refuse to cooperate. If the chamber finds irregularities, it requires the offending agency to inform the chamber of the steps it will take to remedy the problem. Often these replies are not very comprehensive, and failure to comply usually has no costs for the agency.[136] In principle, the chamber can take an agency or its officials to court, but this is not usually done. Between 1995 and 2002, the SCC made only 21 appeals to the courts at the same time as it carried out 32,000 controls. Some urge an expansion of

---

[135] The review was carried out by SIGMA (Support for Improvement of Governance and Management in Central and East European Countries), a joint initiative of the Organisation for Economic Co-operation and Development and the EU.

[136] Poland, Najwyższa Izba Kontroli [Supreme Chamber of Control] (2001a). See also Jerzy Pilczyński, "Korupcja jak trąd" ["Corruption like leprosy"], *Rzeczpospolita*, February 18, 2002, arguing that the government and the legislature do not respond vigorously to the chamber's reports.

criminal penalties for failure to cooperate with audits, pointing to the low fines in force.[137] However, the lack of criminal liability for organizations and the difficulty of collecting evidence suggest the need for alternative strategies. In my interview, the President of the SCC stated that he does not view the agency as a law enforcement body helping the prosecutor. Rather it is an auditing and control body seeking to uncover weaknesses in the system of control and to correct them. This seems consistent with the international image of supreme audit agencies as independent watchdogs seeking to reform rather than to punish state actors.

One way to apply pressure to recalcitrant public agencies is through publicity. According to the 2001 Freedom of Information Act, documentation concerning the course and effects of control as well as the statements, motions, and opinions of the SCC must be publicly available.[138] Although the Freedom of Information Act was a response to the chamber's recommendations, SCC officials protested the provisions concerning the chamber. During the drafting of the act, they argued that making the whole official correspondence public will be harmful for the functioning and authority of the chamber.[139] Nevertheless, even before passage of the Freedom of Information Act, the SCC provided a large amount of public information on its audits and other activities. The SCC's press office issued 5,042 press reports of which 63% concerned audits. In 2001, the SCC audited 3,891 entities and issued 4,207 audit pronouncements. The SCC also publishes a report that includes the results of selected audits (Poland, Supreme Chamber of Control 2002: 26, http://www.nik.gov.pl).[140]

One reason the SCC lacked clout in the past was the weakness of the internal control system inside the government. In response to this problem,

---

[137] Jerzy Pilczyński, "Co wolno NIK" ["What the Supreme Chamber of Control is allowed"] *Rzeczpospolita,* November 6, 2002.

[138] Freedom of Information Act, article 6, section 4, point (a).

[139] See Tomasz R. Aleksandrowicz, Comment on the Statute on Supreme Chamber of Control, Lex Polonica Maxima (electronic resource), Wydawnictwo Prawnicze LexisNexis, 2003.

[140] A particular difficulty that faces the audit offices in Poland arises from tensions between the law of business secrets and the need for transparent accounting for government funds. Some who want to restrict the reach of the SCC in Poland argue that it should be limited to auditing organizations with at least some share, say 25%, of state ownership. Others want to retain the current system under which a firm is subject to audit with respect to its use of state funds – for example, when it administers a public contract. The issue was highlighted in 2002 when the Polish copper company (KGHM) refused to permit access to SCC inspectors. Under a settlement the SCC inspectors obtained entry, and prosecutors dropped a court case. Jerzy Pilczyński, "Co wolno NIK" ["What the Supreme Chamber of Control is allowed"] *Rzeczpospolita,* November 6, 2002.

a July 2001 amendment to the Public Finance Act created a public internal financial control system – an internal auditing process overseen by a general internal auditor who is a nonpolitical civil servant.[141] It is an internal complement to the work of the external Chamber of Control. The impact of the external chamber largely depends on the power and competence of the internal chamber and its interest in following up on problems isolated by the external auditor.

Incumbent politicians criticize the SCC and claim it has a partisan agenda. Such sniping is the natural result of an appointments process that can lead an SCC president, appointed by one government, to serve in another government's tenure. In spite of this criticism, Poland appears to have a professional, established system of external audit that focuses on promoting financial accountability, not referring cases for criminal prosecution. It seeks to conform to international and EU audit standards. As an advisory body, it has limited influence that depends on its own professional reputation and on the interest of the government in responding to the problems it uncovers. From the point of view of policy-making accountability, its problem is not too much influence but too little. It does not have a mandate to review policy making and is mostly focused on performance accountability.

Hungary

An independent audit office existed in Hungary in the interwar period, but in 1949 the regime dissolved the office and assigned its functions within the government. The present State Audit Office (SAO) has had constitutional status since 1989 and was reconstituted in 1994.[142] A parliamentary committee nominates the president and vice president, and they are elected to 12-year terms (with one renewal possible) by two-thirds of the Members of Parliament. The SAO's implementing statute needed support of two-thirds of the members present. The SAO reports to Parliament on its work supervising the central budget and the separate national funds.[143] It audits the final government budget each year for "legality,

---

141 The official title of the Public Finance Act is Ustawa z dnia 26 listopada 1998 r. o finansach publicznych [Statute of November 26, 1998, on Public Finance], consol. text Dz. U. 2003, No. 15, Item 148, with amendments. Mentioned in Commission of the European Communities (2001b: 98).

142 See Hungary, State Audit Office (2002a, 2002b), Karatnycky, Motyl, and Shor (1997: 188), Galligan and Smilov (1999: 121).

143 The SAO is mentioned in the Hungarian Constitution article 19, section 3; article 20, section 5, and articles 27 and 32/C The relevant constitutional text and the act on

expediency, and efficiency" and does 40–50 special ex post audits. It can also investigate institutions holding state property, political parties, and local government to ensure that they have not violated the law. It reviews the property declarations submitted by nonprofit public foundations and other public bodies and audits the use of public funds by such groups and by religious organizations. In 2001, legislation extended its mandate to cover the disbursement of EU funds and to permit it to audit the Central Bank.[144] According to Kovács, the President of the SAO, more than half of its work is mandated by law, and the rest is under the office's discretion. The SAO has a broader mandate than similar institutions in other countries. However, there are some gaps. It cannot audit state work by private companies, the financial sector, private utilities and social service providers, and contracts with private firms to provide public services such as railroads.

The President of the SAO wishes to become the "conscience of the Parliament." This means the SAO not only audits specific government departments but also carries out studies of issues central to the integrity of government such as corruption in public procurement, the privatization process, and political party financing. The President of the SAO is concerned about a crisis of trust. The public is skeptical about privatization deals that put public services in private hands, but they have little recourse. The SAO would like to respond to this problem but faces legal constraints. As in Poland, one weakness is the Parliament's lack of staff capacity. Most committees have only two or three administrative staff and advisors (Supreme Audit Institutions 2001: 66). Thus, Parliament has only a limited ability to act on recommendations of the SAO.

Like most audit offices, the SAO is not designed to investigate and prosecute malfeasance. It may uncover wrongdoing, but it does not make unannounced audits (Act XXXVIII/89 articles 20, 25). Its main goal is to convince those it audits to establish good internal financial controls. However, the SAO can refer cases to the prosecutor. It is not a crime to

---

the SAO (XXXVIII/1989) are available in English at http://www.asz.gov.hu/ASZ/www.nsf/AMain?Openframeset. The nomination procedure and the 12-year terms with one reelection are set out in articles 7 and 8 of the statute. The web site also includes excerpts from all the other statutes that mention a role for the SAO. On relations with Parliament see Supreme Audit Institutions (2001).

[144] The basic act is XXXVIII/1989. A document in English summarizing the legal provisions related to the Audit Office in this and other acts is available at http://www.asz.gov.hu/ASZ/www.nsf/AMain?Openframeset. For summaries of a number of recent audits see http://www.asz.gov.hu/ASZ/jeltar.nsf/Glossary?OpenView.

violate the budgetary law, but fraud and misuse of funds can be prosecuted. In the early years of the transition, Parliament passed hundreds of laws each year, and most public firms collapsed. Thus, if a firm failed, it was hard to determine the reason and to sort out malfeasance from a lack of economic viability. The SAO has sent only a few cases to the prosecutor, who does his own investigation. President Kovács stated that he prefers to prevent problems up front and to highlight places where better systems of financial controls can limit corruption and fraud. In particular, the SAO has recommended public monitoring of the path of public money as far as end users. In 2002, it recommended better public control of contractors in response to firms' attempts to shield themselves from public inquiry over scandals involving road building and a fireworks display. In the area of political party funding, the SAO has argued for stronger accounting controls and for a law regulating lobbying.[145]

The EU finds that the SAO is a strong institution whose staff is undergoing extensive training. The main problem is the lack of follow-up. It issues reports that often do not lead to any action by the state. Furthermore, the audit function inside the government is weak and understaffed, and personnel training is inadequate. The SAO makes a similar criticism, finding that the old system of internal control has disintegrated and that new systems inside the government are developing very slowly. It also criticizes both the financial integrity of local and regional governing bodies and the quality of private sector auditing. In carrying out its own tasks, the SAO points to ambiguities in its legal competence, especially with respect to audits of corporations and foundations with public functions (Commission of the European Communities 2001a: 92–93; Kovács and Lévai 2001; Hungary, State Audit Office 2002b).

In Hungary, the independence of the SAO is facilitated by Kovács' reputation and by a bipartisan understanding that financial integrity is ultimately in the interest of all political groups, however painful it may be in particular cases. Although the SAO dates from just before the end of the old regime, it has been strengthened by the new democratic governments and given more responsibilities. Another source of independence is budgetary. The SAO formulates its own budget and sends it to the Ministry of

---

[145] See Hungary, State Audit Office (2002c) and Kovács and Lévai (2001). In response to missing funds and unbuilt highways under a program administered by the Hungarian Development Bank, private contractors claimed that information on their subcontracting and their activities under the contract were business secrets and did not have to be disclosed.

Finance. It is nominally under the budgetary control of the government, but, in practice, it has considerable autonomy.

Kovács was selected in 1997 for a 12-year term with an 88% majority. Thus, his mandate has already extended through three different governments. However, it is difficult to know if his strong support stems from a reputation for toughness and impartiality or from an unwillingness to stir up trouble for any governing coalition. That it is at least partly the former is indicated by the SAO's frequent criticisms of sitting government practices and its active audit schedule.[146] Nevertheless, the SAO clearly performs a balancing act in which it picks its fights carefully and tries to avoid confrontations that would involve passing on cases to the prosecutor. It has a reputation for integrity and competence but also for seeking structural reforms rather than scapegoats.

Conclusions

Audit offices concentrate on financial integrity and waste in public spending. In the process, they also evaluate the underlying quality of some programs and isolate those that need a substantial overhaul. In Poland and Hungary, these offices have largely maintained a reputation for probity, but they are limited by their advisory role. True, the government and its supporters have accused the Polish SCC of partisanship, but that type of criticism is the predictable result of the SCC's independence of the sitting government. In Hungary, the 12-year term and the two-thirds parliamentary majority required to appoint the president may dampen such criticism. However, the required supermajority may produce a compromise candidate, as in the cases of the Ombudsman for Data Protection and Freedom of Information and the Constitutional Court discussed previously.

The supreme audit offices report to the national parliaments and may refer serious breaches to the prosecutor. In practice, their role is as an advisor on fiscal integrity who can credibly threaten to go public with information on waste and malfeasance. They act almost like consultants because the objects of their concern need not comply with their recommendations. They obtain leverage from opposition politicians who use unfavorable reports to criticize the government or other public organs and from media publicity surrounding their reports. These offices are necessary, but not sufficient, for the development of performance accountability. Like the ombudsman, their reports can be an input into the policy-making process,

---

[146] See, for example, Béla Fincziczki, "Ász to Probe Bank Tender" *Budapest Business Journal,* January 27, 2003.

and public support for government reform is aided by citizens' belief that the audit office will monitor the use of funds. However, an audit office is not itself a source of policy-making accountability. Its role is simply to review the way appropriated funds are being spent and to publicize any problems.

Independent Institutions and Policy-Making Accountability

Poland and Hungary have created similar institutions for government oversight. Both have presidents with some independent power and active constitutional courts. They have ombudsmen, audit offices, and procuracies, and they permit judicial oversight of the administration. In practice, these institutions operate somewhat differently in the two countries. The independently elected Polish president is stronger than the indirectly elected Hungarian head of state. In the early years of the transition, the Hungarian Constitutional Court was more activist than its Polish counterpart partly because of permissive standing requirements combined with the character of the early justices. The procuracy has constitutional status in Hungary but not in Poland. The system of administrative courts is an important institution in Poland and does not exist in Hungary. Nevertheless, the package of institutions in each country provides a similar range of checks on government power. These checks are all important and could be strengthened and reformed. However, they are essentially tools for performance accountability. They do little to enhance the democratic accountability of the policy-making process inside the government.

Both countries have parliamentary governments, a constitutional structure where resistance to government oversight ought to be strong. The unitary nature of the legislative and executive branches limits the political incentives to create independent oversight bodies that may embarrass sitting governments. Yet these countries do have a full range of such institutions. One reason for their existence is the socialist legacy. Oversight institutions that helped maintain Communist Party control and constrain the bureaucracy were carried over into the new regime. At present, they have the same nominal form but very different functions. The procuracy and the audit office were used to maintain Communist Party control over the administration but are now an outside check on the government. They were not discredited like the secret police but, instead, were rehabilitated under the new system.

A second explanation is that these institutions were part of the compromise that produced the peaceful transition. Reformers recognized that constitutional rights would mean little unless individuals had a way to complain if rights were violated. The constitutional courts play this role, especially in Hungary, and ombudsmen help mediate disputes and resolve many without judicial intervention. The nonexecutive presidents were the result of compromises between those who wanted strong presidents and those who wanted pure parliamentary systems. In some cases, incumbent politicians supported oversight institutions as ways to tie their hands and those of their opponents. They hoped to benefit politically from rules that prevented all politicians from responding to pressure from special interests. Furthermore, national politicians seek to control both career bureaucrats at the national level and politicians at other levels of government. This goal can be partially accomplished by creating oversight bodies that report to the national legislature.

Now that these institutions exist, they are likely to remain. Most would need a supermajority to disband, they are popular with citizens, and they comply with EU requirements. Nevertheless, their effectiveness depends on their often fragile independence. Devices such as bipartisan appointment processes, long terms with limits on reappointment, and budgetary independence help insulate incumbents from day-to-day pressures, but their limited mandates and often advisory role constrain their direct impact. Some operate under appointment procedures that can be easily influenced by narrow political considerations, and incumbents are accused of bias by government supporters. Without citizen support, these institutions risk degenerating into a closed system that provides weak or partisan oversight. The audit office, the procuracy, and the ombudsman report to parliament, whose governing coalition controls the executive. The president and the constitutional courts are more independent, but, except for the Polish president, they are selected by the legislature. Even if incumbents are not allied with the current coalition in power, they may have political connections with a past government. In practice, the energy and character of most of the early incumbents in all six offices played a major role in the development of these institutions, and they retain a high level of popular support to this day. However, one should not take that situation for granted.

The oversight institutions discussed in this chapter are essentially institutions of performance accountability. They provide only a limited route for individual citizens and private groups to participate in the monitoring of government, and even there the focus is on the implementation of the law in individual cases, not policy making. Even at their best, they do not provide much scope for popular participation and oversight. The most open institutions are the ombudsmen, the Hungarian Constitutional Court, the Polish administrative courts, and the Polish president.

In both countries, ombudsmen handle individual complaints but only to resolve specific personal claims of mistreatment. The constitutional courts in both countries are open to individual complaints, although to a much lesser degree in Poland than in Hungary. The Polish administrative courts are important sites for individual complaints. Judicial review, however, does not function well as a source of policy-making accountability. There are two reasons for this. First, the caseload is very large, especially in the Polish Supreme Administrative Court before recent reforms. This results in long delays and sometimes in a de facto refusal to decide certain cases. Second, individual access to the courts generally is limited to those who can claim direct harm. Lawsuits against the state are seldom a way to voice a general objection to a policy. This is not true of the Hungarian Constitutional Court, but in that case its role as a government monitor depends on the justices' willingness to take on this role.

In fact, there is good reason not to rely on the courts to play a primary role in promoting policy-making accountability. Rather than insist that citizens and groups work indirectly through the courts or through bringing cases to the ombudsman, the emerging democracies of CEE should consider creating institutional structures that permit direct citizen participation in the policy-making processes of the government. I argue for this in subsequent chapters, but first I consider another type of policy-making accountability – the devolution of oversight and service delivery to local communities.

SIX

Decentralized Political Accountability

If a country's central government suffers from insufficient popular control, one option is decentralization to lower level governments that are "closer to the people." Neither Poland nor Hungary is a federal state, but municipal governments have locally elected governing bodies. Both countries also have broader territorial administrative units that oversee the operation of municipalities and exercise some central government functions. In Poland, these bodies have directly elected councils.

The socialist past has influenced the debate over government structure in both countries. That legacy has led to a distrust of centralized authority, with some observers supporting the devolution of more power downward. However, regional inequalities mean the central government provides considerable funding for lower-level governments and hence must monitor its use. These opposing pressures have produced conflict over government organization and authority in both countries. Debate over the proper division of authority remains contentious.

Data from the European Values Study 1999/2000 suggest a sharp difference in public attitudes between Poland and Hungary (Table 6.1). Poland is more like Central and Eastern Europe as a whole with more than half the respondents preferring more devolution. In contrast, in Hungary there is little support for increased devolution, even though the country is currently more centralized. Apparently, any support for devolution that accompanied the change in regime in Hungary has largely dissipated.[147]

---

[147] The inter-country difference is not an artifact of differences in the sample. In both countries about 70% of respondents lived in towns of fewer than 100,000. See Appendix 2.

Table 6.1. *Public Opinion on Decentralization of Government*

	Would It Be a Good or a Bad Idea to Give More Power to Local Authorities?		
Region	Good (%)	Bad (%)	Don't Mind (%)
Eastern Europe	54	15	30
Central Europe	57	18	25
Poland	55	15	30
Hungary	24	52	24
Western Europe	43	24	33

Source: Question 57H on the European Values Study 1999/2000.

The division of authority is a more important issue in Poland simply because it is much larger than Hungary in both population and land area. Poland has almost 40 million inhabitants compared with just over 10 million for Hungary. In Hungary, an important source of regional conflict is the dominance of Budapest, which contains about 20% of the nation's population and is also the capital city;[148] Warsaw does not have the same degree of dominance. In spite of these differences, the democratic character and public accountability of local governments are central to the debate over the development of democracy in both countries.

The European Union (EU) has weighed in on the side of regionalization (Commission of the European Communities 2003a, 2003b), but its position is fraught with contradictions. On the one hand, the Commission is committed to promoting regional development bodies throughout the Union (Halkier, Danson, and Damborg 1998). These are planning entities that have authority to spend EU development funds. On the other hand, the Commission promotes the creation of democratically elected bodies below the national level in the new member states. Comprehensive development planning and local electoral democracy are not always compatible, and this leads to tensions in EU policy. Sometimes the Commission seems to be pushing for planning bodies that are not associated with democratically elected governments but that instead are composed of experts and representatives of other governments and agencies. These bodies are held accountable not through direct elections but through

[148] The population of the city of Budapest was about 1.7 million or about 17% of the national population of 10.2 million. Including the entire metropolitan region raises the share to almost 24%. Data are from the web site of the National Statistical Office: http://www.ksh.hu.

hearings that canvass the views of the public and of organized interest and advocacy groups. Their priorities may not be the same as those of directly elected self-governments at the local and regional levels.

Increased devolution under any of the models on offer will not solve the problems of public accountability in Hungary and Poland and may exacerbate some existing problems. To see why, one needs to understand the often complex pattern of intergovernmental relations in each country and to see how local democratic accountability can conflict with national policy making and competent bureaucratic performance.

Poland

Poland reformed its system of subgovernment organization several times under the socialist and postsocialist governments.[149] Reforms in 1998 apparently have solved some past problems,[150] but difficulties persist, and the EU remains somewhat dissatisfied.[151] The existing problems are

[149] I am grateful to Maciej Kisilowski and Aleksandra Sznajder for help with the details of the Polish case. Administrative reform occurred in 1972–1975 under the socialist government and created a system of 49 regional administrative units (*voivodships*). The first posttransition reform took place in 1990 and created the municipalities (*gmina*) as the basic local self-government unit. The local governments at first performed well, but, because they depended on the central government for funds, they constantly complained of lack of resources (Taras 1993: 24–25). In 1996, a reform effort attempted to clarify the relationship between the 49 voivodships and the central government and to require them to cooperate with the municipalities (Galligan and Smilov 1999: 213–214 225–227). Cooperation with the central government was difficult, however, because there were several dozen task-specific central government administrative systems with their own boundaries.

[150] The basic statutes are: Ustawa z dnia 8 marca 1990 r. o samorządzie gminnym [Statute of March 8, 1990, on commune self-government], consol. text. Dz. U. 2001, No. 142, Item 1591, with amendments [hereafter The Commune Act], and three acts passed on June 5, 1998: Ustawa o samorządzie powiatu [Statute on County Self-Government], consol. text Dz. U. 2001, No. 142, Item 1592, with amendments. [The County Act], Ustawa o samorządzie województwa [Statute on Voivodship Self-Government], consol. text Dz. U. 2001, No. 142, Item 1590, with amendments. [The Voivodship Act], Ustawa o administracji rządowej w województwie [Statute on Governmental Administration in a Voivodship], consol. text Dz. U. 2001, No. 80, Item 872 with amendments. [The Voivod Statute]. There is also a statute on local referenda of September 15, 2000: Ustawa z dnia 15 września 2000 r. o referendum lokalnym, Dz. U. 2000, No. 88, Item 985, with amendments.

[151] The Director General for Enlargement stated in a 2002 interview that Poland lagged in its administrative capacity, especially with respect to "managing aid to agriculture and to the regions." Andrzej Stankiewicz, "Czeka was wielka praca" ["Big task awaits you"] *Rzeczpospolita*, January 25, 2002 (interview with Eneko Landaburu, Director-General

lack of accountability, unfunded mandates, and disputes over legal authority and political power.

Government Structure

Poland has 16 regional administrative units (*voivodships*), 314 counties (*powiats*), 2,478 *gminas* or municipalities, and 65 cities that combine county and municipal functions.[152] Each level of self-government has its own responsibilities and, in addition, carries out many central government functions. The *voivodships* are both units of the central government and of the self-government structure. At that level, the central governmental administration is headed by a *voivod* who represents the Council of Ministers. The *voivod* can make rules, but they are subject to central government review for conformity not only with the law, but also with government policy. Each *voivodship* also has a self-governing, popularly elected *sejmik* or council that selects a governing board and a chief executive (*marszałek*) to manage self-governing functions. The *powiats* and *gminas* are self-governing unions of people living in a particular territory. The *powiats* have locally elected councils that select boards headed by *starostas*, who manage the executive. The citizens of a *gmina* also elect a council and, since 2003, they also elect the mayor (*wójt, burmistrz,* or president).[153]

Under the constitution, the prime minister and the *voivod* supervise all levels of self-government but only with respect to the legality of their actions; the regional accounting chambers audit them to ensure financial accountability.[154] The elected subnational governments have

for Enlargement of the European Union of the European Communities). The 2003 Commission report concludes that the reorganization "was not accompanied by a clearly oriented, long-term programme for local and regional self-government and this could complicate the further implementation of the decentralization process" (Commission of the European Communities 2003b: 14).

[152] Information obtained from http://www.mswia.gov.pl/index1_b.html (website of the Ministry of Internal Affairs and Administration), last visited April 14, 2004. See Okraszewska and Kwiatkowski (2002: 185–191) for an overview of the sub-government structure in Poland.

[153] See Ustawa z dnia 20 czerwca 2002 r. o bezpośrednim wyborze wójta, burmistrza i prezydenta miasta [Statute of June 20, 2003, on direct election of wójts, burmistrzs and presidents of cities], Dz. U. 2002, No. 113, Item 984, with amendments.

[154] As part of this supervisory authority, the *voivod* and the regional accounting chambers have the right to demand information and inspect the offices of self-governments. The Polish Constitution article 171, section 1, states that: "The legality of actions by a local self-government shall be subject to review." Article 171, section 2, states that

considerable autonomy with respect to both their self-governing functions and their delegated responsibilities. The national government does not directly review the exercise of policy discretion.

In practice, however, the distinction between law and policy is not always clear, leaving some room for central government policy oversight. For example, the regional accounting chambers monitor the use of earmarked funds distributed by the national government. This may require them to make judgments about the appropriateness of self-government spending decisions.[155] The government's review of legality is not a mere formality. The *voivods* can and do invalidate ordinances of local governments that they consider illegal. However, the self-governments can appeal adverse decisions to the administrative court system.[156] In addition to promulgating ordinances, self-governments also adjudicate numerous matters involving individual residents and businesses. The system of appellate review adds another layer of central government control that can conflict with local autonomy.[157]

---

the organs exercising review shall be "the Prime Minister and voivods and regarding financial matters – the regional audit chambers." Nelicki (2001); Poland, Ministerstwo Spraw Wewnętrznych i Administracji (Ministry of Internal Affairs and Administration 1999).

[155] The regional accounting chambers oversee all *gmina* financial matters to ensure compliance with the law; with the exception of the use of earmarked grants, they do not evaluate policy (Okraszewska and Kwiatkowski 2002: 202).

[156] All municipal, *powiat*, or *voivodship* self-government ordinances must be submitted to the *voivod* within 7 days. The *voivod* has 30 days to decide on the legality of the rule. After 30 days if no action is taken by the *voivod*, the action cannot be declared illegal but may be submitted to the administrative court.

[157] Most adjudicatory decisions are subject to routine appeals to the *voivod*. Others can be appealed to a Self-Government Review Board, whose members are selected in a complicated procedure involving public contest, co-optation (opinion of the general assembly of a review board), and appointment by the Prime Minister (on the motion of the president of a review board) (Ustawa z dnia 12 października 1994 r. o samorządowych kolegiach odwoławczych [Statute of October 12, 1994, on Self-Government Review Boards], consol. text Dz. U. 2001, No. 79, Item 856, with amendments., articles 7 and 8). There are 49 boards that consider appeals from the decisions of *gminas, powiats*, and the self-governmental administration of the *voivodships*. Under the Administrative Procedure Code, this review is not limited to legality. The boards have broad, substantive discretion to annul the decisions of the self-governments and to decide cases on their merits. The decision is remanded to the lower level only when there is a need to conduct explanatory proceedings (fact-finding). Once again, decisions can be appealed to the Administrative Court, but the broad scope of review means that narrow considerations of legality are not the only criterion for the reversal of self-governments' decisions [Article 138 of Ustawa z dnia 14 czerwca 1960, Kodeks postępowania administracyjnego (Statute of June 14, 1960, Code of Administrative Procedure), consol. text Dz. U. 2000, No. 98, item 1071 with amendments].

The 1998 reform attempted to balance the self-governments' performance of central government functions with a territorial organization of responsibilities under local democratic control. The law established the new county or *powiat* level, each with an elected council. At the same time, the number of *voivodships* was reduced from 49 to 16 to strengthen regional control over larger geographic areas. A number of special administrative units were retained that continue to operate independently of the decentralized administrative structures.[158] The shift from task orientation to territorial organization included services such as safety and public order (police, fire departments) and compliance with business regulations such as sanitary, veterinary, and construction inspections. However, this aspect of the 1998 reform proved controversial and was cut back in 2002.

Encouraged by the EU, Poland has created Regional Development Agencies (RDAs) that add another complication to the organizational landscape. They are designed to facilitate economic growth at the regional level with the encouragement and financial support of the EU and other international donors. They are not self-governments but instead are independent, incorporated organizations with heavy organizational and financial support from these governments. However, regional enterprises are usually major shareholders. To supplement outside support, the RDAs engage in profit-making activities. Thus, they play a dual role of encouraging the development of their region – especially the promotion of small and medium-sized businesses – and engaging in their own profit-making businesses including renting commercial space, training, printing, and lending.[159]

The RDAs operate on a separate track that overlaps with but is not identical to the self-governments. The RDAs are able to carry out development programs that would be difficult to finance and organize entirely within the self-government structures. A study of Polish RDAs concludes that most play a positive role in promoting regional development. However, the fact that they must raise considerable funds themselves means that in some cases the drive to earn profits dominates, and then "the existence of such a potential clash of interests is either ignored or concealed from public opinion" (Gorzelak et al. 1998: 118). Instead of promoting

---

[158] Examples are the military, taxation, mining, measurement and standards, rivers and waters, customs, ports and seas, border patrols, navigation, and fishing inspection (Wierzbowski 2003: 237).

[159] Most are joint stock corporations, although some are foundations and are partially funded by profits earned from their own enterprises plus outside funding mostly from the EU and the Polish government (Gorzelak, Kozak, and Roszkowski 1998).

overall development of the region such RDAs risk promoting their own financial well-being at the expense of broader community interests. These hybrid public-private entities deserve further study as outside funding dries up. Will they be able to find a valuable niche or will they end up as competitors with private for-profit firms or with self-governments?

This outline of Poland's governmental structure indicates that two models of service provision compete for primacy. Under the first, the central government maintains direct supervision over service delivery. It may decentralize provision to the regional, county, or municipal level, but this is done only for administrative convenience, not to accommodate political imperatives. Under the second, lower-level governments are politically accountable to those living in their own geographic areas under statutes that assign certain tasks and programs to these governments. Although the national government maintains some oversight to control fraud and illegality, the goal is for regional and local political forces to design and operate programs.[160]

Tensions and Conflicts

Because Poland is not a federal state, lower-level governments are ultimately subordinate to the central government as a matter of law. In case of conflict, the central government has the legal authority to preempt subordinate governments. Nevertheless, the legal framework tries to mix the efficient, decentralized delivery of central government services with grants of autonomy to local and regional elected bodies. Clearly, these two goals can conflict if a lower-level unit is corrupt or ineffective in the eyes of the central administration or if it has different policy priorities.[161] Furthermore, tasks that are designated as the responsibilities of one level of government may, nevertheless, impinge on the direct responsibilities of the central government or of other subgovernments. This can lead to confusion and controversy.

---

[160] Kulesza (1993: 37–38), who in 1993 was the Government Plenipotentiary for Public Administration Reform in Poland, makes this distinction in discussing the 1990 reforms.

[161] As an example, consider a law passed by Sejm in January 2000 to limit the earnings of local government officials. A large group of councilors and mayors had been awarding themselves bonuses so that they earned considerably more than parliamentarians, the president, and the prime minister. The law forbade them from earning more than the president or the prime minister. "Local officials protested, and in revenge, Warsaw's councilors prohibited the sale of alcohol in parliamentary restaurants on the grounds that it is illegal to sell alcohol in workplaces" (Constitution Watch: Poland 2000:31). The Sejm responded with a special law permitting sales.

Sometimes intergovernmental tensions spill over into a genuine crisis. If a municipality, county, or *voivodship* council repeatedly violates the constitution or statutes, the Sejm can dissolve it (Polish Constitution article 171, section 3). If the executive board is the source of the violation, the prime minister can dissolve the board and appoint a representative (a so-called, "small commissioner") who must immediately organize elections. Furthermore, the Commune Act (article 96), the County Act (article 83), and the Voivodship Act (article 84) all state that if a self-government shows an overwhelming lack of efficacy with no hope for fast improvement, the prime minister, on the motion of the Minister of Public Administration, can suspend the organs of self-government and appoint a special commissioner who will govern for up to 2 years or until the election of new governing bodies. The Sejm does not have to approve these seemingly more intrusive interventions. However, the administrative courts can review all such actions, thus providing some check on central government overreaching.

Although suspension might seem a drastic measure, it has sometimes been used – most notoriously in the case of the Warsaw city government in 2000. In the Warsaw case, the national government took over the city government offices, leading to a crisis that eventually led to the departure of one party in the governing coalition. The precipitating event was a breakdown in the Warsaw governing coalition that led to a walkout of some members of the city council. The remaining members continued to govern and selected a governing board and mayor. This behavior was declared to be illegal by the *voivod* acting as the national government's representative. The prime minister then installed a commissioner, leading to considerable resistance and lawsuits in the administrative court. Those who had walked out were political allies of the national government and wanted to force a showdown. Thus, the case mixed together partisan wrangling with claims of illegality – a portion of the council governing in the name of the whole and a commissioner installed without waiting for administrative court review.[162]

---

[162] The details are too convoluted to provide here. Of particular interest, however, are the decisions of the administrative court in two cases. The first case (Judgment of June 1, 2000, II SA 1331/2000, Orzecznictwo Sądów Polskich [OSP] [Judgments of the Polish Courts] 2000/9, Item 136) found the prime minister's action installing the commissioner had no binding force because the law gave the *gmina* 30 days to file for administrative court review. Thus, all decisions of the commissioner between May 17, when he was appointed, and June 1 were illegal. The court did not rule on the merits of the takeover. In the second case (Judgment of July 7, 2000, II SA 1246–1253/2000, Orzecznictwo Naczelnego

A less dramatic confrontation occurred at about the same time, in the small *gmina* of Leoncin, about 50 kilometers from Warsaw. In 2000, the *gmina*'s council decided that the village's two primary schools would have only three lower classes. The older children were to attend school 27 kilometers away.[163] Parents disagreed and organized a referendum to recall the council. The recall succeeded, and the prime minister appointed a commissioner. The two cases are similar in that in both a portion of the local populations supported the actions of the prime minister. The national government resolved an internal political dispute. Neither case involved allegations of corruption or fraud. They demonstrate that devolution is not a fixed characteristic of the government structure but can be overridden by political considerations.

Cases in which the central government steps in temporarily to replace a sitting government are only the most dramatic examples of intra- and intergovernmental controversies. Throughout the country, conflicts have arisen both within self-governments and between national political parties

Sądu Administracyjnego [ONSA] [Judgments of the Supreme Administrative Court] 2002/1, Item 14), the same court upheld the decision of the *voivod* concerning the invalidity of the election of the *gmina*'s board. This cleared the way for the prime minister to appoint a new "small" commissioner who was required to organize new elections. They were held in September, with a victory for the parties representing the dismissed board. The Commune Act was amended in 2001 to make appointments of commissioners effective immediately with no 30-day waiting period (Ustawa z dnia 11 kwietnia 2001 r. o zmianie ustaw: o samorządzie gminnym, o samorządzie powiatowym, o samorządzie województwa, o administracji rządowej w województwie oraz o zmianie niektórych innych ustaw [Statute of April 11, 2001, on amendment of the Commune, County, Voivodship, Voivod Acts], Dz. U. 2001, No. 45, Item 497, with amendments.). For background see: "Gmina która wstrząsnęła Polską" ["Gmina that has shaken Poland"], *Gazeta Stołeczna*, September 9–10, 2000; "Zapis wydarzeń" ["The record of events"], *Gazeta Stołeczna*, September 25, 2000; "Zarząd komisaryczny w Warszawie" ["The commissioner's authority in Warsaw"], *Gazeta Stołeczna*, May 18, 2000; "Gabinet komisaryczny" ["Commissioner's cabinet"], *Gazeta Stołeczna*, May 20–21, 2000; "Dzień po ciężkiej pracy" ["A day after a hard work"], *Gazeta Stołeczna*, May 20–21, 2000; "Komisarz atakuje nocą" ["Commissioner strikes at night"], *Gazeta Wyborcza*, May 22, 2000; "Jak doszło do powołania komisarza" ["The appointment of the commissioner: how it happened"], *Gazeta Wyborcza*, May 25, 2000; Iwona Szpala, Jan Fusiecki, "Był i nie ma" ["He was and he isn't"], *Gazeta Stołeczna*, June 2, 2000; JanFusiecki, Iwona Szpala, "Spektakl wyborczy" ["Election performance"], *Gazeta Stołeczna*, June 8–9, 2000; "Prawo z limitem" ["Law with limit"], *Gazeta Stołeczna*, June 9, 2000; "Umorzono komisarza" [Commissioner discontinued], *Gazeta Stołeczna*, August 25, 2000; "Zwycięski, uwikłany" ["Winning, embroiled"], *Gazeta Stołeczna*, September 26, 2000. Research on this case was done by Maciej Kisilowski.

163 "Komisarz też w Leoncinie" ["Commissioner in Leoncin, too"], Gazeta Stołeczna, June 2, 2000; Włodzimierz Pawłowski, "Tęsknota za komisarzem" ["Longing for a commissioner"], *Gazeta Stołeczna*, August 11, 2000.

and local political interests. As a result of case studies of several local governments, Jacek Kurczewski and Joanna Kurczewska (2001: 956) conclude that:

The abolition of Communist rule meant not so much a change of local elites as the disappearance of previous external controls and the assumption of full power of local elites, now openly pluralistic in their general political orientation. . . . [The] unprivileged complain about the irresponsibility of the elite while the elite complain about the mental remnants of a *homo sovieticus* psychology, about passivity and the lack of civic virtue on the part of the civil society. . . . [Moreover, the elite is not much concerned with] negotiating with members of the common local civil society. . . .

If this observation is generally correct, then the claim that decentralization can produce more democratic accountability seems problematic.

Public Participation
Some substantive statutes require public participation in the promulgation of local ordinances. For example, modifications of local land use plans require notice (in the local press, by announcement, and by other customary forms) and a comment period open to local citizens as well as to the authorities of neighboring *gminas* and other organs.[164] Even without formal legal requirements, municipalities frequently establish committees to consider draft rules that include residents both in and outside the council. The rules are adopted in open council sessions, which may involve the participation of individual citizens and organizations (Galligan et al. 1998: 449). Thus, opportunities for public participation exist at the municipal level for local issues that may involve the implementation of central government statutes. However, a hint that municipal practices are not always transparent is suggested by an April 11, 2001, amendment to the Commune Act. This amendment requires that the "activities of *gmina* bodies be open" with limitations imposed only by statute. The law then elaborates the meaning of this phrase: Citizens have the right "to gain information, to gain entrance to the sessions of the *gmina* council and its committees, as well as access to documents related to its performance of public tasks. . . ." (article 1, point 12). The 2001 national Freedom of Information Act applies to self-governments, so this is another route to greater transparency that supplements other requirements. Nevertheless, there is

---

[164] Ustawa z dnia 27 marca 2003 r. o planowaniu i zagospodarowaniu przestrzennym [Statute of March 27, 2003, on land use and planning], Dz. U. 2003, No. 80, Item 717 with amendments., article 11.

no general statute regulating public participation. As a result, citizens and businesses may have trouble finding out what the self-governments are actually doing unless the incumbent officials themselves are committed to openness.

A survey conducted in connection with a project organized by the Open Society Institute suggests that public and group participation are low at the local (*gmina*) level of government. For example, *gminas* can invite local community groups to discuss the planned budget at an early stage in its development. Yet few *gminas* take advantage of this possibility, and these are usually the larger ones. In general, most civil society groups are specialized and get involved only in trying to influence subsidies to themselves and in decisions affecting their area of focus. Local government officials, in turn, do not seem eager to involve such groups in decision making (Okraszewska and Kwiatkowski 2002: 219–226). As for civil society groups, they are heavily concentrated in the larger cities and do not play much of a role in Poland's many small towns and villages. Those that do exist often depend heavily on local governments for financial support. Nevertheless, local *gmina* authorities claimed to do some consultation with business, civil society, and ordinary citizens when making decisions (Okraszewska and Kwiatkowski 2002: 236–238, 255–259).

Funding and Legal Competence

Funding affects the discretion of lower-level governments or administrative units to set their own priorities. In 2002, the voivodships raised 12.8% of their revenue locally; counties raised 10.2%, and municipalities collected 45% of their budget from their own citizens.[165] Subgovernments receive transfers from the central government, many of which are earmarked for particular purposes (Gilowska 2001, for *gminas* see Okraszewska and Kwiatkowski 2002: 195–199). Municipalities can also fix the rates of some local taxes (including a real estate tax) but only up to a statutory limit; in practice, most governments are at the limit.

---

[165] Poland, Główny Urząd Statystyczny [Central Statistical Office], Rocznik Statystyczny Rzeczpospolitej Polskiej [Statistical Yearbook of the Republic of Poland], Warsaw 2003. The counties and *voivodships* cannot raise their own taxes. Each level is instead assigned a fixed percent of personal and business income taxes in their areas. See Ustawa z dnia 13 listopada 2003 r. o dochodach jednostek samorządu terytorialnego [Statute of November 13, 2003, on the income of the units of territorial self-government], Dz. U. 2003, No. 203, Item 1966. The rest of their funds comes from earnings on property owned by the governments and dividends, etc.

Giving more rights to self-governments would require amending the constitution. Article 217 states that "the imposition of taxes, as well as other public imposts, the specification of those subject to the tax and the rates of taxation, as well as the principles for granting tax relief and remissions, along with categories of taxpayers exempt from taxation, shall be by means of statute." Many of the resources from the central government are explicitly targeted to particular tasks. Lower-level governments, especially the newer counties, complain about being assigned responsibilities without being given adequate funds.[166] Targeted funds account for more than three-quarters of county income and more than 50% of the income of *voivodships*; some observers claim they are allocated in arbitrary ways that breed clientelism.[167]

Tensions frequently arise between professional, hierarchical bureaucratic structures that operate nationally and elected self-governments. One response is simply to keep these positions under direct national government control, as has been done with the military and the customs service, or to place them under the control of the *voivod* rather than the *voivodship* self-government.[168] Some national professional services – in particular, police, fire, sanitary, veterinary, and construction inspection – also operate at the lower levels of government. Thus, they are key arenas for observing the tensions between the two models of decentralization – that is, administrative convenience versus democratic accountability. The

---

[166] Andrzej Orzechowski, "Proteza prowizorki" ["Prosthesis for a temporary solution"], *Rzeczpospolita* November 22, 2001. Lack of funds is an especially serious problem in health care. See Witold Kieżun, "Powiaty – fikcja samorządności"["Powiats – fictitious self-goverance"], *Rzeczpospolita*, November 5, 2001. In 2002, 43% of the budget of subnational governments was spent by *gminas*, 36% by cities with *powiat* status, 15% by other *powiats*, and 5% by *voivodships*. Earmarked national government subsidies (including educational subsidies) went 31% to *gminas*, 25% to cities with *powiat* status, 25% to other *powiats*, and 6% to *voivodships*. Calculated by Maciej Kisilowski using data from Poland, Główny Urząd Statystyczny [Central Statistical Office]. 2003.

[167] *Powiats* and *voivodships* obtained 77% and 52%, respectively, of their budgets in the form of earmarked grants in 2002. The share for *gminas* and cities with *powiat* status was about 40% for each (calculated by Maciej Kisilowski from data in the Polish 2003 Statistical Yearbook). See also, Gilowska (2001), Witold Kieżun, "Powiaty – fikcja samorządnosci" [Powiats – fictitious self-governance"], *Rzeczpospolita*, November 5, 2001; Andrzej Orzechowski, "Proteza prowizorki" ["Prosthesis for a temporary solution"] *Rzeczpospolita*, November 22, 2001.

[168] These units include, for instance, police, fire service, trade inspection, inspection for the purchase and processing of agricultural products, geodesic and cartography service, inspection for protection of the environment, inspection for the protection of plants and seed, boards of education (Wierzbowski 2003: 236).

self-government reform in 1998 attempted a compromise. It gave the head of the counties "policy supervision" over the professional units at the county level, including a right to issue binding guidelines that set policy goals.[169] The law gave the elected *starosta* influence over the appointment of the chief of each service. For example, the police chief was appointed by the *voivodship* police commander but only with the approval of the *starosta*.[170] The county received earmarked funding for these services and could supplement them with other funds.

This system caused conflicts between the political interests of the counties and the professional interests of the police. In 2002, the police statute returned power to the police hierarchy to appoint police chiefs and required the police only to obtain an opinion from the *starosta*. Funding responsibility returned to the national government.[171] The amended statutes on sanitary and veterinary inspections went even further and removed the *starostas* from any role in such inspections.[172] *Starostas* no longer participate in appointing the local chief inspectors in these fields, and they also lost the right to make binding guidelines and orders in case of emergency. The *starostas* retain only the powers granted in 1998 for building inspection and fire protection.

Discontent

The Polish mixture of decentralization along some dimensions, continuing central control on others, unfunded mandates, and tied grants has

---

[169] The creators of the reform saw it as a way to balance professionalism and democratic accountability. "The starosta cannot give them [uniformed services such as police and fire protection] concrete commands or official orders, but he can issue binding guidelines that specify a desirable state of public order and collective security...or that point to threats to collective security that should be eliminated. The [choice of] means for executing these orders is a pragmatic matter; it results from the provisions of particular statutes, and its determination belongs to the appropriate commander (head) of powiat's services, inspections and guards" (Izdebski and Kulesza 1999: 197, translated by Maciej Kisilowski).

[170] Ustawa z dnia 24 lipca 1998 r. o zmianie niektórych ustaw określających kompetencje organów administracji publicznej – w związku z reformą ustrojową państwa [Statute of July 24, 1998, on the amendment of some statutes describing the competences of organs of public administration – in connection with a reform of a system of government], Dz. U. 1998, No. 106, Item 668, with amendments., article 62, point 5.

[171] Amendment dated November 13, 2002, Dz. U. 2002, No. 200, Item 1688.

[172] Amendments of August 24, 2001, Dz. U. 2001, No. 128, Item 1407, with amendments., March 1, 2002, Dz. U. 2002, No. 37, Item 329, and February 14, 2003, Dz. U. 2003, No. 52, Item 450.

produced a good deal of discontent. The situation is summarized in a 2002 publication of the Warsaw Foundation in Support of Local Democracy (Regulski 2002: 10):

Decisions regarding the sphere of competence of local and regional government have too often been treated instrumentally. [The] issues [that] have been transferred to the self-government bodies [are those] which created problems and were costly, while at the same time, attempts were made to keep at the central administrative level those spheres related to allocation of resources or personal appointments. Means given by the central budget are increasingly restricted, which creates disillusionment among the citizens, who blame the local government. . . . Financial problems, [including] the problems of financing the tasks of local self-government, make . . . it difficult to engage in local development policy. Strong dependence of self-government on the arbitrary financial decisions of state administration [reduces] self-government to the role of a vassal and the creation of clientelistic relations between the governing group and self-governments. The specificity of current financing methods results in self-government activities becoming increasingly concentrated on managing allocated means. They are increasingly devoid of the potential of engaging in developmental activities, which liberate social energy and increase the income of both local and state budgets.

In spite of efforts to balance local democracy and central control, the competition between levels of government makes it difficult to carry out either central or local government policy. The attempt both to retain central control of funds and to give lower levels of government some freedom of action has produced strains. The underlying problems of funding and the contested interactions between governmental bodies make accountability difficult to establish. Each level of government can blame another for its problems, and citizens seeking to hold the government accountable may be frustrated by the lack of any clear guidance on which authority bears responsibility for particular outcomes. Corruption and favoritism can easily occur at any level of the administration. RDAs can effectively carry out promotional activities for their region, but their own financial imperatives and lack of democratic accountability will limit their role. Furthermore, some scholars see strong clientelistic patronage-based systems emerging at the local level – some built on past links and others that are newly established. The role of ordinary citizens and organized groups varies widely across *gminas*, and mechanisms for receiving and evaluating public input are poorly institutionalized in some subnational governments. These developments suggest that further devolution downward will not lead to more publicly accountable government under current conditions.

Hungary

Hungary, although a much smaller country, has also struggled to balance centralized control against local political autonomy. At present, only local governments have directly elected bodies; regional administrative units operate under national government control.

Structure

In the immediate postsocialist period, the political interests of opposition parties affected subgovernment reorganization. When the first law on local governments was passed in 1990, the opposition was more powerful at the municipal level than at the center and pushed successfully for local political autonomy (Balázs 1993: 77). The socialist regime had a hierarchical structure under which municipalities had little independent power, and county-level officials, who reported to the cabinet, supervised local governments (Balázs 1993: 75–76; Szabó 1993: 96–97). This gave the county level a bad odor among localities, and it was re-created in 1990 as a weak, residual administrative category. The 1990 reorganization went quite far in devolving authority downward and providing block grants to municipalities (Lorentzen 1998: 147; Szabó 1993: 100). The only directly elected officials below the central government were the representative bodies of the municipalities and the mayors, and this continues to be so today.[173] The counties have assemblies composed of municipal representatives, an indication of their subordinate role with respect to local governments.

The law originally gave local governments almost complete freedom to manage their own affairs and created large numbers of municipalities so that every small village became its own self-governing body. There are more than 3,000 local governments, more than in Poland, and many are too small to operate effectively.[174] When this structure proved too weak to permit the central government to administer the country effectively, a 1996 reform strengthened the role of the 19 counties and consolidated and reorganized the central government's power.[175]

---

[173] Mayors are chosen by a direct vote of the citizens in municipalities of fewer than 10,000 people and selected by representative assemblies in larger communities (Balázs 1993: 85).

[174] Interview with Professor Ilona Kovács, Director, Center for Regional Studies of the Hungarian Academy of Sciences, Pécs, conducted in Hungarian by Füzér, October 22, 2002, Pécs.

[175] Hungary, Miniszterelnöki Hivatal, 2000. See the critique of the 1990 structure by Verebélyi (1993: 111–117).

The EU distributes structural funds on the basis of seven regions incorporating several counties. The regions each have Regional Development Councils (RDCs) and planning agencies, but many of them are too small to be effective regional, political, and administrative units.[176] The RDCs bring together national and local government officials across several counties along with representatives of the private sector, labor, and others (Lorentzen 1998: 131). These bodies are supposed to take regional interests into account in making decisions and advising the national government. In the spring of 2004, the EU was pushing Hungary to further consolidate the regions by creating only two or three large units. Citing a study sponsored by the Hungarian government, the Eurpean Commission predicts that regional governments will have both directly elected bodies and public administration offices by the time of the next elections in 2006.[177] However, reorganizing and democratizing the regions would require an amendment to the constitution, which can be done only by a two-thirds vote of the members of parliament, a difficult requirement in the closely divided parliament. In addition, the national bureaucracy and the existing county assemblies oppose such a reorganization, and officials at the regional level are closely tied to the government that took power in 2002 and are not eager to stand for election. Hence, informed insiders doubt that Hungary will create regionally elected governments any time soon.[178] Furthermore, the European Commission seems somewhat

---

[176] See Farkas (2002: 57–58). The Hungarian government is reorganizing some of its other functions in terms of these seven regions instead of the 19 counties. For example, in spring 2004 the government was planning to reorganize the National Statistical Office by abolishing the county offices and setting up seven regional offices based on the regions that are already used for statistical analysis. The regions are Western Hungary, Central Transdanube, South Transdanube, Central Hungary (Buda and Pest counties), Northern Hungary, Northern Great Plains, and Southern Great Plains. However, such reorganizations in other areas are likely to meet resistance from entrenched county leaders (e-mail from Katalin Füzér, March 31, 2004).

[177] Commission of the European Communities (2003a: 12). The study was performed for the Ministry of the Interior by a group headed by Professor Attila Ágh but was not universally accepted by the government, and its recommendations are unlikely to be implemented (e-mails to author from Katalin Füzér, March 31, 2004, and Judit Kálmán, April 18, 2004. The documents from the study are at: http://www.b-m.hu). See especially the study by Ilona Kovács, "Regional Development and Regional Development Policies" that recommends directly elected regional governments to coincide with regional planning bodies but argues for broad-based consultation.

[178] Commission of the European Communities (2003a: 12). Interview with Professor Kovács. E-mail communications from Viola Zentai, Project Manager, Open Society Institute/Local Government Initiative, Budapest, April 5, 2004, from Katalin Füzér, March 31, 2004, and from Judit Kálmán, Open Society Institute, April 18, 2004. Interview

conflicted about increased regional democracy in the spending of EU structural funds. It pushes for more decentralization at the same time as it demands that the central government provide tight fiscal controls for EU funds.

Municipalities are responsible to local electorates, and representatives of the central government administer central government programs along a separate organizational track. The counties and municipalities also carry out delegated central government functions, often with a share of funding from the center. Other individual ministers and national government organs may delegate tasks to regional or county organs with further delegation to state field offices at the local level (Szabó 1993: 96–98).

Some view the Hungarian municipalities as weak, irresponsible, and overly independent. Others criticize the intermediate regional bodies as rigid and bureaucratic and full of holdovers from the old regime with little in the way of policy or technical expertise.[179] Probably both views are exaggerated but capture part of the reality. What does seem clear is that there are democratic deficits at the local level where elections occur as well as at the regional level where they do not.

Local Participation

The Open Society Institute surveyed municipal officials in 2001 to assess the quality of local democracy. The survey reflects the situation outside of Budapest because participation rates were low in the capital city. The authors conclude that most local governments have only minimal organized contacts with local citizens, include few civic associations in decision making, and do not approach journalists on a regular basis. Local representatives do consult voters individually, but few voters initiate contacts. In municipalities where civic associations exist, 62% of these local governments do not consult with them, and 71% do not ask the opinions of local groups on budgetary priorities (Soós and Kálmán 2002: 44–47). Of course, local politicians cannot consult with civic groups unless they exist. Some villages have no groups, and the density of such groups is much lower than average in the poorest and smallest villages. Partly because of special national government funding, civic organizations of minorities are widespread and are important politically in regions of dense minority, particularly Roma, populations. Other groups have been founded and largely

with a knowledgeable opposition Member of Parliament, April 16, 2004, conducted in Hungarian by Füzér.

[179] Interview with Zentai, November 14, 2002, Budapest.

financed by local governments; they are unlikely to provide independent voices. In all, 36% of municipalities have set up at least one such organization. In a given locality, the average proportion of civil society groups receiving some local government funding is above 80%, and most local governments have contracts with at least one civil society organization (Soós and Kálmán 2002: 76–79).

Consistent with these data, Professor Ilona Kovács, Director of the Center for Regional Planning in Pécs, claimed in a 2002 interview that it is a myth that local governments, particularly those in small villages, encourage the participation of "civil society." Instead, those in power try to isolate themselves as much as possible from citizen pressures. In reaction, especially in the 1994 and 1998 elections, many independent candidates ran for local assemblies. Although municipal council meetings are open to the public, local governments often do not provide much transparency with respect to contracting and fail adequately to oversee the operation of service providers (see also Soós and Kálmán 2002: 30–31).

A 1994 revision of the Act on Local Governments requires local governments to maintain a list of local nongovernmental organizations (NGOs) that have a right to be consulted and who may attend assembly meetings.[180] Kovács believes many local governments invite only those NGOs that "will not talk too much." NGO representatives also may serve on local government committees, but, especially in the larger cities, political parties allocate membership as a reward to their supporters. Nevertheless, for some issues consultation with NGOs occurs simply because it is politically valuable to get their opinions.[181]

In an interview, Ferenc Bércesi, a central government official who heads the Administrative Office of Baranya County in southern Hungary, claimed that participation was particularly well developed in the areas of consumer protection, environmental protection, and guardianship, but his experience is mainly with policy areas largely under the control of the national government.[182] Localities do frequently have public hearings and representatives of civil society organizations often serve on local and regional committees or are elected to local councils. Bércesi gave two

---

[180] LXV/1990, article 8, section 5; in addition, section 13 mandates an annual public meeting of the local assembly where citizens and organizations can pose questions.

[181] Interview with Professor Kovács.

[182] Interview with Ferenc Bércesi, head of the Administrative Office, Baranya County, December 3, 2002, Pécs. Interview conducted in Hungarian by Katalin Füzér. Bércesi has written widely on administrative law subjects since 1990.

examples of public participation in his region, one involving a battery recycling plant and the other, the proposed site of an airport.

The Act on Regional Development and Physical Planning (XXI/1996), setting up the RDCs, includes provisions that require consultation with nongovernmental groups. The regional planning process is supposed to be "a dynamic bottom-up movement of both initiative and resource mobilization" (Lorentzen 1998: 150) that involves government bodies and private sector representatives. In practice, the participation of chambers of agriculture, artisans, and industry and trade is more regularized than that of other groups, although, even for the chambers, there is wide interregional variation. The chambers are bodies established by law on a regional basis in 1994 (Lorentzen 1998: 154), and this legal status gives them an advantage. Other groups are dissatisfied with the opportunities available. For example, environmental organizations point to wide disparities across the regions and to the overburdened regional agencies (Proposal 2002). Some of the old centralized structure remains from the past, and new regional development agencies are not always able to coordinate (Lorentzen 2002).

Even when participation does occur at the RDCs, it is difficult for interested groups and individuals to get information, consultation comes too late in the process, and the time allowed to craft a response is very short. Several environmental groups have proposed changes in the law to enhance the opportunities for public participation (Proposal 2002). They urge more detailed rules for public participation in the Act on Regional Development and would require the participation of certain groups with regional mandates, including membership in important committees. Thus, the new RDCs are not providing strong fora for public participation and consultation outside a few regions and a few types of organized groups.[183]

This overview suggests that both at the level of local governments and in the RDCs participation by civil society groups is weak and episodic

---

[183] One response is to create Subregional Development Councils (SRDCs) to perform some functions now carried out by the 19 counties and by the RDCs. A government decree created 170 SRDCs, but they will have little power without legislation that allocates regional development funds to that level. The creation of such councils would likely facilitate local public participation in the planning process but would, of course, risk undervaluing planning issues with broader geographical impacts such as some kinds of environmental issues. SRDCs could be established and funded through ordinary legislation requiring only majority support, but the proposal is at an early stage. Katalin Füzér interview with opposition member of parliament, April 16, 2004.

and varies widely across municipalities and regions. Municipalities and RDCs have considerable policy-making authority, but most suffer from democracy deficits.

National Government Oversight

In principle, the national government's authority to oversee the legality of local government actions constrains local governments. However, that control is, in practice, quite weak.[184] Since 1996 the State Audit Office has had the authority to audit local governments. However, it obviously cannot audit some 3,000 municipalities each year, and in any case its oversight mainly concerns fiscal integrity, not performance evaluation (Soós and Kálmán 2002: 32). As in Poland, the County Public Administration Offices oversee the municipalities with respect to the ex post legality of their actions, not their policy content. If a municipality refuses to go along with a finding of illegality, the commissioner's only recourse is to appeal to the courts; he or she has no direct administrative authority over county and municipal governments (Act on Local Government LXV/1990, as amended, article 98). Nevertheless, some criticize these offices for making politically partisan decisions especially when their party affiliation differs from that of the local government. In Budapest under the government in power from 1998 to 2002, the official with jurisdiction over Budapest vetoed several decisions of the mayor with each claiming the other was partisan. This dispute appears to be a less intense variant of the contretemps in Poland between the national government and the Warsaw government in 2000.

Bércesi, the central government official, reveals the difficulties of central government oversight.[185] At the local level a "notary" acts as both "the executive organ of local government and exercises state administrative competences" (Balázs 1993: 79, 85; LXV/1990, article 36).[186] Notaries are supposed to be the liaison between these two levels of government. However, the mayors control their working conditions and benefits, many notaries are political associates of the mayors (Bércesi estimates that 30% leave office when the mayor changes), and the mayors resist consultation efforts. Because of the difficulties of such a dual role, the central

---

[184] Interview with Professor Kovács.
[185] Interview with Bércesi.
[186] The term in Hungarian is *közjegyző* which translates as "public notary" although the position is very different from the English or American notary. The German term is *Stadtdirektor*.

government has also established independent local organs in areas such as public health, tax administration, and consumer protection.[187]

Bércesi's office has the authority to review local ordinances and decisions and to disapprove those that conflict with national law. In practice, the local government notaries, who are responsible for sending the records to his office, often miss the 15-day deadline, and in the meantime the local governments have taken steps to lock in their decisions. Hence, Bércesi stressed the importance of consultation before a local government issues a decision or decree; after an action is taken, it is almost impossible to reverse. There is nothing his office can do to discipline the notaries, and the mayors obviously have no incentive to do so. The central government cannot effectively control the activities of local governments but can only supervise or review their actions. To illustrate the problem, Bércesi mentioned a case in which the major city in his jurisdiction shut down a facility for intoxicated people thus shifting the cost to hospital emergency rooms run by the county. This was a clear violation of a law forbidding one government from shifting costs to another. A lawsuit challenging this decision has been going on for 3 years to no effect, an indication of the general weakness of the courts in resolving public law disputes. Changes in the law to modify the relationship between local and national governments are unlikely because there are almost 50 mayors who are members of parliament. Thus, Bércesi concentrates on ex ante consultation and on programs of education and publicity.

Funding

As in the Polish case, the real authority of subgovernments cannot be understood without a discussion of their resource base and their responsibilities to provide services. In 2000, locally raised income accounted for only 33% of municipal budgets. Less than half of this comes from local taxes;[188] the rest comes from other local income sources and capital accumulation. The local share of the national income tax and national government grants make up most of the remaining two-thirds.[189] Local

---

[187] Balázs (1993: 79). Originally, county governments, which also have notaries, did not carry out delegated tasks, but that was changed by the 1996 reforms (Hungary, Miniszterelnöki Hivatal 2000).

[188] The national government permits municipalities to levy five types of taxes, with a tax on businesses being the most important (Law LXV/1990, article 82, section 1; Law C/1990; Soós and Kálmán 2002: 27).

[189] The rest is as follows: 17% from national taxes that remain at the local level, 29% from state transfers, 18% from the health fund, 3% other (Várfalvi 2001: 2). A breakdown

government spent about 12% of gross domestic product (GDP) in 1999–2000, down from almost 17% in 1994. In addition to annual transfers, these governments received a "disproportionately large share" of state assets during the transition period (Balázs 1993: 85; Várfalvi 2001).

Thus, there are two sources of cross-jurisdictional inequities (Szalai 1995–1996; Verebélyi 1993). First, devolution led to large differences in the tax base across governments, with most local taxes collected by Budapest and its districts (Soós and Kálmán 2002: 27). Second, with the change in regime much of the capital stock devoted to the provision of social services was simply given to the local governments (LXV/1990, article 107). The socialist government had "rationalized" service delivery by concentrating services such as schools, health clinics, and hospitals in larger towns. This meant that municipalities began the transition period with very different levels of infrastructure in greater or lesser degrees of disrepair. As Júlia Szalai (1995–1996: 51) concludes: "Administrative authority became a base for property, while historical deprivation from it developed into lasting and legitimate exclusion."

At the same time as property was distributed, the central government began to make grants to municipalities from the state budget. These funds were supposed to be disbursed by a formula that favored poor communities and those with large dependent populations. However, over time the state has adjusted the formula to downplay the automatic portion based on need. A survey of the actual disbursement of funds in 75 municipalities in 1993 showed that wealthy communities with fewer old people received more funds than other communities (Szalai 1995–1996: 47, 54). However, the wealthier communities also inherited more property than others and needed to invest a good deal in dealing with deferred maintenance. Thus, in practice, the actual transfers to the needy tended to be higher in the capital-poor communities that lacked other demands. Those that had inherited property also inherited programs and the employees who provided services. They faced political pressure to keep these facilities open, pressure that reduced the funds available for the needy (Szalai 1995–1996: 49–50). This led to some awkward compromises. One author states that "one never can know when opening the door of the local nursery, whether one will find there the kids in day-care, or the outside office of

---

for earlier years is provided by Soós and Kálmán (2002: 25). The pattern is similar, although the share of own revenue has risen from a low of 22% in 1994. According to these authors, the relative stability of the total shares hides a good deal of instability in the underlying programs over the period (Soós and Kálmán 2002: 24–25).

a nearby factory, paying rent and overhead to the head mistress" (Szalai 1995–1996: 50).

Many of the services devolved are redistributive services that political economists recommend for central provision because of free rider problems and the possibility of exit. Local governments are responsible for both health and education, and one important central government grant program consists of funds earmarked for health care (Soós and Kálmán 2002: 26). About 18% of municipal budgets comes from the health fund (Várfalvi 2001:2). In fact, the share of grants that are designated for particular programs has risen over time (Soós and Kálmán 2002: 28). Thus, it is not surprising that entrepreneurial municipalities have tried to divert resources to provide services that benefit the middle class and attract business. Witness the case of the closed detoxification facility outlined earlier. Even the pet projects of local mayors get priority over broad public needs.[190] The joint pressures both to maintain existing programs using inherited capital and employees and to boost the local economy meant that the larger towns tended to neglect the problems of the needy. In smaller villages, there was not much for the government to do except help the needy, but the level of service provision was low and considerable funds were spent on subsidizing transportation to neighboring centers (Szalai 1995–1996). The national government does not do much to influence overall municipal spending priorities, although it does influence municipal behavior through tied grants. Unfortunately, the tied grants seldom cover the full cost of mandated programs. This increases budget pressures on municipalities and has led some to offload service delivery, particularly in education, to NGOs such as religious bodies. The State Audit Office has jurisdiction over municipal finances but cannot do in-depth audits of all municipalities each year and in any case focuses on the misuse of funds, not spending priorities and implementation deficits.[191]

Problems of Accountability and of Policy

In Hungary below the national level there are problems both of accountability and of substantive policy. The accountability problem arises from

---

[190] A case study of one medium-sized city discusses the struggle of the mayor, a devotee of water polo, to build a high-quality public swimming pool in the city along with other projects to promote tourism and civic pride (Szalai 1995–1996: 66–73).

[191] Interviews with Kovács and Bércesi. Telephone conversation with András Sajó, August 2, 2004.

the same kinds of uncertainties as arose in the Polish case. Citizens may not know which level of government or which agency is responsible for which function. Even if the procedures are clear, local government exercise of tasks delegated by the central government may be lax or may be used as a source of local patronage or payoffs. As an EU report concludes: the "over-decentralized structure of local government complicates fiscal discipline. The high number of local authorities, the slow implementation of larger regional units, the lack of own resources, and the absence of effective monitoring mechanisms continue to distort government accounting" (Commission of the European Communities 2001a: 32).

If national level oversight is weak, grassroots citizen involvement might compensate. However, in practice, participation opportunities are highly variable at local, county, and regional levels. Even if local and regional governments do create participation opportunities, the nonprofit organizations' weaknesses limit their impact. My interviews with environmental nonprofits suggest that it was often difficult for such groups to find many people willing to attend and participate in local public meetings.[192]

Monitoring of municipalities both by the national government and by local citizens seems weak. The extent to which local governments favor narrow groups and the cronies of elected officials is not known, but the general weakness of local citizens' organizations suggests that one should not be too optimistic about municipal politics as a substitute for more participation at the national level. A strengthened regional level of government with democratically elected councils might help overcome the problem of too many very small government units. However, the democratic regional governments supported by the EU risk placing elections at a jurisdictional level that may attract little citizen interest or loyalty. Adding more democracy at that level may just replace entrenched bureaucrats with elected politicians who have narrow support bases.

The second problem concerns substantive policy and involves the unequal distribution of social benefits and services. This is a problem both of the unequal distribution of resources across governments and of the pressures inside local governments that downgrade these programs in some communities more than others. Local governments may be accountable to the majority of their citizens, but the end result can be very unequal provisions of social services across the country and within individual communities.

---

[192] See the interviews with representatives of Danube Circle and Green Future.

Limits of Decentralized Accountability

The postsocialist countries inherited a legacy of resentment and distrust from their overly centralized and bureaucratic socialist states. A natural response was to decentralize local service provision down to the municipal level. Neither Poland nor Hungary appears to have considered going so far as to create a federal state and neither seems at risk of splitting apart like Czechoslovakia or the former Yugoslavia. Instead, both have worked to give more authority to elected local governments. They have also struggled to find an appropriate role for governmental and administrative units in between national and local governments. They have tried to balance domestic political and administrative concerns with European Commission pressure to establish regional planning bodies that are appropriate to receive EU structural funds. Local democratic accountability, on the one hand, and fiscal control and professional competence, on the other, are frequently in tension as Hungary and Poland struggle to create a viable system of self-governments and public administration.

Whatever the aims of decentralization, in both countries it faces difficulties familiar to any student of intergovernment relations. First, in a country with a national media, many citizens may be more involved in national than in local issues, leaving the local issues to those with narrow interests. Second, even if citizens want to be engaged, a small self-serving group may capture local or regional governments and effectively block the democratic process. Third, even if most local governments are inclusive and democratic, their ability to satisfy local demands may vary widely depending on the local tax base. Without central government help, standards of service delivery may vary widely. Fourth, if the central government provides equalization funds, it will want to monitor their use, a process that will reduce local autonomy. Either the center will provide services on its own, or it will require the municipalities to submit to audits and central oversight. It cannot rely on local citizens to take care that municipalities use central government funds effectively. Fifth, the mobility of businesses and households limits the actions of municipalities eager to attract businesses and wealthy households. This may, as some claim, limit self-dealing, but it also may lead to special deals with mobile business at the expense of the public (Engel and Rose-Ackerman 2001; Rodden and Rose-Ackerman 1997). In short, local oversight is often weak, and, even when it is strong, it will not be a sufficient overall check on government.

Poland and Hungary need to make some hard choices about how and where to devolve authority and funding. Both countries need to recognize that sometimes devolution to local governments can encourage corruption, produce less public accountability, and lead to low-quality service delivery. They should resist pressure for devolution from the EU insofar as the EU lacks a realistic understanding of the local situation. Decentralization can have valuable benefits, but it is not a substitute for citizen and civil society oversight at the national level.

SEVEN

Public Participation in Policy Making

Government Procedures

The institutions of accountability discussed so far have weaknesses both in principle and in practice. Even those that promote performance accountability are of little help in ensuring the accountability of government policy making. Thus, we need to consider a final group of mechanisms that call on citizens and organized groups to participate in central-government policy making. The aim is not impartial external control but an active effort to incorporate the views of the public and of organized groups into the policy-making process.

Some political leaders in Central Europe have recognized the value of such participation, but their understanding of the possibilities has often been limited to consensual processes involving labor, business, and the government. These politicians have indeed identified an important democratic value, but they have an overly narrow conception of the options. To take one example, consider the following quotation from Péter Medgyessy from 1988 at the beginning of the transition period when he was Deputy Prime Minister of Hungary; he was Prime Minister between May 2002 and mid-August 2004:

What we [the government] should do is to make use of interest reconciliation, to base our decision-making on the consideration of the viewpoints of all those concerned.... [I]t is in the public interest that the country have not only responsible government, but [also] one which is in a position to take action and is able to act in difficult situations.... Today the government can achieve this position, through involving people in the preparation of decisions, sharing its information and concerns, and discussing its envisaged measures with them, making use of their comments. It was based on this approach that the government decided to establish the new institution of interest reconciliation – the National Council for the Reconciliation of Interests [NCRI].[193]

Of course, within a short period of time after Medgyessy made this statement, the transition process put in place a representative democracy with an electoral system that gave incumbents a reason to canvass public opinion. However, other forms of government accountability have languished. Those who see the need to extend public accountability beyond the periodic election of representatives have kept close to the interest reconciliation model exemplified by the NCRI.

In modern democracies, there are three common types of participation. The first is the tripartite process mentioned by Medgyessy, involving labor unions, employers' associations, and the government.[194] These procedures build on neocorporatist models that are most fully developed in the Scandinavian countries where labor union membership is high.[195] The government selects the types of groups to be represented and may even name the specific organizations. These bodies may be able to make binding decisions in some areas of labor market policy if they can come to a consensus. Even if they have no formal legal authority, in practice, the government promises to abide by a group consensus.[196] The substantive issues on the table involve labor market policy, such as minimum wages,

---

[193] Interview with Medgyessy published in *Magyar Hírlap*, October 4, 1988, Budapest. Translated and quoted by Héthy (2001: 9).

[194] Iankova (1997: 47) in her analysis of the Polish and Bulgarian cases provides a good working definition. To her: "Corporatism is mainly and predominantly a bargained exchange over employment, wage and incomes policies. The exchange process is fostered by the domestic and international interdependence of interests. At the policy level, the process of bargained exchange is often assumed as a process of concertation. Concertation means mainly consultative but also decision-making responsibilities of integrated interest organizations in shaping the economic and social policy of the government." See also Iankova (2002: 3–15).

[195] On the Norwegian case see Olsen (1983); on the decline of corporatism in Sweden see Lewin (1994).

[196] In some cases, governments delegate policy choices entirely to nongovernmental groups under co-determination procedures. Rothstein (1998: 109–112) labeled these processes "user oriented" and seemed to have in mind service-providing organizations such as day care centers. However, the co-determination model also applies in some regulatory areas. Sometimes this occurs by default as when an industry engages in self-regulation in the absence of a statute. Alternatively, a statute may explicitly grant regulatory or programmatic authority to an official body, such as the professional association of doctors, which may itself have been created by statute. Some of the groups that participate on advisory commissions and corporatist bodies are of this type and have the right to govern the affairs of their own members.

working hours, and conditions for overtime pay, but they may also include broader economic and social policy issues. Some describe the process as social dialogue and the participants as social partners to emphasize the idea of cooperation in furthering common ends. However, in practice, the procedure cannot avoid facing the reality that labor and business often have opposing interests and that conflicts occur within the labor and business sectors. Furthermore, trade unions may poorly represent many workers if union membership is low. The process differs from ordinary industry-level collective bargaining because there are no strike threats and government has a seat at the table.[197]

The second, sometimes called "civil dialogue," extends the social dialogue model to public policy decisions where the interests are not exclusively economic and some may be poorly organized (Armstrong 2002). Nevertheless, it retains the first model's view that participation should take the form of permanent committees composed of stakeholders. Those who participate do not represent political parties; members participate as experts and as representatives of particular interests and points of view, not as party members. Those excluded from the committee have no legal right to demand to be heard or to challenge the committee's makeup unless the challengers are named in the implementing statute. These committees have a purely advisory function; the government is ultimately responsible for deciding policy and does not bind itself to follow the group's recommendations. This civil dialogue model is a common response to demands for public participation in Poland and Hungary. Although it is a step in the direction of consultation with groups outside the governing coalition, it is essentially a closed-ended process under the control of the relevant ministry.

The third option of open-ended public participation differs from both social dialogue and civil dialogue. On the one hand, unlike civil dialogue, the government establishes no permanent advisory group and does not determine which groups participate; on the other hand, like that model and unlike a pure corporatist process, the final decision remains in the hands of the government. Participants have no decision-making responsibilities. Rather than negotiations of the affected interests, participation must be available to a wide range of civil society groups – be they advocacy organizations, ideologically driven groups, or professional associations. The

---

[197] See Armstrong (2002) and Barnard (2002). Some countries, such as Germany, Austria, Switzerland, and Japan, have systems with only weak government participation (Iankova 2002: 15).

government organizes the process under legal constraints and issues a final decision in the form of a binding regulation or a legal guideline. This then may be subject to court challenges by the same organized groups or by anyone affected by the policy. However, judicial review is limited to checks on the procedures followed and on the rule's conformity with substantive statutes and the constitution. The courts cannot review the issue de novo and hence cannot impose their view of good policy on government decision makers. Under this third type of public participation, administrative law sets out the required procedures, and the administration leaves a record of its actions that can be compared with that standard. Both the creation of procedural standards and the routine production of useable public records represent major new tasks for the postsocialist countries. Furthermore, under current conditions groups that might provide competent advice and oversight are few and must struggle to remain financially viable.

The social dialogue model is prominent in Poland and Hungary. Tripartite commissions are in place in both countries in the area of labor-management relations. Each also has a number of formal advisory committees that follow the civil dialogue model and include both members of official interest organizations – representing economic groups such as business chambers, labor unions, and professional associations – and representatives of civil society groups. However, open-ended public participation outside of elections is not well institutionalized in either country. Although both have administrative codes and recognize the need for reasoned decision making within the government, neither requires the publication of draft rules or gives outsiders general participation rights. Both the Hungarian and Polish governments make some draft rules available on the Internet and invite comments, but this practice is not universal and is not required by statute.[198] Formal hearings open to the public are uncommon and, even when they do take place, appear to be of limited importance. Both countries require the publication of central government rules with legal force but do not require written justifications and do not require publication of informal rules or resolutions, although, in practice, most are made public. The courts, including the constitutional courts, have been of little impor tance in opening up government processes to participation and oversight.

---

[198] Interviews with István Somogyvári, Administrative State Secretary, Ministry of Justice, December 12, 2002, Budapest, (Katalin Füzér helped with translation) and Botond Bitskey, Head of Department, Constitutional and Legal Department, Office of the President, November 29, 2002, Budapest.

Both Poland and Hungary have some laws with consultation requirements, but the statutory language does not always translate well into the
day-to-day practice of the government. Groups and individuals that want
to participate in the policy-making process can seldom assert the right to
be consulted unless they are specifically named in a statute. Instead, they
must argue that it is politically expedient for them to be heard or that their
involvement will produce more effective programs. Unless the constitutional rights of individuals are at stake, there is little judicial oversight of
the operation of the government as it makes policy under existing statutes
or proposes new laws.

There are fundamental differences between corporatist processes and
open-ended public participation. Decisions of the former obtain their legitimacy from the consensus of those around the table. The body, like
a legislature, need not justify its decisions in technical or moral terms.
Agreement of the members is sufficient. In contrast, under open-ended
public participation, government officials – bureaucrats and political appointees – make the final decision; the legitimacy of their decision has
three sources. The first is the accountability of the cabinet and the higher
civil service to the legislature. The second is the information they have
gathered from the concerned public – be they civil society activists, business groups, labor unions, ordinary citizens, or professional chambers.
However, because neither the legislature nor the concerned public is directly charged with making the decision, the third source of legitimacy is
the government's public explanation for the policy choice, an explanation
that must draw upon the public input as well as the government's own
expertise and political judgment. The ultimate decision must be publicly
justified because that is the only way the electorate can hold decision
makers accountable and test the relationship between the government
policy and the underlying statutory mandate.

Because of the speed and depth of the transition, the debate on public
participation and the role of organized groups has concentrated mainly on
their role in drafting legislation. The focus may shift to normative acts of
government as the pace of statute writing slows. Over time, as Poland and
Hungary move to consolidate the democratic transition, policy making
inside the government is likely to become an increasingly important locus
of public concern. One of the goals of this study is to increase the salience
of this issue in discussions of democratic consolidation.

To proceed, one needs to know both what procedures the government
actually follows in making policy and how civil society groups function.
The former is the subject of this chapter; the latter is considered in the

chapters that follow. I first outline the neocorporatist processes in labor-management relations and then summarize and critique other forms of consultation including the role of advisory committees.

Neocorporatism and Social Dialogue

The institutions for social dialogue in both Hungary and Poland are an outgrowth of their recent history, but they are also a response to pressure from the European Union (EU). The Commission has been an enthusiastic supporter of social dialogue at both the level of the EU and in member states.[199] The EU created a European Employment Strategy based on a corporatist model of dialogue and consensus among member states. In addition, the EU can promulgate labor law directives by involving only the Commission, the "social partners" from labor unions and the business community, and a qualified majority of the Council.[200]

There are some important differences between the Polish and Hungarian cases. Hungary established a tripartite institution before the end of the socialist regime. Poland did not create a tripartite body until the transition was well established. Both countries, however, shared the initial problem of ensuring strong and representative participation from both business and labor, and internal divisions in the business and labor camps are a continuing source of conflict (Iankova 2002: 4–16, Ost 2000). The most serious difficulty at present is the low level of union membership in the workforce. This means the labor unions do not directly represent most workers.

Poland

Poland did not create a formal tripartite institution until 1994. Before the 1989 elections, the high level of societal consensus meant the first

---

[199] See Iankova and Turner (2004) and Iankova (2002: 27–29). Some member states such as the Netherlands, Belgium, and the Scandinavian countries have strong corporatist traditions in labor-management relations (Gorges 1996: 116). However, some claim that corporatism is declining in Western Europe and that Europe is approaching American-style pluralism. For an analysis based on the case of Sweden, where labor union membership remains over 80% of the workforce, see Lewin (1994).

[200] See Chapter 4, Bercusson (1999), and Barnard (2002). One reason for encouraging accession countries to develop processes of social dialogue is to ensure that the EU process retains its legitimacy in the eyes of the EU courts. In the 2003 Commission report on Hungary, one motivation for encouraging social dialogue, especially at the sectoral level, is to prepare the way for participation in EU level processes (Commission of the European Communities 2003a: 35).

democratic government carried out a program of "shock therapy" with broad public approval. In the early years of the transition, leaders of the Solidarity Labor Union had a direct role in the government, and civil society was unified behind the new state and its policies.[201] By 1992, the consensus had evaporated in a wave of strikes. Protest actions by various groups of workers followed by negotiations with government were common. There was no established procedure for resolving disputes, and protestors frequently listed policy goals that went far beyond ordinary labor issues of wages, benefits, and working conditions (Ekiert and Kubik 1999: 135–157; Iankova 1997, 2002; Iankova and Turner 2004: 87–88).

In 1994, partly because of the disruptive nature of these protests and after an attempt to establish a state enterprise pact failed in 1993, the government issued a resolution in February 1994 establishing a Tripartite Committee on Socio-Economic Issues with representation of government, labor, and employers.[202] In December, the Sejm passed a law on the negotiated determination of the growth of wages, which gave the committee the competence to operate by consensus to set minimum wages, determine target maximum wage increases, and decide other related matters.[203] If the committee could not reach an agreement, the Council of Ministers made the decision. The wage decisions had to be submitted to the Sejm before they became official government policy.[204] The Ministry of Labor and Social Policy was also required to consult with national labor and employer groups about other policy issues affecting labor, although the ministry had ultimate decision-making authority. The process did not go smoothly. Even though the Solidarity Labor Union was closely tied to the government, its leaders often had sharp disagreements with ministry

---

[201] The history of Poland's social dialogue since the transition from socialism was outlined for me by Irena Wóycicka of the Institute for Research on the Market Economy, Warsaw. She was advisor and then Deputy Minister at the Polish Ministry of Labor, 1989–1994 and 1997–2001. The interview took place in Warsaw on December 5, 2002. For more details see Iankova (2002: 92–122) and Iankova and Turner (2004: 87–89).

[202] Uchwała Rady Ministrów Nr 7/94 z 15 lutego 1994 r. w sprawie powołania Trójstronnej Komisji do spraw Społeczno-Gospodarczych [Resolution of Council of Ministers No. 7/94 of February 15, 1994, on establishing Tripartite Committee on Socio-Economic Issues], unpublished.

[203] Ustawa z dnia 16 grudnia 1994 r. o negocjacyjnym systemie kształtowania przyrostu przeciętnych wynagrodzeń u przedsiębiorców oraz o zmianie niektórych ustaw [Statute of December 16, 1994, on negotiated determination of the growth of average wage compensation and on amendment of some statutes], Dz.U. 1995, No. 1, Item 2, with amendments.

[204] Interview with Wóycicka. See also Iankova (2002: 92–113), Iankova and Turner (2004: 88–89), and Matey (1997: 146–147).

officials. In addition, there were disagreements between Solidarity and other unions and within Solidarity. During this period, the Confederation of Polish Employers, which represented employers, was dominated by the large state firms and was not a strong counterweight to labor. For example, in one case, both the unions and the employers' association supported an increase in the minimum wage that the government opposed.[205]

Between 1997 and 2000, the process of social dialogue stopped. In 2001, the parliament adopted a law reestablishing the Tripartite Committee on Social and Economic Affairs. The law establishes the general rules for the representation of trade unions and employers' organizations and the scope and rules of negotiations. It also regulates the institutional framework of the social dialogue. As a result of the law, a new Tripartite Committee on Social and Economic Affairs was established in June 2002 with broader employer representation. The committee includes the Polish Confederation of Private Employers, a group, formed in 1999, that is a more effective representative of private employers.[206] The Business Center Club also recently became a member; this is a group created in 1991 as an elitist club of business people that lobbied for strong liberal positions. Its decision to join the committee is a reflection of the new importance of the tripartite process.[207] In 2002, unions and employers negotiated the liberalization of the labor laws with the government acting as a mediator. However, a draft law on revisions in the labor code has led to conflict.[208]

The main difficulty with the Polish tripartite committees has to do with representation. There are multiple employer and union organizations, and they do not always agree among themselves. Furthermore, only about 20% of the workforce is a member of any union so it is not obvious that

---

[205] Interview with Wóycicka. See also Iankova (1997, 2002). The weakness of the Confederation of Polish Employers was partly due to the government's refusal to encourage business to organize until almost 5 years after the first noncommunist government took power. This meant the Confederation was not broadly representative, was dominated by large state-owned and privatized firms, and suffered from internal disputes. One study found that, even though the Confederation was the only group with the right to be represented on tripartite bodies, its influence was limited, and it was frequently marginalized and ignored by the government (McMenamin 2002: 306–308).

[206] Interview with Wóycicka. Other tripartite institutions dealing with employment also exist at the national, regional, and local levels (Supreme Employment Council and *voivodship* and *powiat* employment councils). See Iankova (2002: 158–171).

[207] See Rafał Kalukin, "Marsz ku Komisji [The March to the Committee]", *Gazeta Wyborcza*, July 8, 2002, Rafał Kalukin, "Żeby Troje Chciało Naraz," *Gazeta Wyborcza*, November 22, 2001.

[208] Interview with Wóycicka; see McMenamin (2002: 313–315).

the interests of nonunion workers are well represented by either unions or the government.[209] In interviews conducted by Umut Korkut (2002) in the spring and summer of 2001, both labor and business groups claimed that the government operated on the basis of widespread patronage links. This led some business organizations and labor unions to find ministries very accessible and others to find them closed. Korkut argues that part of the appeal of both street protests and extremist parties comes from the weakness of social dialogue. However, because of the low level of union membership, it is hard to see how reform of that process, tied as it is to labor union representation, could overcome the alienation of many members of the labor force.

Hungary

As the quotation from Medgyessy indicates, Hungary has had a tripartite National Council for the Reconciliation of Interests (NCRI) since December 1988 at the end of the socialist regime. It survived the transition period under a variety of different names and with a variety of functions. The NCRI is legally recognized by the Hungarian Labor Law, but the statute does not specify its precise composition. The NCRI is the only group that legally must be consulted on many issues.[210]

In a January 9, 2003, interview, László Herczog, Deputy Secretary of State in Charge of Employment Policy, Ministry of Economic Affairs, provided an overview. He is a public official who has been deeply involved

---

[209] See McMenamin (2002: 304). In my interview with her, Wóycicka estimated that union membership was about 20% of the workforce and falling because it is concentrated in the large state firms that are going out of business. Many small enterprises are not unionized and the restructuring of industries such as mining has led to many closed firms. Earlier estimates of trade union membership place it at 30%–40% of the workforce, but the difference may simply represent a trend over time (Karatnycky et al. 1997: 181, 283). Survey evidence found that 18.2% of those surveyed reported trade union membership in 1990; this had fallen to 7.4% in 1996. Of course, this survey included many people not in the labor force so it is consistent with other data (Kurczewski and Kurczewska 2001: 943). This is a problem in the EU as a whole where union membership is also falling (Barnard 2002: 93). There are allegations that some employers actively discourage union organization in their workplaces. Aleksandra Sznajder uncovered examples in her dissertation research in Poland and Romania.

[210] Labor Code XXII/1992, articles 16–17, 38, 53, 75, 144. The most complete history of this and related groups until 1999 is by Lajos Héthy (2001). See also earlier work by Héthy (1994, 1995). He was the architect of the original 1988 council and the government's chief negotiator in 1994–1998. He presents an insider's view that is both supportive of the overall goals of tripartism and critical of many aspects of the Hungarian case. He gives one a sense of the frustrations of sitting at the negotiating table when he writes: "I followed three principles: to make believe that I was indifferent as to the final outcome of the talks, not to get irritated whatever was said by my partners, and not to set any time limit for the negotiations, even for myself" (Héthy 2001: 111).

with these processes since the beginning of the transition. The NCRI has had its ups and downs over the transition period linked in part to the party coalition in power and its relative sympathy toward labor or business. Nevertheless, it has never been disbanded even when the government was relatively unsympathetic. The NCRI suffered its greatest challenge under the social democratic government in 1994–1995 when the government tried and failed to use the process to produce a comprehensive social and economic agreement (Héthy 1995, 2001: 101–114).

The most difficult task facing Herczog over the years has been managing the disagreements within the subgroups of labor and business representatives. The labor union movement split over rival unions' cooperation with different political parties and different groups of employees. Tensions exist between the union confederations based on the old socialist unions, a group of autonomous unions, and a confederation of high school and university teachers and researchers. These tensions date from the early years of the tripartite process. The business associations represent very different types of firms with quite disparate interests. As in Poland, the predominant business association originally represented large state-owned and partly privatized firms; other groups represent cooperatives and agricultural enterprises. At first, the business representatives were weak. In the first major negotiation in 1992, business representatives were quite passive and did a poor job of representing employers as a whole.[211]

The right-of-center government that was in power between 1998 and mid-2002 reorganized the process. A National Labor Council continued to attempt labor-management interest reconciliation but did not deal with broader economic issues. The government created a new Economic Council but limited its role to consultation. The council included representatives of banks, foreign investors, professional associations, and the stock exchange as well as domestic employers and labor. The government was not very sympathetic to labor union demands so it is not surprising that the union leaders interviewed by Korkut (2002) were unhappy with their limited access to the ministry. Business leaders were largely satisfied. However, although those he interviewed believed the council did play a role in policy making, they still believed that whatever political coalition was in power played favorites in providing access.

The left-of-center government elected in May 2002 strengthened the Interest Reconciliation Council to include macro-economic issues and

---

[211] See Greskovits (1998: 160–164), Héthy (2001: 41–62), and Korkut (2002).

limited its membership to business associations and labor unions. The Economic Council no longer functions. The council continues to include six trade union representatives and nine employer representatives, although this is nowhere specified by statute. With one minor exception, the groups represented continue to be those that attended the first meeting called by the first postcommunist government. If all three parts agree, it can set minimum wages. If they cannot reach consensus, the government sets the level. It also must be consulted on a range of issues affecting labor, such as health and safety regulation. The government aims not just to consult the social partners but also to reach negotiated agreements.

However, there is a deeper problem. As in Poland, no more than 25% of the workforce is a union member. This means that any claims of the member unions to speak for the labor force are severely compromised by the overall weakness of unions. For business, a different problem of representation arises. Since 1995, a Hungarian statute has required that businesses join an official, statutory body or chamber of commerce (McMenamin 2002: 304, 315). These chambers might seem the logical bodies to serve on the tripartite commission. However, that is not the case. The membership was determined on the basis of the organizations that happened to exist and to be in the room when the process was organized in the early years of the transition. Many of these are only marginally concerned with national labor-management issues (Héthy 1995, 2001). Nevertheless, at least one of the business groups, the Alliance of Hungarian Manufacturers and Employers, does appear to be strong and well organized with a staff of 60, access to a large pool of experts, and an office near the parliament and the Economics Ministry (Access Initiative, part III, 2002: 2).

Conclusions

Tripartite commissions for social dialogue give organized groups a decision-making role and sometimes a de facto veto over the final outcome. These groups may mirror political party divisions in countries where a labor party faces one with strong business links. Nevertheless, labor unions represent only the interests of their workers, not the broader public, including nonunionized workers and consumers.[212] Employers' associations may not be a balanced sample of the business community and may not be good proxies for consumers and the neighbors of industrial

---

[212] In the Hungarian debate over the constitution, some favored an upper house with an explicit corporatist structure. Religious and populist parties on the right supported a Senate based on churches and unions (Arato 2000: 204).

plants. The government represents only the political parties in its coalition. Thus, some groups will be left out – supporters of interests not well represented either by the governing coalition or by the labor and management groups at the negotiating table.[213] If, as in Hungary and Poland, the state uses corporatist institutions for some issues, such as labor-management issues, and not others, there may be an imbalance in the relative power of different groups. Furthermore, there may be a tendency to give more responsibilities to existing commissions without considering if they are truly representative.[214] The role of cooperative processes is uneven across issue areas. Some have consultation processes in which groups have real power to make policy and in other cases consultation is informal and merely advisory.

The mixed record of tripartite processes in Hungary and Poland casts doubt on their value as a model for citizen and group participation in policy making. The problems are not just growing pains. Questions about the representativeness of those included and the difficulty of reaching consensus will remain even if the particular groups at the table change to reflect current realities. Even when all parties understand the issues at stake, disagreements will often persist, delaying the resolution of pressing policy issues. Processes that do not lock in a fixed set of participants and that are open to newly developing interests will better serve the long-run interest of democratic consolidation. Furthermore, if the standard of success is consensus of those at the table, this condition can thwart democratic mandates approved by a parliamentary majority. Consensual processes can be effective in limited situations in which representation is unproblematic and negotiations focus on a set of options that dominate the status quo for everyone at the table. Otherwise, they are not a general solution to the problems of collective action.

Poland: Civil Dialogue and Public Participation

In Poland policy making occurs within the government in many areas not covered by tripartite negotiations. Constitutional provisions and statutory law circumscribe these processes but provide only limited space for

---

[213] According to Greskovits (1998: 86–87), strikes have been uncommon in Central and Eastern Europe, and, in addition, many workers have exited the formal sector with its unionized firms. Neither the poor nor the workers in the informal sector are represented in tripartite negotiations.

[214] This happened in Hungary during some portions of the transition where labor and business negotiators were asked to review and seek consensus on broader issues of income policy and the government budget (Héthy 2001).

open-ended public participation. Most procedures fall into the civil dialogue category.[215]

Legal Constraints: Regulations

The Polish Constitution of 1997 specifies a closed list of sources of "universally binding" law: the constitution, statutes, ratified international agreements, and regulations (article 87, section 1).[216] Regulations can be issued
only if authorized by statute and only by certain organs specified in the
constitution. That list includes the president, the Council of Ministers,
the prime minister, Ministers with Portfolio, and the National Council
of Radio Broadcasting and Television (NCRBTV).[217] The authorizing
statute must specify which organs can issue the regulations, the scope of
the matters to be regulated, and guidelines on their content (article 92).[218]
The closed list of sources of law and the limited organs authorized to issue
regulations are a reaction to the communist government's use of independent resolutions to govern the country.

   The blind spot in the constitutional text is a failure to balance the need
for legal regularity against the need for flexibility in administration of
the law. This creates difficulties when the Constitutional Tribunal faces
challenges to an agency's regulatory authority. Thus, when the Central
Bank issued resolutions that it sought to enforce as binding law, the Constitutional Tribunal struck down three resolutions claiming that they were
de facto "universally binding normative acts" and that the bank had no

---

[215] I am particularly grateful to Maciej Kisilowski for help with some of the material in this
section.

[216] The list in the constitution also includes regulations issued by the president under a
state of emergency (article 234) and laws established by certain international organizations (article 91, section 3), essentially the EU. See also Judgment of the Constitutional
Tribunal of December 1, 1998, K. 21/98, OTK ZU 1998/7, Item 116. Local laws are
also binding in the territory of the organ issuing the enactments (Polish Constitution
article 87, section 2).

[217] Polish Constitution article 142, section 1; article 146, section 4; article 148, point 3;
article 149, section 2; article 213, section 2.

[218] Article 92 states: "1. Regulations shall be issued on the basis of specific authorization
contained in, and for the purpose of implementation of, statutes by the organs specified
in the Constitution. The authorization shall specify the organ appropriate to issue a
regulation and the scope of matters to be regulated as well as guidelines concerning the
provision of such act. 2. An organ authorized to issue a regulation shall not delegate
its competence, referred to in section 1 above to another organ." The Constitutional
Tribunal has held that the statutory specifics required depend on the subject matter of
the statute. Criminal matters and other "repressive" regulations require more details in
the statute than other areas (Judgment of November 9, 1999, K. 28/98, OTK ZU 1999/7,
Item 156).

authority under the constitution to issue such acts.[219] This decision implies that no agency that operates independently of the Council of Ministers, except the NCRBTV, can issue legally binding norms but must function through case-by-case adjudication and by issuing guidelines with no binding legal force.

The constitution does not permit open-ended grants of regulatory authority to the government or to independent agencies. It does not acknowledge that such grants might be counterbalanced by procedural requirements for transparency, public accountability, and judicial review. Under the constitution, there is only one route for public input at the national level – through the election of representatives to the Sejm, which has the power to enact statutes.[220]

Regulations can be issued without giving notice or holding a public hearing. However, final regulations must be published in the *Journal of the Laws of the Republic of Poland* (*Dziennik Ustaw*) before they go into effect. The only constitutional constraint is the possibility of a referral to the Constitutional Tribunal for a ruling on the constitutionality of the regulation or indeed of any "legal provisions issued by central state organs" (article 188, point 3). A referral is possible only after the legal provision has been promulgated. Only a limited number of bodies (the president and the ombudsman) can refer any issue to the Tribunal; other bodies (churches, labor unions, employers organizations) only can refer issues in the scope of their authority (article 191).[221] The Code of

---

[219] Judgment of June 28, 2000, K. 25/99, OTK ZU 2000/5, Item 141.

[220] Article 87, section 2, of the Polish Constitution also states that enactments of local law shall also be universally binding in the territory of the organ issuing the enactments.

[221] Individuals also have access to the tribunal to challenge the constitutionality of statutes and other normative acts but only if they believe that a final decision of a public body violates their individual constitutional rights or liberties. The entities listed in article 191 are as follows: "the President of the Republic, the Marshal of the Sejm, the Marshal of the Senate, the Prime Minister, 50 Deputies, 30 Senators, the First President of the Supreme Court, the President of the Supreme Administrative Court, the Public Prosecutor-General, the President of the Supreme Chamber of Control and the Commissioner for Citizens' Rights, the National Council of the Judiciary, to the extent specified in Article 186, section 2; the constitutive organs of units of local self-government; the national organs of trade unions as well as the national authorities of employers' organizations and occupational organizations; churches and religious organizations; the subjects referred to in Article 79 to the extent specified therein."

Article 79, section 1 gives "... everyone whose constitutional freedoms or rights have been infringed... the right to appeal to the Constitutional Tribunal for its judgment on the conformity to the Constitution of a statute or another normative act upon which basis a court or organ of public administration has made a final decision on his freedoms or rights or on his obligations specified in the Constitution."

Administrative Procedure is concerned solely with implementation of the law in individual cases. It does not apply to the procedures used to issue regulations and guidelines.[222]

There is no general statutory provision requiring the administration to provide reasons for its regulations. The only obligation comes from the internal rules of procedure of the Council of Ministers, but they are not "universally binding law" and apply only to the ministers.[223] These rules include vague requirements, such as that the justifications must include an analysis of the influence of the regulation on public finances, on the labor market, on the internal and external competitiveness of economy, and on the regions. Ministers also are supposed to report on any consultations that took place.[224] However, these documents are not routinely available to the public so they operate only as internal instructions to government agencies. With certain exceptions, the law "does not require that drafts . . . be referred for consultation to political parties, associations, other formal or informal citizens' groups, or experts" (Galligan et al. 1998: 446). Of course, consultation does frequently occur, and citizens and organized groups can seek to initiate rule-making processes and express opinions (Galligan et al. 1998: 446, 449–450).[225]

---

[222] Ustawa z dnia 14 czerwca 1960 r. Kodeks postepowania administracyjnego [Statute of June 14, 1960, Administrative procedure code], consol. text. Dz. U. 2000, No. 98, Item 1071, with amendments.; Galligan et al. (1998: 85–89, 445–446).

[223] Uchwala nr 49 Rady Ministrów z dnia 19 marca 2002 r. regulamin pracy Rady Ministrów (Resolution No. 49 of the Council of Ministers of March 19, 2002, The proceeding rules of the Council of Ministers), M.P. 2002, No. 13, Item 221, with amendments. The lack of procedural rules for drafting governmental documents played a role in one of the biggest political scandals in recent Polish history, concerning the proposed amendment of the broadcasting law. As a special parliamentary investigatory committee later revealed, crucial parts of the project were drafted in an atmosphere of struggles between the ministries, media executives, and interested politicians from the ruling party. A well-known businessman approached the CEO of one media company, claiming that he represented the prime minister and offering to make changes in the project in exchange for a large bribe. When the cabinet finally proposed the bill, an unknown person attempted to change its text during the editing process that precedes the sending of a bill to the Parliament.

[224] Article 10, section 6, points 2 and 3.

[225] The lack of transparency and of public participation in the process of issuing decrees can lead to allegations of corruption and favoritism. For example, in the late 1990s a government decision to ban the import of gelatin on the grounds of avoiding mad cow disease was shown by journalists to favor the only major national producer. Some alleged that the decision was made to favor the firm in return either for past campaign contributions or for bribes. The expertise used by the government came from material prepared at the request of the company. The prosecutor's investigation of the affair ended before reaching a clear outcome. See "Gdańsk przejmuje materiały o finansowaniu AWS" ["Gdańsk takes over the materials about AWS financing"], *Rzeczpospolita*, April 27, 1999.

For example, case studies of rule making in the Ministry of Labor and Social Policy and the Ministry of Internal Affairs found that when they drafted statutes and rules, officials frequently consulted experts. These experts were lawyers, other professionals, and "persons not associated with the ministry . . . [who] asked to aid in drafting certain legal acts" (Galligan et al. 1998: 458). The last phrase raises questions about the biased access of interested parties. The Ministry of Labor and Social Policy always consulted national labor union and employers' associations. There was less consultation with other social organizations. The ministry did not publish draft rules and did not give the addressees of the regulation a hearing (Galligan et al. 1998: 458–459). A study of business associations found that some had legal rights of consultation, and others were included in ministry deliberations because of the influence of their members. However, at least one group with a legal right of review claimed that it was given too little time to do so responsibly. In contrast, the other groups could more carefully pick and choose where to put their lobbying energies (McMenamin 2002).

Freedom of Information Act

The 1997 Constitution gives citizens the right to privacy and the protection of personal information (article 47) as well as the right to obtain information from the state without having to show that their individual rights have been violated.[226] At first, the focus was on privacy, and an act implementing that part of the constitution was passed in 1997 (Majtényi 2001b: 327–329). A statute governing the freedom-of-information provisions took longer. In 2000, the Sejm passed an act giving the public access to information about the environment, but, at that time, there was no general statute implementing the freedom-of-information provision

---

[226] Article 61, paragraphs 1–3 state:

A citizen shall have the right to obtain information on the activities of organs of public authority as well as persons discharging public functions. Such right shall also include receipt of information on the activities of self-governing economic or professional organs and other persons or organizational units relating to the field in which they perform the duties of public authorities and manage communal assets or property of the State Treasury.

The right to obtain information shall ensure access to documents and entry to sittings of collective organs of public authority formed by universal elections, with the opportunity to make sound and visual recordings.

Limitations on the rights referred to in paragraphs 1 and 2 above may be imposed by statute solely to protect freedoms and rights of other persons and economic subjects, public order, security, or important economic interests of the state.

(Hańderek 2002: 54). In September 2001, the Sejm finally adopted a Freedom of Information Act, but it has provoked controversy with some claiming that the law is weak and inadequate and others arguing that the law is stronger than the main alternative draft.

The main criticisms of the statute are that it can be trumped by other laws restricting access in particular situations, that no oversight institution exists so the only recourse is to the overburdened courts, and that the law is vague, thus giving a good deal of discretion to individual public officials.[227] In one interview, a legally trained official complained that the law was "drafted by journalists." In contrast, the Adam Smith Research Center, which played a major role in drafting the law, views it as a strong and effective response. The center emphasizes that the law refers to information, not documents, and thus can be interpreted to require that information be provided even if it does not exist as a "document."[228] Beginning in January 2004, the law gave the public access to information about the "intentions" of legislative and executive authorities and the drafting of normative acts [that is, in particular, government regulations] (Freedom of Information Act article 6, section 1, point 1). Of course, the act deals only with access to information, not process, but these provisions may help open up the administrative process.

Resolutions and Orders
The government can achieve some flexibility by issuing resolutions and orders, but these are not sources of binding law (Polish Constitution

---

[227] Teresa Górzyńska quoted in Żaneta Semprich, "Jawność – zasadą, tajność – wyjątkiem" ["Disclosure – the Rule, Secrecy – the Exception"], *Rzeczpospolita*, July 26, 2001; Hubert Izdebski, "Jawne prawie wszystko" ["Almost everything is disclosed"], *Rzeczpospolita*. October 29, 2001; Andrzej Rzepliński, "Opinia o ustawie z dnia 25 lipca 2001r. o dostępie do informacji publicznej (dla senackiego Biura Informacji i Dokumentacji)" ["Opinion on statute of 25 July 2001 on access to public information" for the Senate Bureau of Information and Documentation)], Warsaw, July 30, 2001. The constitution also gives individuals access to information pertaining to themselves (article 51). The law does not cover this type of information. Furthermore, the Administrative Procedure Code permits media and nongovernmental organizations to file complaints and suggestions to the appropriate administrative organ, and it is required to respond within one month, or the administrator could face liability. (Ustawa z dnia 14 czerwca 1960 r. Kodeks postępowania administracyjnego [Statute of June 14, 1960, Administrative procedure code], consol. text. Dz. U. 2000, No. 98, Item 1071, with amendments, articles 248 and 249). Depending on how these provisions have been interpreted, they could perform some of the functions of a freedom-of-information law.

[228] Interview with Andrzej Sadowski, Director of the Adam Smith Research Center, and material supplied by Wojciech Przybylski of the Center, December 3, 2002, Warsaw.

article 93; Garlicki 2002). They lack external legal force but are recognized in the constitution as a part of the administrative system. The Constitutional Tribunal has held that the constitution permits the Sejm to authorize any public entity to issue internal acts and gives public authorities flexibility in the forms these internal acts can take. The list is open, not closed; the "resolutions" and "orders" mentioned in article 93 are just two possibilities (Judgment of Dec. 1, 1998, K. 21/98). In practice, given the limited scope for legally binding regulations, such rules are very important in guiding the administration of laws. This raises questions about the government's freedom to decide what form of executive action to use in particular cases and about citizens' access to such rules if they have not been published. Informal legal norms are a particularly sensitive issue in Poland because they were widely used by the former communist government to compensate for "the incomplete and unsatisfactory condition of legislation." (Galligan et al. 1998: 503). Ordinary citizens often see them as unfair. Thus, there is strong support for treating such norms as supplementary rules that are inferior to statutes and formal rules, and the constitutional text reflects that view (Galligan et al. 1998: 503–504). Whatever they are called, they must conform with the basic requirements of article 93; that is, they (1) are binding only on organs "organizationally subordinate" to the entity issuing the act, (2) must be grounded in statutory authority, (3) must conform with universally binding law, and (4) cannot be used as grounds for a decision against citizens and legal persons (Polish Constitution article 93; Judgment of the Constitutional Tribunal of Dec. 1, 1998, K. 21/98).[229]

Like formal rules, informal rule making is subject to no procedural constraints. In particular, as with formal rule making, agencies need not announce their plans to issue such rules, need not publish drafts, and do not have to engage in public discussion. They are commonly drafted by officials with no mandatory inclusion of citizens or associations (Galligan et al. 1998: 506, 511). Since 2000, such rules, like formal regulations, must be published in the official journal (the *Polish Monitor*) or in similar journals issued by individual ministries.[230] This is an improvement over the

---

[229] The strains of the current system are indicated in the Central Bank case cited above. In addition to striking down three resolutions as de facto regulations, the tribunal held that the bank could issue resolutions designed to bind private banks, which were held to be "subordinate" to the Central Bank for such purposes. Judgment of June 28, 2000, K. 25/99, OTK ZU 2000/5, Item 141.

[230] Ustawa z dnia 20 lipca 2000 r. o ogłaszaniu aktów normatywnych i niektórych innych aktów prawnych [Statute of July 20, 2000, on promulgation of normative acts and some

past when publication was not required (Galligan et al. 1998: 505). The new Freedom of Information Act may play a role here in encouraging consultation under provisions that mandate access to information on executive intentions and draft normative acts and the implementation of government "programs" (article 6, section 1, point 1).

Civil Dialogue and Rule Making

At present, the civil dialogue model governs consultation in some agencies through ongoing institutions that include stakeholders. The Social Insurance Agency has a Supervisory Board that includes retirees, employer and employee representatives, and the Ministry of Labor. A National Advisory Council for the Disabled includes representatives of unions, employers, government, and the disabled. There is also a tripartite Council of Statistics that advises the Central Statistical Office. One of the responsibilities of these groups is to comment on draft normative acts and on petitions to improve regulations. A Council of Higher Education includes students as members. These councils and boards are modeled after the Tripartite Committee discussed earlier, but they have only supervisory competence in a specific area. The parallel, however, is embodied in the fact that the government has simply labeled the associations of disabled workers and pensioners "unions" and included them in advisory bodies.[231] In all these advisory bodies an institutionalized group of stakeholders has a role in the administrative process; the process excludes others with an interest in the outcome but who lack a connection with the specified groups.

A limited move toward open-ended public participation began October 1, 2001, when the European Union pressured the accession states to prepare Strategic Environmental Impact Assessments (EIAs) at all levels of government. The EIA process must include "social consultation with all interested subjects, not only with those who can prove their legal interest" (Hańderek 2002: 53). If it works effectively, this broadening of the sphere of consultation will make it possible for civil society groups to be part of the process. This is one area where the Freedom of Information Act can interact with a more open process to facilitate

---

other legal acts], Dz. U. 2000, No. 62, Item 718, with amendments., articles 10 and 12. Article 2, section 2, of that act does permit statutes to exclude some internal laws from publication.

[231] Interview with Irena Wóycicka, Institute for Research on the Market Economy, Warsaw, and advisor and Deputy Minister at the Polish Ministry of Labor, 1989–1994, 1997–2001, on December 5, 2002, Warsaw; Galligan et al. (1998: 511).

the involvement of nongovernmental organizations (NGOs). However, the governing statute is vague about how to structure the participation process, with NGOs urging that it permit meaningful participation early enough to affect the outcome (Hańderek 2002: 55–56). It remains unclear how the process will work in practice, and, in any case, it does not appear to be subject to judicial review.

Conclusions

The relative lack of transparency and public input in the promulgation of both formal regulations and other legal enactments suggests the importance of proactive efforts by NGOs and individuals to use the Freedom of Information Act to find out what the government is doing. The limited scope for formal regulations pushes public entities to use more informal methods. The skepticism about government discretion reflected in the constitutional text may be producing a situation with three problematic features. First, some statutes may be difficult to implement effectively because the government cannot issue binding rules. Second, the government may administer others through informal acts and case-by-case adjudications that make it difficult for the public to understand government policy and to play a role in its formation. Third, although some judicial review of government policy making occurs even without a law on rule making, this review is, in practice, seldom effective. The Constitutional Tribunal signaled a new, possibly more aggressive stance in decisions in 2002 and 2004, but the impact of these decisions remains to be seen.[232]

Citizens and interest groups have no levers to challenge their exclusion from the policy-making process. They can challenge the application of a law or regulation only in a particular case, and such challenges will not usually raise broader issues concerning the representative character, transparency, and competence of government rule-making procedures.

Hungary: Civil Dialogue and Public Participation

As in Poland, Hungarian law provides no general, legally enforceable participation rights in the drafting of rules and statutes. Some statutes include participation requirements mostly in the form of advisory committees.[233] Some participants, such as the Ombudsman for Data Protection

---

[232] See Chapter 5.
[233] For example, the Environmental Act (LIII/1995), the laws dealing with education, the Regional Development and Country Planning Act (XXI/1996), and, of course, the Hungarian Labor Code (XXII/1992).

and Freedom of Information, some legal academics, and several environmental groups have urged more transparent and legally accountable procedures, but, at present, consultation is mainly under the control of the government and can change dramatically when the political coalition in power shifts. The government that came to power in 2002 has made some tentative moves to increase information and access, but these have not been codified into law.[234]

Constitution

The constitution authorizes the issuance of decrees by the government (that is, signed by the prime minister), by cabinet ministers, and by local representative bodies. Decrees must not conflict with statutes or with higher ranking legal norms (Hungarian Constitution article 35, section 2; article 37, section 3; article 44/A, section 2). Thus, under the constitution, decrees do not have to be authorized by statute; it is sufficient that there is no conflict. They can perform a gap-filling role. Of course, as more areas of public life are covered by statutes, this open-ended grant of rule-making authority has become less important. The courts supervise the legality of government decrees and of any other actions of the public administration. The Constitutional Court has interpreted these portions of the constitution to limit the power of the government in several ways. For example, in 1991 in a case dealing with abortion, the court held that it was unconstitutional to regulate a fundamental right through an executive decree. However, the decision accepted the need to use executive decrees in many cases to avoid overburdening the parliament.[235] As another example, in 1997 the court upheld a statute that delegated regulation of the medical profession to the Hungarian Medical Association (HMA).[236] However, the court held that the HMA's authority was limited by the constitutional right to free choice of employment and occupation and by a requirement

---

[234] "With You or Without You: Including the Civil Organizations in Legislation," *Magyar News*, April 17, 2003 (translated by Csilla Kalocsai) [hereafter "With You or Without You"].

[235] The court held that because the regulation of abortion required a judgment on the meaning of the constitutional right to life, a legislative judgment was required [Decision 64/1991 (XII.17) on the Regulation of Abortion, excerpted by Sólyom and Brunner (2000: 178–199). See similar language in Decision 3/1997].

[236] Sometimes executive power is delegated by statute to self-governing professional associations. The associations' rules can be nullified by the minister in the appropriate subject area, but the associations can appeal such decisions to the courts. Interview with Professor Antal Ádám, School of Law, University of Pécs, October 12, 2002, Pécs, conducted in Hungarian by Katalin Füzér.

for judicial review for conformity with the constitution. The court held that this review must involve both the facts and the law.

Supervising the legality of the decisions of public administration therefore cannot be limited constitutionally to reviewing only the formal legality of decisions.... In an action for judicial review of an administrative decision the court is not bound by the facts of the case as determined by the public administrative body; further the court can also review the legality of administrative discretion. Deciding on the merits of the case is not against the fact that the court instructs the administrative organ...to conduct a new procedure.[237]

Law on Normative Acts

A distinctive feature of the Hungarian legal system is the Law on Normative Acts (XI/1987) passed at the end of the socialist period. The act provides that decrees must not conflict with statutes. This was a concession by the socialist government that used decrees extensively.[238] The law also specifies the procedures to be used for issuing decrees, although it leaves some crucial features unspecified. The minister is responsible for promulgating the decree, but "citizens – directly or through their representative bodies – participate in the preparation and creation of legal regulations [i.e., normative acts] affecting their daily life" (article 19). Furthermore, before promulgating a decree, "jurisdictional bodies, social organizations, and interest representative organs have to be involved in the preparation of draft legal regulations which either affect the interests represented and protected by them or their social relations" (article 20).[239] Jurisdictional bodies are local and regional governments and other ministries that may be involved in implementing a regulation; social organizations include groups such as environmental and women's groups with policy agendas; interest representative organizations are trade unions and business and professional associations. Unfortunately, the act does not specify how ministries should organize the consultation process or if they must make the results public. Because draft rules need not be published, the

---

[237] Decision 39/1997 (VII.1), On the Judicial Review of Administrative Decisions, excerpted by Sólyom and Brunner (2000: 368).

[238] The act attempted to put some order into the chaotic state of legal rules and decrees that characterized the late socialist period. Interview with Prof. Dr. József Petrétei, Professor, Vice Dean and Head of Department, Department of Constitutional Law, Faculty of Law, University of Pécs, November 15, 2002, Pécs. Katalin Füzér translated questions and answers; see Galligan and Smilov (1999: 117) and Galligan et al. (1998: 421).

[239] Based on translations by Katalin Füzér and Csilla Kalocsai. Interview with Prof. Petrétei. See also Galligan et al. (1998: 423).

government and its ministers generally will have considerable leeway to manage participation by deciding who is to receive the draft and how much time to allocate for comments.

In its original form, the act contained broad requirements for consultation with social groups and self-governing associations. The first democratic government repealed these provisions in 1990 (XXXI/1990) on the grounds that they were purely window dressing enacted by the previous government to try to enhance its democratic credentials, and that they would undermine efforts to create a functioning multiparty democracy. This suspicion of interest-based representation remains in Hungary and surfaces periodically in debates over the role of nonparty groups in political life.

The Law on Normative Acts includes no provisions for judicial review so these consultation requirements do not create any rights that groups and individuals can enforce in the ordinary courts. My interviews suggested that the law is not taken into account by groups seeking to participate in policy making. Its provisions are essentially internal orders to the bureaucracy and the ministers. The only possibility for judicial review would be to claim constitutional violations. Because Hungary has permissive standing requirements for some kinds of constitutional challenges, such allegations can provide a route to the Constitutional Court.[240]

However, the court has not been sympathetic to attempts to build consultation requirements into the constitution. One exception concerns consultation with local governments and affected organizations under the Act on Regional Development and Country Planning (XXI/1996). In deciding a challenge to that law, the court held that county governments must consult with these bodies before drawing up a plan (Decision III/1997). However, this decision was very closely tied to particular clauses in the constitution dealing with local government. Other cases deal with the process of drafting national statutes. In 2001 the court held that, in spite of the language of the Law on Normative Acts, consultation was not constitutionally required unless the groups to be consulted were explicitly listed in the statute. Unlike the Regional Planning Law, the Law on Normative Acts mentions no specific groups, thus no one could claim a right to be heard.[241] In other words, the court refused to read the act as carrying out

---

[240] Interview with Prof. Petrétei. "Anyone" can ask the court to rule on the constitutionality of legal rules, to adjudicate alleged violations of constitutional rights, or to eliminate unconstitutional omissions (Hungarian Constitution articles 33–36, 51). However, the court is not required to decide all questions put to it in a timely fashion so many cases remain unresolved for years.

[241] Decision 10/2001; see also Decisions 7/1993, 16/1998, 50/1998, 39/1999.

constitutionally mandated rights. As a result, no one can legally enforce the clauses in the act that mandate public participation.

Information Rights and Consultation

The constitution includes a right of citizens to learn and disseminate information of public interest (Hungarian Constitution article 61, section 1). A 1992 Act on Protection of Personal Data and Disclosure of Data of Public Interest (Act LXIII/1992) codified this right and established the Commissioner for Data Protection and Freedom of Information with the dual role of ensuring the right to privacy and furthering government transparency.[242] According to the first incumbent of this office, the purpose of the act is "rendering the State transparent for the public and the citizens aloof from scrutiny" (Majtényi 2001b: 330). As well stated by a lawyer on the commissioner's staff: "freedom of information amounts to asserting control over government as a citizen's right. In other words, it means the citizen has a judicially enforceable privilege to be informed about the activities of government bodies that use the taxpayers' money to exercise public power" (Kerekes 2001: 288). The Environmental Protection Act also contains a freedom-of-information provision.[243] Both acts permit anyone to obtain access to information. There is no need to show a personal or legal interest.

There are two difficulties in practice. First, given the legacy of the one-party state, there is considerable popular distrust of the government's collection of personal data but less concern with ensuring openness and transparency. Most petitions to the commissioner concern data protection and privacy so such cases dominate the commissioner's work. As of 2001, the ordinary courts had decided no more than two dozen freedom-of-information cases with about the same number of cases decided by the Constitutional Court at the instigation of the commissioner. Overall, public access were only about 10% of the commissioner's caseload.[244]

---

[242] The act has a status in between an ordinary statute and an amendment to the constitution. A two-thirds vote of those present is required to amend the statute. Amending the constitution requires a two-thirds vote of the members (Majtényi 2001a).

[243] LXIII/1992, http://www.obh.hu/adatved/indexek/AVTV-EN.htm and LIII/1995. The court must hear cases brought under the Freedom of Information Act promptly. This ability to jump the queue is important because routine cases can take years to be resolved. Telephone interview with André Farkas and György Kalas, REFLEX, January 10, 2003, Győr.

[244] See Kerekes (2001: 289), interview with László Majtényi, the first Ombudsman for Data Protection and Freedom of Information, October 14, 2002, Budapest.

By combining the protection of personal data in a single statute with freedom-of-information provisions, Hungarian law highlights the possible tension between the two. Some data that concern the operation of government will refer to individuals and be personal in nature (Kerekes 2001: 290). One source of tension has been confronted by the Constitutional Court [Decision 60/1994 (XII.24) AB; Kerekes 2001: 291]. The court held that government officials and those holding public roles in politics have a narrower sphere of privacy than ordinary people. "Access to such personal data is essential not only for an informed discussion of politics, but also for a correct perception of government authorities and for substantiating the trust placed in them" (Kerekes 2001: 291). However, controversies continue to arise when the commission argues for the release of information about public officials' personal ties with government contractors and economic interests (Kerekes 2001).

Second, even when requests are made, information is not always easily available. Interviews conducted by the Environmental Management and Law Association found that in seeking environmental information, "people have to know the sources well, they have to make some special efforts to cope with the bureaucracy, and those with the best chances...have some direct personal connections to the authorities possessing the information." Furthermore, contrary to the intent of the Freedom of Information Act, authorities tend to ask the reason for the request and might deny a request if they judge that the requester is not "interested enough" (Environmental Management and Law Association 2002: 10–11). Nevertheless, many requests are filled. The Office of Public Information of the Environmental Ministry handles 650 requests per month; the total rises to about 1,000 if one includes other bodies that handle requests for environmental information (Environmental Management and Law Association 2002: 16–17).[245]

The treatment of Freedom-of-Information-Act requests can affect public participation in policy making. Civil society groups have tried to use these acts to increase their influence by pushing for the disclosure of drafts prepared by the government or its various ministries. The portion of the act dealing with freedom of information has an exception in article 19, section 5, stating that: "Unless otherwise provided by law, working documents and other data prepared for the authority's own use, or for the purpose of decision making are not public within 30 years of

---

[245] See also the material on Hungary put together by the Access Initiative with heavy input from the EMLA at http://www.accessinitiative.org.

their creation. Upon request, the head of the authority may permit access to these documents or data." The government has sometimes used this paragraph to limit effective outside review of draft laws or regulations. Because the Law on Normative Acts does not require publication of draft statutes and rules, it is not clear whether drafts can be disclosed when the government asks outside groups and individuals for comments. It is also unclear whether a civic group has the right to publish a draft it receives for comments.

In 2000, a national umbrella organization objected that some ministries sent drafts of decrees for comment but stipulated that the drafts could not be made public for 30 years. The organization pointed out that this effectively prevented its member organizations from participating in a discussion of the drafts. It brought its complaint to the ombudsman who oversees the administration of the act, although in a purely advisory capacity. He supported the position of the civic organization in connection with a draft proposal dealing with the government's strategy against corruption. The ombudsman pointed out that some ministries treat drafts circulated to outsiders as exceptions under article 19, section 5, although others do not. He argued that the line between public and private drafts needs to be clarified in light of the public interest in understanding and debating proposed rules and laws.[246] In his advisory opinion, he supported a policy of greater openness so that documents would not be circulated only to those with inside connections. Nevertheless, there is, at present, no legal requirement to publish proposed rules and statutes.

Actual practice appears to vary. In the environmental area, draft laws and rules are routinely available to the public. The official National Environmental Council, discussed later, receives draft statutes and rules for review, and some members of the council post draft laws and rules received on an open web site called Green Spider that provides environmental information and is maintained by several environmental groups. The Ministry for Environment does not object to this practice and posts drafts itself on the ministry's web site.[247] The principle articulated by those who post drafts is that once a draft has been made available to someone

---

[246] 2000 Annual Report of the Parliamentary Commissioner for Data Protection and Freedom of Information, Hungary, http://www.obh.hu/adatved/index/2000. See Kerekes (2001: 298).

[247] Interview with György Erdel, Deputy Under Secretary for Legal and Public Administration in the Ministry for Environment and Water, reported in "With You or Without You."

outside of government, then it should be available to anyone in order to facilitate debate.[248] In addition, the Aarhus Convention on procedural environmental rights[249] and the EU Directive on Freedom of Information with respect to the Environment [90/313/EEC, 1990 OJ (L 158)] both encourage open treatment of environmental policy making. In this area a number of fairly well-established groups monitor the government and are influenced by American and Western European models of public involvement.

Note that in the ombudsman's case discussed earlier, the petitioning organization was not complaining about the denial of a request for information. Instead, it asserted that the government had an obligation to make draft proposals public at the time it sought comments from outside groups. The group attempted to link the provision of information to the possibility of effective participation by outsiders. A next step is to claim not only that the government should provide information but also that it should facilitate broad public consultation. Instead of relying only on advisory committees with fixed membership, it also should hold public hearings open to a wide range of participants.

This possibility was raised in connection with negotiations with Slovakia over the Bős-Nagymaros dam on the Danube. The controversy began before the change in regime, and the project is an ongoing source of dispute. A civic organization claimed that Hungary was required to have nationwide public hearings on projects with international environmental consequences such as the dam. The Commissioners for Citizens' Rights and for Data Protection concluded that environmental issues required not just public access to information but also the participation of citizens and their organization in decision making. However, the particular type of nationwide hearing supported by the civic organization was not required by either Hungarian or international law. Nevertheless, the commissioners went on to argue for an amendment to the Environmental Act that would require such hearings. The Minister of the Environment issued a draft decree in 2000 on environmental impact statements that

---

[248] Interview with Sándor Fülöp, executive director of the Environmental Management and Law Association, October 29, 20002, Budapest.

[249] Its formal title is the Aarhus Convention of 25 January 1998 on Access to Information, Public Participation in Decisionmaking and Access to Justice in Environmental Matters (available at http://www.unece.org/env/pp/treatytext.htm). Rose-Ackerman and Halpaap (2002) discuss the failure of many Western European countries to ratify the treaty, although they were among the original signatories. Most of the Central European countries have ratified the treaty.

included a requirement for an open forum on any development with an environmental impact across national borders.[250] However, it does not appear to have been implemented.

Advisory Councils: Civil Dialogue Model

Instead of open-ended public participation, a number of Hungarian laws call for the creation of advisory councils. These councils are permanent bodies with shifting individual membership that review a range of government proposals and sometimes initiative studies on their own. As in Poland, they seem loosely based on the Tripartite Commission in the labor-management area but without any government commitment to implement their recommendations.

A general pattern repeats itself in a number of policy areas. An advisory council is set up with the types of members specified in the statute but with the selection of persons left to particular organized groups. The ministry or the government must consult with the council but is not subject to penalties if it fails to do so. The government decision makers are under no obligation to consult more broadly or to consider if particular interests are poorly represented on the councils. Because the government need not permit broader participation, there may be little or no opportunity for input from those outside these organized bodies. The ministry may consult only with those outsiders that it knows and trusts. Furthermore, even when public participation is mandated, as it was during the reform of the pension system in Hungary, the process may be handled poorly.[251] Any access groups or individuals have outside the advisory council route is unregulated and ought to benefit those with more resources and stronger organizations. The ultimate decision is in the hands of the government, however, so a minister, in principle, can compensate for any perceived bias in the councils. To some extent, of course, biased communications are inevitable, as studies of the rule-making process in the United States indicate, but at least these biases could be countered somewhat by requiring open-ended hearings and permitting court review of the policy-making process. At present, most consultation with civil society groups

---

[250] 2000 Annual Report and 2000 Cases Involving the Disclosure of Data of Public Interest and the Conflict Between Various Informational Rights, A Joint Recommendation by the Parliamentary Commissioner of Citizens' Rights and the Data Protection Commissioner on Public Hearings and the Disclosure of Information Related to the Environment, http://www.obh.hu/adatved/indexek/2000.

[251] On pension reform, I am relying on Eszter Kósa who wrote a Central European University doctoral dissertation on the topic.

is purely at the discretion of public officials. Several examples illustrate these broad regularities.

In the environmental area, an established process exists for government consultation with the National Environmental Council (NEC), an advisory group that includes 21 people from outside the government plus the Minister for the Environment.[252] The government is required to send all draft laws and rules with an environmental impact to the NEC, and the NEC can initiate its own evaluations and projects. Created by the 1995 Act on the Environment (LIII/1995, section 45), the NEC is meant to "simultaneously guarantee public participation, scientific basis of the decisions and reconciliation of economic and social interests" (Hungarian National Environmental Council 2000–2001, 2002). It consists of seven members representing the environmental movement, seven representing the scientific community, and seven from business. The members are volunteers chosen by each of the three groups – that is, the National Gathering of Environmental and Nature Protection Nongovernmental Organizations, the Academy of Sciences, and the National Association of Hungarian Manufacturers.[253] The selection process removes the government from any role in appointing members. Thus, the NEC has the potential to be truly independent.

However, in practice, the NEC has some structural weaknesses that limit its effectiveness. Although the government is obligated to provide drafts to the council and give it time to respond, this does not always happen even though a Constitutional Court decision held that the NEC could obtain any draft it found relevant. Simply mandating consultation cannot make it effective. The advisory role of the NEC is limited by its small staff (four professionals in late 2002) and by the short time limits imposed by the government when it sends the council draft laws and regulations. Frequently, the time to respond is a week or two even though the act specifies 30 days for the review of environmental assessments [LIII/1995, section 44(2)]. The deadlines are often too short for any real discussion among the members, and even a 30-day window would not be sufficient for the members to develop independent data or analyses.

---

[252] The NEC advises the prime minister, not the environmental ministry, which gives it somewhat more influence than a group reporting to a single ministry. This is important because environmental issues arise in the administration of agricultural and transportation programs and in programs involving the Ministry of the Interior.

[253] Hungarian National Environmental Council, 2000–2001(2002); Commission of the European Communities (2001a: 75); Access Initiative (2002, part IV.B.1.c), and interview with Miklós Bulla, Secretary General, NEC, December 20, 2002, Budapest.

Formal meetings of the council are held only once a month, but the cabinet meets weekly. This means some issues are resolved by subcommittees in between plenary sessions, with the rest of the group simply signing off on the decision.[254] More fundamentally, the NEC cannot be characterized as a public forum and is not equivalent to an open-hearing process. Rather the interests and the people consulted are defined ex ante, not issue by issue.

The leaders of the environmental movement in Hungary have a mixed evaluation of the NEC. Some environmentalists advocated for the creation of such a group during the negotiations over the 1995 act. Two of the people I interviewed, Sándor Fülöp, Executive Director of the Environmental Management and Law Association, and, András Lukács, President of the Clean Air Action Group, were environmental members of the body in 2002 and obviously find it valuable to be part of the process. Lukács, however, does not believe the body has much influence. Others were even more skeptical. György Droppa of Danube Circle, worried that "structured" consultation risked cooptation and the weakening of environmental voices. Both he and Ada Ámon, Executive Director of Energia Klub, had opposed the creation of the NEC when the law was drafted in 1994. Barnabás Bödecs, President of HUMUSZ, an alliance concerned with waste management, was a member for 1 year and then resigned after voting no on a proposed hazardous waste management law. Both he and Ámon saw the NEC as ineffective because it reviewed too many drafts too late in the process with too short deadlines. Bödecs believes the use of the media along with efforts to seek a negotiated compromise with the government are better routes to influence.[255]

Others pointed to the partisan nature of government-NEC relations. Under the right-of-center government that lost power in 2002, relations

---

[254] One critic of the NEC complains that the environmental groups do not get any feedback after the NEC reviews a draft rule or law. She claims that information on drafts is not, in fact, available to anyone. Interview with Zsuzsa Foltányi, director of Ökotárs Foundation, in "With You or Without You."

[255] Interviews with Fülöp and András Lukács, President of Clean Air Action Group, December 20, 2002, Budapest; György Droppa, member of the board of directors of Danube Circle, Co-chairman of the Green Party, November 27, 2002, Budapest; Ada Ámon, Director of Energia Klub, December 2, 2002, Budapest; and Barnabás Bödecs, Chairman of HUMUSZ and one of the three founders of HUMUSZ in 1995, January 4, 2003, Budapest. In an interview, István Farkas, Director, National Society of Conservationists, stated that he believes the NEC is not a good model for future efforts to improve public participation, December 18, 2002, Budapest. See Chapter 9 for more information on these organizations.

were frosty but considerably improved under the new government. Nevertheless, the very existence of the NEC may have constrained the right-of-center government. Whatever the political complexion of the government in power, however, the basic structural weaknesses of the process remain. However, the EU has expressed an interest in the NEC model so it is important for future research to determine whether the NEC's problems are the growing pains of a new institution or whether they are more fundamental.[256]

In other areas as well, advisory committees comment on draft laws and regulations and provide policy advice. These committees include representatives from interested state bodies, citizens' representative organizations, and scientists and professionals with expertise on the issue. The required participants are organizations of citizens or other interests; individuals seldom seem to be involved directly (Galligan et al. 1998: 423–425). One example is the advisory Economic Council mentioned previously. In the social welfare area, a number of councils advise the Ministry of Social, Health, and Family Welfare. They include councils for issues affecting the handicapped, elderly people, and social issues in general. However, in many areas active client groups do not exist so that clients are "represented" only by service providers.[257]

In the field of education formal consultation bodies exist both for higher education and for primary and secondary schooling. There is no explicit provision for judicial review of the consultation processes, and their role is purely advisory. The Act on Public Education (LXXIX/1993, articles 96–98) establishes four permanent bodies: a National Council on Public Education (NCPE), a Council on Public Education Policy (CPEP), a National Committee of Minorities (NCM), and a National Council of Student Rights (NCSR). The NCPE is an advisory group of 23 appointed by the minister who must obtain its opinion on policy matters. The minister picks 3 members, teachers' associations pick 10, teacher training

---

[256] In addition to the interviewees mentioned in the text, my discussion of the NEC is based on the interview with Bulla and on Hungarian National Environmental Council, 2000–2001 (2002). The NEC report on its activities in 2000–2001 stated that government consultation with the NEC had reached a nadir at the end of the previous government.

[257] Interview with Kinga Göncz, Political State Secretary, Ministry of Social, Health and Family Welfare, December 28, 2002. See "With You or Without You," which also includes an interview with Göncz. In the mid-1990s, Robert Jenkins studied the Social Council at the Ministry of Welfare that was created by decree in 1990 (1990/1060) and includes representatives of central and local government, employers, employees, and social policy organizations. He argues that, in spite of its formal structure, the council was not central to social policy formation (Jenkins 1999: 189–191).

schools pick 6, the Hungarian Academy of Sciences picks 2, and the national employers' associations select 2. Except for the 3 appointed by the minister, terms are 5 years so the members may have some independence from the minister. The act sets up quite detailed criteria for election of the representatives of teachers and teacher training schools. The other committees also advise the minister. The CPEP has members from each of the groups affected by education policy including representatives of national organizations of parents and students, local governments, minority self-governments, private schools, teachers, and ministry representatives. It seems doubtful that this group can function as an effective voice for its component groups, especially parents and students. The NCM consists of representatives of the minority self-governments and must be consulted on educational matters relating to minorities. The NCSR has nine members with six selected by national student organizations.

The Higher Education Act establishes a Higher Education and Research Council (article 76–79) to advise the minister.[258] It deals with general policy matters at the request of the minister and "shall publish" its opinions and recommendations. It has 21 members – 10 elected by higher education institutions and 10 by groups that hire graduates (professional chambers, employers, scientific bodies, and local governments). The minister appoints the remaining member. All serve 3-year terms. The language of the statute suggests that, on broad policy matters, the council "shall" advise the minister whether or not he or she asks for its help.

Water Management Councils, which make proposals on managing water supply, exist throughout the country as a result of a 1998 government decree [5/1998 (III.11) KHVM]. The members are local and county governments and related bodies, industrial and engineer chambers, water management cooperatives, and other water and sewage enterprises. Members of the public and environmental NGOs participate to some degree but have no legal entitlements (Environmental Management and Law Association 2002: 12).

The Act on Regional Development and Spatial Planning and an accompanying regulation (XXI/1996, 184/1996) set the framework for "partnership" in planning and programming. Regional Development Councils include only government and local government representatives. The

---

[258] LXXX/1993, accessible through: http://www.om.hu. The act (articles 80–81) also establishes an accreditation committee that has real authority to regulate aspects of individual institutions' degree granting activity. It operates like a quasi-independent regulatory agency within the ministry.

councils can invite business and social partners to attend the meetings, and these groups have a right to be consulted. Most regional councils do not invite NGOs. The National Regional Development Council advises the government and seeks to reconcile the disparate interests of local and regional governments, trade unions, and business. The official members are from the several government ministries, seven regions, business, trade unions, and some of the 19 counties. It has no obligation to include NGOs, but it regularly invites an NGO representative to attend meetings and receive drafts for comment ahead of time. Furthermore, the National Society of Conservationists, an NGO umbrella group with 86 members, was asked by the government to organize public hearings on the National Development Plan, but they did this at the request of the government, not as a result of any legal right.[259]

Conclusions

Mechanisms for consultation exist in Hungary, at least in some ministries. They mostly take the form of consultation committees with an advisory role that have more or less independent membership. If they have a statutory basis, the Constitutional Court has held that they must be consulted under article 2, section 1, of the constitution, which states that Hungary is a state operating "under the rule of law." The court found unconstitutional a government decree issued without consulting with the NEC (Decision 30/2000). On the other side of the ledger, there is the 2001 case that refused to grant constitutional status to participation rights in statutes unless specific groups are mentioned, such as the NEC or local governments (Decision 10/2001). The court also distinguishes between "organizations of public authority" and other groups. The former are established by law and include bodies such as the Academy of Science, the associations of medical doctors and lawyers, business chambers, and local governments. Consultation rights are frequently incorporated into their founding statutes, and these have been upheld by the Constitutional Court. In contrast, civil society groups have no official status and no legal right to be heard. Overall, there are no general legal requirements governing notice, participation, and reasoned justification with respect to government policy making and the issuance of decrees and rules.

Judicial review of government policy making is limited except where constitutional rights are at stake. The Constitutional Court has decided a number of important cases and was a focus for popular discontent in the

---

[259] See Farkas (2002: 59–62); interview with I. Farkas.

early years of the democratic state because of generous standing rules and an activist court.[260] However, the court has not provided much guidance on judicial review of "the legality of decisions of public administration" (Hungarian Constitution article 50, section 2) that involve conformity with statutory schemes rather than asserted violations of constitutional rights. Individuals or groups have very limited means to challenge rules and decrees. If a constitutional issue is at stake, plaintiffs can bring constitutional challenges, but such cases may languish on the court's docket for years, and those cases that have been decided do not suggest much judicial sympathy for expanding participation rights.

The government elected in 2002 has made a few moves in the direction of openness. The Ministry of Justice published a draft law on minorities on its web site and invited comments. In drafting revisions to the Criminal Code, 52 organizations sent in their suggestions.[261] The ministry also has encouraged other ministries to publicize draft laws and regulations and accept comments.[262]

The Ministry of Social, Health, and Family Welfare has begun a process of broader consultation. In June 2003, its web site included several draft laws and other decision documents and plans. It sends draft laws to a mailing list of about 600; however, about 6,100 organizations work in related fields so it is obviously omitting many, probably smaller, organizations.[263] Of course, this ministry will have difficulty developing effective consultation programs for the beneficiaries of programs that serve the poor, the infirm, and the handicapped simply because these groups are likely to be poorly organized and informed. Thus, effective consultation in this policy area will require more proactive behavior by the ministry than in other areas where well-organized groups already exist. In fact,

---

[260] Kim Scheppele, September 3, 2003, e-mail.

[261] "With You or Without You." The article reports that material from the Hungarian Helsinki Committee and the Society for Liberty was rejected as biased. Of course, no government department has an obligation to incorporate all the suggestions it receives, but with no judicial review there is no check on ministry discretion.

[262] Interview with István Somogyvári, Administrative State Secretary, Ministry of Justice, December 12, 2002, Budapest.

[263] Interview with Göncz. In June 2003, Csilla Kalocsai reported that the following material was on the ministry's web site under the heading "Laws and Decrees": draft law dealing with modifications of the social law; draft law on some aspects of the legal position of medical doctors and other health workers T/3780 and the justification of the draft law; parliamentary decision about Decade of Health and the Béla Johan National Program; questions and answers about the law on institutions; code and point system for patient treatment; and parliamentary decision draft on social security between Hungary and Canada, H/3840. The web address is http://www.eszcsm.hu/indexelit.html.

Kinga Göncz, Political State Secretary in the Ministry of Social, Health and Family Welfare, an official with considerable experience in the voluntary sector, expressed some frustration with the process of developing productive means of public participation and consultation, although she is clearly sympathetic to these developments. Part of the problem seems to be different expectations about what participation is meant to accomplish. Some civil society groups expect a negotiating process such as the tripartite processes that prevail in labor-management relations. The ministry appears to envisage a process of consultation, similar to the rule-making process in the United States, in which the government retains ultimate authority to draft the law or decree.[264]

In addition, the Ministry of Justice claims that the guidelines on submitting opinions on proposed laws and normative acts need to be updated. It has proposed a substitute for the Law on Normative Acts under which all drafts should be available on the Internet with a 15-day comment period. To balance the increased opportunities for public participation, the ministry draft proposes that legal professionals should codify the legal texts. This type of structural reform, however, is unlikely to pass because it would require a supermajority in the parliament and thus would need the support of some opposition party members.[265]

Conclusions

In spite of some salient differences, the Polish and Hungarian governments face similar challenges in developing more accountable policy-making procedures. Reliance on advisory committees and corporatist processes of social dialogue are not sufficient. The difficulties with current procedures fall into four categories: public knowledge, open processes, government justifications, and judicial review.

Proposed regulations and statutes are not routinely made public when they are still under consideration. Hungary is moving toward broader internet access for drafts, but many agencies still circulate proposed rules only to a select list that is not permitted to circulate the draft further. Even when plans and proposals are made public, few laws require open-ended hearings or information gathering from the public. Instead, agencies limit

---

[264] "With You or Without You" and interview with Göncz.

[265] "With You or Without You" and interview with Prof. Dr. Géza Kilényi, D.Sc., Pázmány Péter Catholic University, Budapest, former justice of the Constitutional Court, December 18, 2002, Budapest.

consultation to pre-set advisory groups or a select group of insiders. In practice, consultation through these routes is sometimes quite broad, but the advisory committees' composition limits the amount of consultation, and the government often is not very interested in hearing from those outside the national government. The law does not require public, written analyses providing legal and policy justifications for normative acts (regulations) in either country, and such analyses are seldom prepared.

Freedom-of-information acts in both countries require public agencies to provide information to citizens without a showing that their own rights are at stake. This provision for citizen access, which is the core of a freedom-of-information act, can help increase government accountability and transparency. The act in Poland is too new to evaluate with confidence. Petitioners can use the Hungarian act to demand more government openness, but the act has not produced a major change in the operation of the administrative process, and officials do not always satisfy requests promptly. Nevertheless, the underlying laws in Hungary and Poland are an advance over standard practice in many countries in Western Europe where even the EU directive concerning freedom of information on environmental matters has been hotly contested.[266]

The judiciary has not imposed procedural constraints on rule making. In Hungary, court challenges to the administrative rule-making process are seldom successful. Access to the Constitutional Court is open to all citizens who want to challenge the constitutionality of a law, but the court has been unsympathetic to claims concerning process unless the particular substantive statute is very clear. Nevertheless, the openness of the Constitutional Court to citizens' complaints means it does respond to substantive constitutional concerns. The court has also directed that parliament regulate certain issues by statute; it judged that government decrees were insufficient. In contrast, in Poland access to the Constitutional Tribunal is more limited and is seldom open to individuals, but the tribunal recently struck down aspects of two laws. In addition, Poland has an administrative court system, but it mostly deals with the implementation of the law in individual cases. Although it does sometimes rule on the meaning of

---

[266] See Rose-Ackerman (1995: 114–115). Germany has no general freedom of information act and diligently guards bureaucratic prerogatives. However, there has been some movement at the state (*Länder*) level in Germany. Brandenburg, formerly part of East Germany, adopted a freedom of information act in 1998 that borrows from the Hungarian model. As in Hungary, the regulation of access to current documents is combined with provisions that deal with access to old secret police files, a very different issue. Berlin and Schleswig-Holstein have followed the lead of Brandenburg (Dix 2001).

statutory terms, it is unlikely to be faced with a case in which the procedures used to promulgate a general legal norm are at issue. Furthermore, in both countries, delays, costs, and the small chance of winning keep lawsuits by NGOs to a minimum. Nevertheless, to some extent, broad access to the administrative courts in Poland substitutes for Hungary's open access to the Constitutional Court as an outlet for citizens' complaints about government.

In both countries, the basic process of producing legal norms and decrees inside the government risks being either an insular exercise carried out by ministers and their top assistants acting alone or a neocorporatist process that involves a few outsiders serving on an advisory committee and a few groups with special access to the relevant ministry. These procedures may work well in particular cases, but they make it difficult for those who feel excluded from the process to do anything about it. They have no right to demand to be heard or to insist that the government defend its policies short of a claim of unconstitutionality. In neither country is the constitutional framework sufficient to manage the policy-making processes of these newly democratic states. Statutory reform is needed but may be difficult to achieve. As the first Hungarian Commissioner for Data Protection and Freedom of Information stated as his term came to an end: "The official urging his government to abide by the law and the constitution may easily find himself out of a job. The political forces tend to regard the entirety of the administration as their sole possession, and senior officials are often more committed to the cabinet than to the law and constitution that put them in power" (Majtényi 2001b: 338–339).

Obviously, formal law reform is not sufficient. Expanded requirements for notice, hearing, and justifications will mean nothing unless some groups in the population care about the results. If only business associations and labor unions come forward to participate, reform in this area will be a failure. Thus, it is important to understand how organized civil society functions. This is too large a task for this study, but I make a start with an overview of the nongovernmental sector followed by reports on advocacy-oriented environmental NGOs in Hungary and on student and youth organizations in Poland.

EIGHT

Civil Society Groups

Overview

Participation rights mean little unless organized groups exist that are willing to be part of the process. If groups simply organize street protests or engage in self-help, a more open administrative process will have minimal impact. Enhanced participation rights are not a viable option if few individuals and organizations would take advantage of the opportunity offered and if those few represent a biased set of interests and expertise.

This concern is a real one in Central Europe. Business firms and trade unions have umbrella organizations, some with official status. Statutory self-governing institutions exist for regions and municipalities and for groups such as students, the professions, and academic researchers. Religious bodies sometimes take positions on contemporary policy debates, especially the Catholic Church in Poland.[267] Organized political parties contest elections, and those in opposition are active critics of the incumbents. Nevertheless, there is one important weakness. Only a small portion of the nonprofit sector engages in advocacy, and it is poorly funded and lacks broad-based membership.

The Central European countries distinguish between three different types of organizations – other than political parties – that play a role in policy making and implementation processes.[268] The first group includes "jurisdictional" organizations, mostly self-governing local and regional

---

[267] On the role of the Catholic Church in the debate over abortion in Central Europe, see Gal and Kligman (2000: 15–36).

[268] This distinction has already been introduced in the discussion of the Hungarian Law on Normative Acts and in the composition of various advisory committees in Chapter 7.

governments, but the category also includes groups such as university students and sometimes even government agencies that will be affected by the policy in question. They are consulted mainly because they will play a role in implementing the policy. Sometimes the concept of "self-government" is extended to include groups of special concern such as minorities in Hungary who have several hundred self-governments that are somewhere in between a local government and a civil society group.

Second are "interest groups," but that term may be misleading because it has too broad a meaning in ordinary American usage. In this context, the term refers to organizations that represent the economic interests of particular groups. As mentioned in Chapter 7, these organizations are sometimes called "social partners." Often, this category simply refers to labor unions and business associations, as in the tripartite processes discussed.[269] Occasionally, the category is bent to include groups, such as the old and the disabled in Poland, that are given the status of "unions" to justify their inclusion in advisory committees.

Professional chambers for groups such as lawyers and doctors and the Academy of Sciences mix these two categories. These groups are statutory bodies that regulate their respective groups and frequently draft the rules that will govern their actions subject to government approval.[270] Thus, they have some features of the self-governments included in the jurisdictional category and are sometimes referred to by that term. All members of the profession or category are automatically members; professional groups usually control the process of certification, and they govern their own internal affairs. However, they also represent the economic interests of their members in government consultative processes. Often the implementing statute requires consultation on laws and regulations related to

---

[269] On the Polish statutory definition of social dialogue see Ustawa z dnia 6 lipca 2001 r. o Trójstronnej Komisji do Spraw Społeczno-Gospodarczych i wojewódzkich komisjach dialogu społecznego [Statute of July 6, 2001 on Tripartite Committee on Social and Economic Affairs and voivodship committees on social dialogue], Dz. U. 2001, No. 100, Item 1080 with amendments, article 1 section 1. See also website of the Ministry of Economy and Labor at http://www.mgpips.gov.pl/_dialog.php?dzial=15&poddzial=18&dokument=454 which reads that "Social dialogue is every relationships between labor unions and employer organizations, as well as their relations (bipartite and tripartite). There is no single, universally binding definition of the social dialogue in the governmental and self-governmental administration." (last visit, Nov. 4, 2004).

[270] Maciej Kisilowski (2004) lists the 19 groups with their own self-governments in Poland, all created by statute. They are attorneys, legal advisors, notaries, court collectors, physicians, nurses and midwives, pharmacists, veterinarians, patent specialists, auditors, tax advisers, judges, probation officers, diagnosticians, psychologists, architects, engineers and urban planners, managers of state-owned enterprises, and students at all levels.

the interests of the group. They are both jurisdictional organizations and economic interest groups.[271]

Many consultation processes in Hungary and Poland are limited to these two sometimes overlapping groups, but it is the third category of "civil society" organizations that interests me here. These groups, which are sometimes still referred to as "social organizations" following communist nomenclature, include those representing more diffuse interests that are poorly institutionalized and cannot call on membership fees to fulfill their budgetary needs. Although economic and professional interests may be involved, the groups have policy goals that will affect people not directly part of the group. Examples of such groups are those that focus on the environment, poverty, and human rights. Groups concerned with women, students and youth, the disabled, the old, and disadvantaged minorities seek economic and social benefits for the groups they represent, but they also have broader goals and attract members who will not benefit personally. Sometimes these groups have socialist era counterparts that have reinvented themselves in the current environment, but such groups are not able to claim a monopoly in the way that is still possible for organizations such as the chambers of law and medicine.

The Central European states are not well equipped to handle open-ended procedures that give widespread access to interested civic groups and individuals. As outlined previously, in Hungary and Poland the state often tries to organize participation by limiting access to a few "recognized" groups. Open hearings are uncommon, and when they do take place, may be poorly attended. Public officials appear to want the various civil society interests to organize themselves on the model of labor unions and business associations. Of course, in practice, neither of these two "social partners" is monolithic in any country, and existing organized groups may not be representative, but, at least, they are fairly well established and have reasonably well-defined interests.[272] In contrast, the disabled are split into diverse factions defined by disability. In the environmental area, a wide range of organizations are grouped under that title from homes

---

[271] Kisilowski (2004) provides Polish examples. The statute creating the self-governing body for attorneys gives the supreme council of the self-government the right to give opinions on normative acts and statutes, and the Ministry of Justice must consult with that body before issuing regulations that set the minimum fees for lawyers. Other statutes give notaries, physicians, and the student parliament consultation rights.

[272] Even here, of course, issues of representativeness arise, and the interests of groups nominally representing "labor" and "business" diverge. See Héthy (1995) on Hungary and the discussion in Chapter 7.

for abandoned animals, to eco-agricultural groups, to groups with policy concerns for air, water, and wildlife. In Hungary, the annual National Gathering of Environmental and Nature Protection Nongovernmental Organizations brings together the most important environmental groups, and one of its tasks is to pick members of the National Environmental Council (NEC) to serve with business and academic members. The NEC is an example of an effort to take the standard advisory committee model, drawn from the labor-management area, and apply it in a new context. As we have seen, the NEC has several weaknesses, and some members of the environmental community are skeptical of its value. However, this case shows how an underlying model of consultation with organized "interest" groups affects the state's dealings with civil society groups even when there is a poor fit between the interest reconciliation model and a policy-making process that incorporates less well-organized points of view.

To introduce my case studies, this chapter provides some information on the nonprofit advocacy sector in Poland and Hungary. The strength of civil society advocacy organizations can be gauged both by considering data on public participation and by looking at the organizational landscape. Along both dimensions, the sector seems quite weak. Citizen participation is low, and most groups have few funds and depend on public sector funding.

However, to understand the role of civil-society groups in policy making, summary statistics are insufficient. The role of nonprofits as advocates and gadflies varies by policy area and is in its infancy in Central Europe. Hence, one needs a more fine-grained sense of what advocacy organizations actually do and whom they claim to represent. To begin that exploration, the following chapters focus on two areas with relatively well-established nonprofits – environmental protection organizations in Hungary and student/youth organizations in Poland. Environmental issues are a traditional focus of civil society advocacy. The case of university students in Poland highlights the tensions between the self-government model of interest representation and one based on the organization of disparate private groups. Interviews with leading members of many of the most important Hungarian and Polish groups in these fields provide an instructive window into the strengths and weaknesses of nonprofit advocacy in transition.

Individual Participation

The 1999/2000 European Values Study includes some background information (Table 8.1). It reports data on membership and volunteer work

Table 8.1. *Membership and Volunteer Work for Nongovernmental Organizations*

Region	Welfare Org	Religious Org	Cultural Activities	Trade Unions	Political Parties/ Groups	Local Community Action	Third World Devt/Human Rights	Environ-ment	Prof Assoc	Youth Work	Sports/ Recreation	Women's Groups	Peace Movement	Voluntary Health Org	Other Groups	None
							Percent Reporting They Belong To									
EE	1.6	3.0	1.8	23.8	1.1	1.1	0.2	0.7	1.1	0.8	3.1	0.6	0.1	0.9	1.3	67.1
CE	4.3	9.8	6.0	16.3	4.1	2.7	0.9	2.8	5.0	2.7	7.9	1.7	0.5	2.8	5.3	68.8
Poland	3.1	5.4	2.1	10.0	0.9	1.9	0.3	1.4	4.0	1.4	2.8	1.3	0.4	1.6	3.1	75.0
Hungary	2.3	12.8	3.6	7.2	1.7	1.2	0.4	1.9	3.9	0.9	3.9	0.3	0.3	2.1	2.9	69.2
WE	6.6	12.0	11.4	9.8	3.8	2.8	3.4	5.2	5.3	3.7	16.6	2.3	1.0	3.7	5.7	54.0
							Percent Working Unpaid For									
EE	0.7	1.3	0.9	3.9	0.6	0.8	0.1	0.6	0.5	0.5	1.1	0.4	0.1	0.5	1.9	90.4
CE	3.1	7.3	4.5	8.4	3.3	2.0	0.7	1.8	2.5	2.1	5.0	1.1	0.2	1.8	4.2	80.6
Poland	2.3	3.6	1.7	2.4	0.6	1.3	0.2	0.7	1.2	0.7	2.2	0.6	0.1	0.7	5.0	86.1
Hungary	2.6	5.5	3.3	1.2	0.9	1.2	0.2	2.0	1.8	1.3	2.7	0.2	0.4	1.4	7.7	84.6
WE	6.5	6.3	5.7	1.8	2.2	2.5	2.4	2.9	3.3	5.4	7.6	1.8	2.2	3.9	5.1	71.1

Source: Calculated from the European Values Study 1999/2000, Questions. 5a A-O, 5b A-O. EE, Eastern Europe (Russia, Belarus, Ukraine); CE, Central Europe; WE, Western Europe. Regional data calculated from country-specific surveys weighted by population size as share of regional population. See Appendix 2.

for a range of organizations; the table includes interest groups such as trade unions and professional associations and civil society groups. It also includes groups that may be involved in political activity only incidentally such as sports and recreation groups and religious organizations. With the exception of trade unions, political parties, and religious organizations in Hungary, the proportion of the surveyed population belonging to or volunteering for a particular type of group is higher in Western Europe and sometimes much higher. The share belonging to no group is 54% in Western Europe and 69% in Central Europe (75% and 69% in Hungary and Poland, respectively). The share doing no volunteer work is 71% in Western Europe and 81% in Central Europe (86% and 85% in Hungary and Poland).[273] When asked elsewhere in the survey if they use clubs or voluntary associations, close to 40% of both Central and Western Europeans say they spend time either every week or once or twice a month, compared with only 12% of Eastern Europeans (Russia, Belarus, Ukraine). Although few Poles belong to religious organizations, two-thirds claim to attend church every week compared with 34% of Hungarians and 13% of Western Europeans (European Values Survey 1999/2000, questions 6C, 6D). Thus, there is broader participation in non-governmental organizations (NGOs) than is indicated by Table 8.1, but such participation is likely to have little relationship to political involvement. There appear to be no broad-based mass organizations outside the Catholic Church in Poland and even that seems to have a mostly passive membership. Thus, the immediate potential for government openness to tap an existing pool of citizen participation seems to be low.

Later I examine in some detail the operation of the environmental movement in Hungary. As Table 8.1 indicates, the environment seems to be on the high side, at least with respect to volunteering. The share reporting that they volunteer is two-thirds of the Western European level. The second group of organizations that I study is student and youth groups in Poland. These groups do not have a separate listing in the table, but they are probably included in the categories for youth work and sports and recreation. In both, the share of Poles belonging to or volunteering for such groups is much lower than in Western Europe.[274]

---

[273] Salamon et al. (2004: 297) provides a similar figure for Poland (stating that 12% of the population did some voluntary work in 1997), but a much lower number for Hungary. According to their data only 3% of Hungarians volunteered in 1995.

[274] This difference may partially be due to demographic differences. According to the European Values Study, 6% of those interviewed in Western Europe were students compared with 4% and 3% in Poland and Hungary, respectively.

Organizational Structure

In Central Europe, a wide range of civic and voluntary organizations exist that vary in size, effectiveness, and professionalism.[275] Only a few, however, are primarily engaged in policy advocacy, and, in general, they have few staff and limited funds. The difficulty of creating and sustaining groups in a period of economic and political turmoil has tempered initial optimism about the development of a vibrant civil society.[276] According to Gill (2002: 116), several factors explain the demobilization of some of the groups that played a key role in the transition. These include the weakness of the economy, the elite focus on political party development, the shift of some leaders into political careers, and conflicts and funding shortages inside the groups.

The NGO sector is relatively small in Central Europe. Excluding religious worship, the share of nonagricultural employment was 0.9% in Hungary in 1995 and 0.6% in Poland in 1997 compared with 6.3% in the United States and about 3.5% in France and Germany. As a share of gross domestic product (GDP), the cash expenditures of the sector were 2.8% of GDP in Hungary and 1.3% of GDP in Poland (including religion), both far below the shares of 7.5%, 4%, and 4% for the United States, France, and Germany, respectively. For Hungary, the only country in the region with data for 1990, the share of GDP increased from 1.2% to 2.8% in 5 years. This makes Hungary comparable to Austria's 3%.[277]

Hungary had about 4,700 organizations per million people in 2000; Poland had 2,500 per million in 2002, of which about 15% were religious organizations, or 400 per million people. This reflects the role of the Catholic Church, a major social force that is much more important than

---

[275] The Johns Hopkins University Nonprofit Sector Project directed by Lester M. Salamon has gathered revenue and employment data on Hungary and Poland among others. The project's web page is http://www.jhu.edu/~cnp. Hungary also has quite detailed data gathered by the Central Statistical Office. Interview with Éva Kuti, Head, Section on the Voluntary Sector, Central Statistical Office, Hungary, November 14, 2002, Budapest, and Hungary, Központi Statisztikai Hivatal [Central Statistical Office] (2000, 2002). For an overview in English see Kuti, Králik, and Barabás (2000).

[276] Millard (1998: 147), in discussing Poland, argues that early optimism had by the time of her writing given way to "a recognition that the pronounced weakness of such [civil society pressure] groups was likely to remain a feature of the post-Communist political process for some time."

[277] The data in this paragraph are from Salamon et al. (1999, 2004). In Poland in 1993 the sector's share was 0.2% of gross national product, but this number excludes the Catholic Church and has surely grown since then (Gliński 2002: 60).

religious organizations in Hungary where such organizations constituted under 3% of the total number in 2000.[278]

Financing comes from a diversity of sources. Private monetary donations are not the primary source of funding. The government operates in partnership with nonprofits in many sectors, and many nonprofits obtain substantial government funding. Fees, charges, and the sale of goods and services are also major sources of revenue. In 2000 in Hungary the NGO sector as a whole received 28% of its funding from the state and 16% from domestic private donations and membership fees. Grants from foreign sources were 6.3% of revenue. Service fees, sales, unrelated business income, and income on capital were over half of total revenue.[279] The Polish nongovernmental sector seemed to rely even more on fees, which in 1997 amounted to 60% of total revenue. The actual share from fees may be even larger because fees are often disguised as donations for tax purposes. Donations are 15% of the sector's income (Salamon et al. 2004: 286). A tax law in both countries permits filers to allot 1% of their tax bill to a registered charity of their choice. Poland enacted the law just recently, and it remains to be seen what effect it would have. A survey conducted in 2003 demonstrated that only 39.4% of Poles were willing to use the option, and almost 85% did not even know about it prior to the survey (Dąbrowska et al. 2003: 4). In Hungary, the tax credit collects less than half of what could be given at no cost to the taxpayer. Most contributions are made to churches and to organizations that provide services, such as schools attended by the taxpayer's children (Kuti et al. 2000).[280] The tax credit amounts to less than 1% of the revenue flowing to the sector. Thus, even if its use doubled, it would not be a major funding source. Adding together private donations and the 1% check-off, only 3% of the sector's

---

[278] Hungarian data are from Hungary (2002). Polish data are based on a survey organized by the major organization researching and lobbying for the nonprofit sector in Poland: Klon/Jawor Association: Dąbrowska et al (2002) as well as on Poland, Główny Urząd Statystyczny [Central Statistical Office], (2003). The Klon/Jawor survey focuses primarily on the organizations incorporated as associations and private foundations. In 2002 there were 41,859 of such organizations. The figure in the text, also takes into account voluntary fire brigades (12,468), social committees (6,655), trade unions (15,704) and economic and professional associations (4,260). See Dąbrowska et al (2002: 4).

[279] Hungary, Központi Statisztikai Hivatal [Central Statistical Office] (2002: 36).

[280] In mid-2003, the government introduced an amendment to set aside 1% of total taxes for nonprofit organizations whether or not taxpayers specifically earmark a charity. A new body would be established to allocate the funds not earmarked by taxpayers. "Developing the Civil Society," *Magyar Narancs*, April 3, 2003, "More Money and Influence for the Civil Organization," *Magyarország*, www.magyarorszag.hu (translated by Csilla Kalocsai). See Kuti et al. (2000) for a comprehensive analysis of the 1% tax.

funding is the result of individual Hungarian household choices not connected with the payment of dues or the purchase of services. The share is even lower for environmental and human rights groups.[281]

Another source of private support is volunteer labor. It appears to be relatively unimportant overall but is a key to the survival of some groups. As a share of the economically active population, it was 0.2% in both Hungary and Poland (in 1995 and 1997, respectively). In comparison, the shares are 3.7% in France, 2.3% in Germany, 3.6% in the UK, and 3.5% in the US in the same period (Salamon et al. 2004: 41, 44, 53). As Table 8.1 demonstrates, about 85% of the population engaged in no voluntary labor at all in 1999–2000 compared with 71% in Western Europe. Paid employment in NGOs is low as well, and the share of volunteering in total nonprofit employment is negatively correlated with its size. In Hungary, which has the largest sector, volunteers made up 19% of full-time equivalent workers in the sector in 1995; in Romania, where the sector is very small, volunteering accounted for 57% of the full-time equivalent workers. (In Poland the share was 17% in 1997.) In Hungary, between 1990 and 1995, the size of the sector as a share of GDP more than doubled, but volunteer labor fell from 1.5% of nonagricultural employment to 0.2%. This appears to represent an absolute decline in volunteering not just an increase in overall employment (Salamon et al. 1999: 305–24). Nevertheless, many individual organizations are highly dependent on volunteers. In Poland, for example, 47% of NGOs work with volunteers to some extent (Dąbrowska et al. 2002: 10).

It is important to distinguish between volunteer participation that has a political or policy goal and that which is done for recreation or to provide charity. The data suggest there is relatively little of the former. In both Hungary and Poland environmental and advocacy organizations accounted just for 3% of total paid employment in the sector (in 1995 and 1997, respectively) (Salamon et al. 1999: 315; 2004: 284). Some observers suggest this is a legacy of the past because, under the former regime, many weekend days were given up to activities labeled "voluntary" by the regime but that actually were hard to avoid. A further reason for the low level of volunteering is economic. As Kim Scheppele (2001) puts it: "If your official job cannot possibly provide the income to support you,

---

[281] Overall in 2000, earmarked individual gifts were 3% of the total with 2.3% from donations and 0.7% from the 1% tax writeoff. For environmental groups the share was 2.2% and for human rights groups 1.6% (Hungary, Központi Statisztikai Hivatal [Central Statistical Office] 2002: 36, 115).

you have to spend your time outside your official job doing something else that will pay you to survive." Nevertheless, a small group of people, including some of my interviewees, manage to do both.

The independence of civic and policy-oriented organizations depends upon their sources of financing. If most of their funding comes from the government, they may have difficulty playing the roles of advocates and gadflys. If their support is largely from foreign foundations, they may be more accountable to international donors than to local citizens (Cirtautas 2001: 83). Hungary has detailed data by organizational category, Consider environment and human rights groups where a relatively large number of organizations have advocacy as one of their goals. A report on environmental NGOs in 1998 found that about half did some lobbying, and advocacy is a central concern of human rights groups. A few predate the change in regime. In 2000, of the 1,019 environmental groups and 561 in the field of human rights, 183 of the former and 59 of the latter were founded before 1991. This includes some very old groups from the 1970s and 1980s. Grants from domestic governments were more than 20% of the budget of both types of groups. In some fields, especially the advocacy areas that are my focus, considerable funding comes from foreign donors. In 2000, human rights groups received almost 60% of their funds from abroad; environmental groups got almost 10% of their resources from these sources. These external sources of funds were often critical to the groups' establishment and survival.[282] Unrelated business income accounted for 23% of total revenues of environmental groups in 2000. This may be a legacy of the past which left some groups with income earning property. The groups I interviewed raise funds through, for example, a recycling business, conference fees, and the sale of books and training materials. The general category of environmental groups includes a number of eco-agricultural enterprises that push up the overall business income share. Domestic private donations and dues from individuals and business firms are only 5.6% and 5.3% for environmental and human rights groups, respectively. The 1% tax checkoff provides less than 1% of these groups' revenue (Hungary, Központi Statisztikai Hivatal [Central Statistical Office] 2000, 2002: 115).

To have staying power, advocacy organizations need professional staff and a budget with some stability. Only a small number of organizations appear to be in that category. This means that on any given issue the group

---

[282] Hungary, Központi Statisztikai Hivatal [Central Statistical Office] (2000, 2002: 115) interview with Kuti, and data supplied by her. Outside funding is also important for advocacy groups in Poland. See Leś et al. (2000: 20).

of organizations capable of monitoring government and participating in policy making is likely to be small. In the environmental area in Hungary there was broad agreement among those I interviewed on the most important groups and umbrella associations. There are 10 to 12 in the top group, and overall, 20 to 25 form the core of the movement. Even those organizations have a precarious financial existence given the low level of private domestic donations.[283] As the environmental cases discussed later indicate, professional advocacy, beyond grassroots mobilization over particular issues, is weak and may face more serious problems in the near future if foreign support falls without an increase in domestic funding.

In Poland, the data are less complete and somewhat contradictory. According to Lester Salamon's data, civic and advocacy organizations receive only 4% of their income from the government, in comparison to 45% from fees and 51% from private donors including foreign foundations (Salamon et al. 2004: 288). The data, however, appear to omit the many advocacy NGOs that are incorporated as private foundations and appear as a separate category in Salamon's study. Furthermore, the meaning of such terms as fees, governmental support, or donations depends upon the particular context. Contributions by individuals are very low.[284] Private donations primarily represent support from major domestic and foreign foundations as well as disguised service charges collected from business corporations or individual customers.

In addition, transfers from the many state-owned companies count as donations. This source of income may constrain the sector's independence even more significantly than government grants because the decisions are made by politically-appointed managers not bound by the procedures concerning public spending. Consider, for example, organizations of students and youth. Two major groups are loosely affiliated with political parties – one of them reconstituted from the old official student group under socialism. Their leaders admit that the political composition of the government significantly affects the well-being of their groups. One of the activists recalled that when "their" party lost elections in the mid 1990s, this caused not only a large decrease in governmental support, but also a decline in the income from private firms and foundations.[285] The group

---

[283] This is not a new phenomenon. See O'Toole and Hanf (1998: 100), who also note the organizations' lack of access to decision makers.

[284] One study points out that, in 2002, donations of private persons accounted for 10.3% of the income of the nonprofit sector. Income from fundraising campaigns totaled just 0.9% of revenues (Dąbrowska et al. 2002: 13).

[285] Interview with Witold Repetowicz, a former official of the Independent Students' Association, Warsaw, Poland, December 30, 2003.

allied with the current governing majority seems to be heavily sponsored by the state-owned firms. In addition, there are several student and youth groups with a professional orientation, such as groups of law, medical, or business students that are associated with the corresponding professional chambers. According to some of their leaders, the patronage of professional interest groups may constrain the organizations' independence in the very areas of their specialty.

Both types of groups interact with the official university self-governments that have a formal role in university governance. Paradoxically, although sponsored predominantly from governmental sources, self-governments seem to enjoy the most financial independence, at least at the university level where they combine advocacy functions with significant statutory powers.

At present, in both Hungary and Poland the initial wave of external support is drying up, but private domestic giving has not filled the gap. Groups increasingly depend on funds directly or indirectly distributed by the government and on revenue generated by the sale of products and services. A few effective individual organizations exist, but they are not capable of handling more extensive participation opportunities without more resources and staff. These limitations must be taken into account in assessing the value of increased public participation in the process of drafting laws and regulations.

NINE

Environmental Advocacy Organizations in Hungary

Activists began to establish environmental groups in Hungary in the late 1980s when they were given space to operate by the rather progressive communist leadership that took power in 1987.[286] The growth in these groups occurred partly in response to a law legalizing free associations passed in 1989 (Harper 1999: 58–93; Pickvance 1998: 75–76 Pickvance and Gábor 2001: 105). During that period a core group of activists mobilized large numbers of people to protest particular issues. These mobilizations continued into the democratic transition (Pickvance and Gábor 2001). According to Pickvance and Gábor (2001: 105), the emergence of environmental groups in the mid-1980s was tolerated when other types were not:

because they were not viewed as a potential threat to the regime.... This led to a situation in which before the regime change environmental issues attracted politically minded people who either blamed the regime for the lack of responsible policies or joined green movements to express their discontent without running the risk of a direct confrontation with the regime.[287]

---

[286] Of the 973 environmental organizations that existed in 1998, 141 or 14.4% were founded before 1990. Almost all are nonprofit associations, not foundations. Some groups date from the 1970s, but they had recreational and social purposes such as bird watching. For example, Birdlife Hungary was established in the early 1970s as a volunteer organization dedicated to the protection of birds.

[287] See also O'Toole and Hanf (1998: 99), who claim that the activism of the 1980s "was based on real public concern but was also used opportunistically by both citizens and those with political ambitions as a vehicle for opposing the regime more generally." Millard (1998: 145) argues that in Poland at the end of the communist period environmental organizations were permitted because the issue was seen as a "safe" issue that provided a safety valve.

During the 1990s, citizens founded large numbers of new groups, but most were small, volunteer organizations with few funds (Kuti et al. 2000: 15–16). Nevertheless, several more professional organizations currently play a key role in government policy-making processes. Some of these date from the socialist period; others are more recent creations. The most active are several specialized umbrella organizations dealing with issues such as air pollution, waste management, energy, and nature protection. The key members of most of these groups know each other well and have interacted for most of the transition period. They have an annual National Gathering of Environmental and Nature Protection Nongovernmental Organizations and are advised by an Environmental Management and Law Association (EMLA).[288] Even these groups, however, depend on the energy of a few committed people, have few funds, and rely on grants that may be canceled after a few years.[289]

The types of problems covered by these groups range from local waste disposal problems, to a major dam on the Danube, to national issues such as air pollution. Case studies by Pickvance (1998) and Pickvance and Gábor (2001) in the mid-1990s and my own interviews confirm that it is possible to establish nongovernmental organizations (NGOs) that gain the attention of political bodies through a reputation both for expertise and for responding to genuine citizen concerns. Relations with public officials are sometimes rocky, but the groups' access to the media and public sympathy for their efforts have helped sustain them and given them some influence. Top political appointees in the Ministry of the Environment and some members of Parliament have often supported these groups as a way to increase the salience of environment issues inside the government, and there is some movement of people back and forth between government and NGOs (Pickvance 1998: 150–155). Nevertheless, some groups distrust the state, limit their dealings with public officials, and claim to be apolitical (Harper 1999). In my own interviews, however, I focused on groups that actively engage in the policy-making process.

---

[288] EMLA also has a Local Environmental Action Program that helps local governments to manage environmental responsibilities. EMLA is small (three lawyers in 2002) and largely funded by grants from non-Hungarian foundations and the Hungarian government. Environmental Management and Law Association (2002), interview with Sándor Fülöp, Executive Director EMLA, October 29, 2002. Web site: http://www.emla.hu.

[289] For a general discussion of the way the dynamism and vitality of the nongovernmental organization sector in Hungary is combined with financial uncertainty and "lack of organizational maturity," see Kuti et al. (2000: 29). See Harper (1999) for case studies of environmental activism in Hungary. She reports that in the mid-1990s most groups had 25 or fewer members and operated with only volunteer labor (Harper 1999: 43).

Nonprofits face three interlocked difficulties. These are problems of financial and human capacity, problems of credibility, and problems of effective access to the policy-making process. I discuss each of these difficulties in the light of interviews I conducted in the fall and winter of 2002 with leading members of many of the major policy-oriented groups and umbrella organizations, all but one based in Budapest. The groups I interviewed fall into six broad categories: a group in decline that was a key player in the transition (Danube Circle), a moderate membership-based group founded in the midst of the socialist period (Birdlife Hungary), the branch of a moderate international environmental group (World Wildlife Fund-Hungary), umbrella groups with subject matter foci and professional staff (HUMUSZ, Energia Klub, Clean Air Action Group, National Association of Conservationists), local groups with national visibility (REFLEX, Green Future), and a law firm providing services to the others (EMLA).[290]

Financial and Human Capacity

As a rough approximation, the Hungarian government, on the one hand, and foreign foundations and public bodies [mostly in the European Union (EU)], on the other, provide equal financial shares, and a small share comes from individuals and domestic businesses. Typically, neither membership fees nor the 1% tax checkoff are a major source of funds. Multinational firms with business in Hungary provide some project funding to a few groups. Some groups run related businesses that bring in considerable revenue.[291] None appeared to have a sizable endowment.

Government funding comes from several grant programs administered by the Ministry of the Environment with nonprofit input and from project funds from various ministries, the government, and the parliament. In 2002, the two programs administered by the environmental ministry totaled 414, 300 million Hungarian forints (HF) (about $1.7 million).[292] The

---

[290] On the similar case of Poland, see Gliński (2001) and Millard (1998).

[291] In the environmental sector as a whole about one-third of funds comes from the government, 14% from domestic donations (including individual gifts, 1.1%; corporate gifts, 2.7%; grants from other NGOs, 9.3%; and the 1% tax credit, 1.1%), almost 10% from foreign donors, and the rest mostly from service fees (13%) and unrelated business income (23%) (Hungary, Központi Statisztikai Hivatal [Central Statistical Office] 2002: 115).

[292] Here and for the figures following, I use an exchange rate of 0.004106 Hungarian forint per dollar, the interbank rate on November 1, 2002.

larger environmental ministry program, called "Green Source," awarded grants totaling 356 million HF in 2002 and operates through a 15-member committee that makes the selections based on applications from environmental groups. Seven members are from the NGO community, and they review all applications and report to the larger committee, which usually accepts their recommendations. The NGO representatives rotate with terms of 1 to 2 years and are chosen by a national committee of NGOs, not the ministry. The ministry must sign the contracts with the NGOs, but in practice the program is administered independently. Of course, the issues of representativeness and impartiality shift in this case to the composition of the NGO committee.[293] The largest individual grants were 2.8 million HF or about $11,500. However, some groups received multiple grants. Birdlife Hungary together with its local affiliates received about one-seventh of the grants under one of the programs.

The consequences of failing to receive government funds can be harsh. For example, consider Danube Circle, a well-known group established under the socialist government to protest the building of a dam on the Danube that mobilized mass protests in the 1980s (Jancar-Webster 1998: 71; Pickvance 1998; Pickvance and Gábor 2001). Some of its members were important participants in the Roundtable that negotiated the transition, and some of them entered politics. In the fall of 2002, it had no paid staff, a small membership base, and an annual budget of about 1.5 million HF (about $6,000), and it shared an office with an animal protection group. It failed to receive government funding for professional development in 2002 and did not apply for Green Source funds, but it does accept funds from Parliament. It sees its mission as being a critical voice that provides competent technical assessments of policies and projects. Nevertheless, however independent its stance, it has a limited impact simply because of lack of funds. It produces evaluations of some policies – for example, on management of the Tisza River – and individual members of the group testify at local and national hearings concerning public projects and policies. However, it does not have the resources to educate the public so as to develop grassroots support for its positions. As was the case with all the groups I interviewed, membership fees are very

---

[293] The data on the allocation of grant funds are available from the web site of the Ministry of the Environment. This is the source of the additional data presented later. Details on the allocation process are from a telephone interview with István Farkas, Director, National Society of Conservationists, by Csilla Kalocsai, June 16, 2003.

low, and the group receives very little private charity from Hungarian citizens and businesses.[294]

The other groups I spoke to were all struggling financially, but none was in as weak a condition as Danube Circle. Consider a few examples.

Birdlife Hungary (also called the Hungarian Ornithological and Nature Protection Association) was founded in the 1970s during the socialist period. It has strong connections with similar organizations in Western Europe, and it was the only organization I interviewed that obtains substantial funds from membership fees and private donations from individuals and Hungarian businesses. It has many local affiliate groups. In 2000–2001, about 7% of the group's funds came from 1% tax contributions and membership. Nevertheless, it too receives almost 40% of its funds from the national government and 20% from foreign donors, both public and private. One-quarter of the foreign funds were passed through to local groups to finance the purchase of land for wildlife habitats.[295] These local groups also receive government funding. Birdlife Hungary is beginning a more ambitious effort to tap private sources of funds inside Hungary but, as with the others I interviewed, had not had success by the fall of 2002.[296]

World Wildlife Fund-Hungary (WWFH) is a relatively large organization in the Hungarian context, with 24 staff in the fall of 2002. It is one-third supported by the international World Wildlife Fund, which has been very active in the region since 1989, and one-third supported by corporations and foundations. It does both policy advocacy and field research.[297] It has also received EU funds for special projects. Its publications are more professional and colorful than those of other groups, and some are funded by special purpose grants from multinational firms active in Hungary. WWFH is involved in a range of nature conservation projects and

---

[294] Based on an interview with György Droppa, member of the board of directors of Danube Circle, November 27, 2002. He is Co-chairman of the Green Party and ran for Mayor of Budapest in the fall of 2002, receiving less than 5% of the vote. He is trained as a researcher and worked on river rehabilitation for the government.

[295] Foreigners cannot purchase rural land in Hungary so this program uses funds from international conservation groups to purchase wildlife habitats.

[296] Interview with László Jánossy, Director, MME/BirdLife Hungary, Budapest, December 9, 2002, and Annamária Orbán, "Case Study 3, Hungary: BirdLife Hungary," background paper for CEU project on "Technologies of Civil Society: Organization, Representation, Accountability," 2002.

[297] A general description of WWFH involvement in the region is provided by Waller (1998: 41–42).

political and policy debates involving wildlife and natural resource use. It obtains government funds (5.6 million HF or about $23,000 in 2002 from the environmental ministry's grant programs) but is less dependent on these funds than many other groups. Instead, it is constrained by being part of an international NGO that helps set the priorities of the Hungarian chapter. WWFH receives almost no domestic private charity, but, similar to Birdlife Hungary, it is beginning to consider local private fund-raising in the face of reduced support from the international WWF.[298]

Now consider the umbrella organizations. Umbrella organizations have a special advantage in the national political arena. Groups that want to be on the list to receive draft statutes from parliament need to have at least one local affiliate outside of Budapest. Thus, groups that want to be included in national debates benefit from having affiliates whatever their actual status within the umbrella organization.

The National Society of Conservationists (NSC) was founded in 1990 and now has 86 member groups, including some of the other groups I interviewed. One-half are purely volunteer groups, and one-half are more formal organizations with staff and legal status. It had nine paid staff in 2002 and works mainly on nature protection, climate change, industry and environment, and regional issues. It receives about half its budget from the government in the form of both general support from the Ministry of the Environment and project funds.[299] Because of its work on regional development and EU accession, it has received substantial support from the EU. Corporate donations are about 3% of the budget, and individual gifts are 1%. Asked how the organization maintained its independence with such a high level of government funding, the executive director argued that the process of allocating environmental ministry support was kept largely separate from a group's policy positions through the operation of the seven-member evaluation committee that includes two NGO representatives.[300] Other funding, however, is not allocated by this method.

Another umbrella organization is the Clean Air Action Group (CAAG) with 126 member groups, most of which are small and local with no staff and minimal budgets. CAAG was founded in 1988 by three Budapest groups with an interest in urban transport. It originated in

---

[298] Interview with Ferenc Márkus, Conservation Director, WWFH, November 18, 2002, Budapest.

[299] It received 4.9 million HF ($20,100) for Green Source projects and professional development.

[300] Interview with István Farkas, Director, National Society of Conservationists, December 18, 2002, Budapest, and Farkas (2002: 66).

several university green clubs (Pickvance 1998; Pickvance and Gábor 2001). CAAG has 10–12 paid staff and (in 2000) a budget of more than 30 million HF (about $123,000). As with the NSC, CAAG is more than 40% funded by the Hungarian government – mostly the Ministry of the Environment and the Ministry of Foreign Affairs (for EU-related projects).[301] A multiyear grant from the Rockefeller Brothers Fund covered more than 25% of its budget in 2000 with additional funds coming from other grants, some with an EU connection, and income from business activities. It receives a small amount of corporate contributions – in 2000, one grant was 1.4% of the budget. CAAG is actively involved in commenting on draft laws and regulations. In response to the question of whether the group's dependence on government funds affected its independence, the director answered that he believed the government supported CAAG because it wanted to have independent organizations reviewing its drafts. Most of the criticism the group faces comes from local governments. Nevertheless, project funding obviously affects the way the organization allocates the time of its staff.[302] With more than one-quarter of its budget from a single foundation grant, CAAG risks a major budget cut when the grant expires, resulting in even more dependence on public funds. With government grants about 40% and the Rockefeller Grant 25% of the budget in one year, if the Rockefeller grant fell to zero with no change in public money, CAAG would be more than 50% state funded.

Energia Klub, a group founded in 1991 that focuses on antinuclear advocacy and other energy policy issues, is in a similar situation, although its sources of external funding are more diversified. The bulk of its funding is from Western European and American foundations, the EU, and the Hungarian Environmental Ministry.[303]

HUMUSZ (The Hungarian Waste Management Working Group), a waste management alliance of 18 environmental groups, began as a group of volunteers with no paid staff. In early 2003, it had seven staff, a 35-square-meter office, and budget of about 30 million HF (about $123,000). It has a reputation for being more confrontational than the NSC or

---

[301] In 2002, Green Source and professional development grants totaled 8.9 million HF or almost $36,500.

[302] Interview with András Lukács, President of Clean Air Action Group, December 20, 2002, Budapest. Additional information from Annamária Orbán, "Case Study 2: Hungary: Clean Air Action Group (CAAG)" background paper for CEU project on "Technologies of Civil Society: Organization, Representation, Accountability," 2002.

[303] Interview with Ada Ámon, Director of Energia Klub, December 2, 2002, Budapest, and a brochure in English about the organization.

CAAG, often staging public media events that combine humor with a serious policy objective. In 2002, about 60% of its budget was from various government sources in the Ministries of the Environment and the Economy, about 30% came from its recycling and waste separation businesses, and 10% from foreign foundations. Thus, HUMUSZ also lacks a domestic charitable base, but it is generating some funding locally from its green business activities.[304]

In general, the funding picture that emerges with respect to the major environmental groups is not very secure. Domestic private donations from individuals provide only a tiny share of revenue with the exception of Birdlife Hungary, the one membership organization in the group. Business support is generally weak as well and is mostly project based. Support from abroad, both from official sources and from foundations, is critical for several groups but has no long-run staying power.[305] Government support is essential and likely to grow in relative importance. Even if government funds do not have strings attached, these groups still may find it difficult to carry out independent advocacy activities. They must attract more local private funds if they are to survive into the future as strong voices for environmental issues.

Credibility: Popular Support, Media Access, and Expertise

The groups all want government officials to take them seriously in policy debates over environmental issues. The groups I interviewed followed two types of strategies. First, they cultivated sources of grass roots support and educated people about environmental problems. Access to the media is a key resource here, and several groups have used it creatively. Second, a group can gain credibility through the provision of expert opinions. Of course, the two overlap. On the one hand, expertise can help mobilize ordinary people, and, on the other, a group's expert views may be taken more seriously if it can point to a constituency of support and a media willing to publicize its positions.

The major environmental groups are not mass organizations, but most of them work to mobilize public support and seek publicity in the media

---

[304] Interview with Barnabás Bödecs, Chairman of HUMUSZ and one of the three founders of HUMUSZ in 1995, January 4, 2003, Budapest. Bödecs is an accountant with Ernst and Young.

[305] The involvement of foreign NGOs and foundations in supporting Central and Eastern European environmental groups and projects in the early transition years is discussed by Waller (1998) and Jancar-Webster (1998).

to increase the salience of issues. Only Birdlife Hungary is a membership organization, with 6,000 members paying annual dues of under $10 each and with numerous local chapters. The umbrella groups – that is, the NSC, CAAG, Energia Klub, and HUMUSZ – all appear to have some member organizations that are local citizen groups. However, consultation with policy makers seems to occur through their Budapest offices, and many of their member organizations are poorly institutionalized. Thus, their claim to legitimacy in the policy-making process rests on two factors. First, they have the potential to mobilize citizens, generate media attention, and stir up opposition politicians around particular issues. Second, their staff and advisory councils contain experts with a specialized understanding of the policy issue on the table. In the case of environmental policy, the justification for consultation is not only to be sure that a range of voices is heard but also to be sure the government's policy is scientifically competent.

Elite groups and umbrella associations commonly mobilize the public around an issue and then create events that are covered by the media. In its early years, this was the successful strategy of the Danube Circle. The mass rallies it organized involved environmental issues but had the broader political purpose of challenging the old regime. At its peak in 1988–1989, the Danube Circle organized rallies in Budapest against a proposed dam on the Danube that attracted more than 40,000 people. Even 10 years later, in 1999, it was able to mobilize a crowd on the same issue (Pickvance and Gábor 2001: 106–107; Jancar-Webster 1998: 71). It is not clear that it currently has such a capacity, and in its work on the Tisza River in eastern Hungary it has focused on providing expert testimony.

Green Future was founded in 1989 to raise awareness of the problem of hazardous pollutants, especially heavy metals and fuel oil, in an industrial/residential district of Budapest. The scientists who established the group tried to alert local residents to the risk factors but found them suspicious of outsiders. It then tried to persuade people of the health problems, working with two local NGOs and a sociologist. Eventually, Green Future attracted large numbers of neighborhood residents to its meetings and held an open meeting to counter the local government's closed meeting on the district's environmental problems. Thus, the strategy was to educate the public and then rely on the citizens' outrage to give local environmental issues political salience. Although the group continues to try to mobilize people around particular issues, it is not a mass membership or client-based organization. Instead, it has 20–30 members of whom 8–10 are active. It operates with a small budget of 1–3 million HF ($4,000–$12,000), organizes forums on environmental themes, and invites the public and the press. In the environmental ministry's books, it received 1.9 million HF (almost $8,000) in 2002 from Green Source and for professional development. This is most of its budget. In addition, like some other groups, they had a young person working with them as an alternative to military service who was paid by the government.[306] Thus, like Danube Circle, Green Future is a thin organization that may be able to tap volunteer help on particular issues that challenge local governments. Because local governments have considerable independence with respect to environmental problems in their jurisdiction, Green Future can serve a valuable catalytic and information provision function. However, in practice, its effectiveness is limited by its lack of funds and professional staff.

The alternative strategy of providing expert advice and critiques of draft laws and regulations is the focus of the umbrella groups and WWFH, although they also often combine their work on particular draft policies with public events and forums. WWFH has enough resources to carry out original research designed to put new issues on the agenda of parliament and the government. For example, it prepared an action plan for endangered forests that critiques government policy and gave the report to journalists. It has done similar policy-oriented work on wetlands preservation and restoration and on sustainable agriculture. WWFH also carries out projects to restore habitats for endangered species, and that work is sometimes coordinated with efforts to influence policy. The group's staff works with parliament, government ministries, the National Environmental Council, local governments, and national parks and testifies at hearings both in parliament and elsewhere. The group organizes conferences and produces very professional-looking publications. The main form of direct public involvement is the use of volunteers to help carry out projects such as efforts to preserve the habitat of endangered species in hills on the outskirts of Budapest. Thus, WWFH involves the public in concrete environmental projects rather than in rallies and marches.[307]

HUMUSZ, the waste management alliance, has a strong interest in changing public attitudes and behavior through education, but, like WWFH, it also seeks to change public policy. For example, in the fall of 2002 it was working toward a new waste and packaging law. It is more of a purely advocacy group than WWFH, with less of a research component.

---

[306] Interview with Professor Péter Mészáros, Budapest Institute of Technology, November 28, 2002, president of Green Future; Pickvance (1998) and Pickvance and Gábor (2001).
[307] Interview with Márkus.

HUMUSZ will go to the media only if it has been so unsuccessful in the internal process that it believes its concerns have not been addressed. HUMUSZ does not just issue press releases; instead, it is well known in Hungary for its clever and humorous media events. In November 2002, it organized a demonstration, discussed later, to protest the weakness of the government's draft packaging and waste law.[308]

Less likely to engage in the street theater that is the trademark of HUMUSZ, the other umbrella groups have similar strategies that combine public education and open events with efforts to affect policy through the provision of expert advice to government officials. Thus, the NSC organizes forums with public administrators, members of parliament, and NGOs; helps to educate and build the capacity of member groups; works with the press; and provides information and opinions to governments. The CAAG also does technical studies designed to affect policy. It prepares an annual report on the government budget as it affects the environment and has done studies on EU accession and transport, on railroads, and on public transport in Budapest.[309]

Relations with Government

The Act on the Environment (LIII/1995) provides for public consultation outside the realm of formal advisory committees such as the National Environmental Council. The basic statute requires consultation, as does an implementing executive decree.[310] For example, article 93 of the act requires that the inspectorate conduct a public hearing after receiving an environmental impact assessment on a particular project. After giving notice, the hearing is held in the premises of the local government of the communities most affected and must include environmental and social organizations. These portions of the act appear to have been partly motivated by Constitutional Court decisions that held that the constitutional right to environmental protection can be carried out only through access to information and participation by the "people concerned."[311] In addition, a few other statutes require public notice and hearings for decisions with environmental consequences. For example, the construction

---

[308] Interview with Bödecs.
[309] Interviews with I. Farkas and Lukács.
[310] LIII/1995, arts. 1(2)(f), 10(1), 93, 97–100. See also Government Decree 152/1995 (XII.12)].
[311] Decision 996/G/1990 AB and a holding that the State must offer "legal and institutional" guarantees, Decision 28/1994 (V. 20) AB.

law mandates public notice and hearings when municipalities draw up organizational plans. Public participation is also required in the beginning phase of power plant planning. The power plant designer must create a committee to inform the affected public and to accept public opinion and comments.[312]

The most detailed provisions concern participation in decisions about individual projects at the local level. Legal provisions for participation in environmental policy making are vague and not judicially enforceable. For example, section 10(1) of the Act on the Environment states that a long list of organizations and interests "shall cooperate in the protection of the environment" and that this obligation shall extend to "all phases of achieving the environmental objectives." Just what this means is not clear.

However, international pressures also encourage participation. In 2001, Hungary ratified the Aarhus Convention on Access to Information, Public Participation in Decisionmaking and Access to Justice in Environmental Matters of the United Nations Economic Commission for Europe. This convention requires strengthened democratic environmental governance.[313] The EU also requires the provision of information to the public and the preparation of environmental impact statements (Caddy 2000; Rose-Ackerman 1995: 108–119). Thus, in the environmental area relatively good opportunities exist for participation, and they may strengthen over time.

This legal framework sets the stage in which environmental groups operate. Their relations with the government are a function of background legal and political practice and the shifting personalities in key positions inside governments at all levels. Because it is relatively weak, the environmental ministry has sometimes welcomed the publicity for environmental issues that NGOs can generate. In general, NGO leaders have greater problems getting a hearing for their concerns in other ministries that lack an explicit environmental mandate, such as ministries that deal with transportation and the siting of public works.

The president of HUMUSZ described the process of government consultation as it affected his group, but it is consistent with others' reports,

---

[312] Access Initiative (2002, part I.A.2).

[313] The text of the treaty, which was signed on January 25, 1998, is at http://www.unece.org/env/pp/treatytext.htm. (See also Rose-Ackerman and Halpaap 2002.) Furthermore, Government Decree 148/1999 (X.13) also provides for public participation if a project has international impacts. http://www.obh.hu/adatved/indexek/2000/text4.htm.

so I summarize it here. First, he tells the relevant minister that he wants to see the draft. In the past, drafts were not posted on the Internet for anyone to see, but he does have a right to receive drafts and is often also given internal documents. If the ministry stalls, he can go to the media, and the threat of bad publicity has been effective. For example, in the case of the draft law on packaging and waste management, HUMUSZ built a catapult and threw pieces of throw-away packaging at the ministry for the benefit of the TV news. This action produced the Deputy State Secretary, draft in hand. The government urges ministries to post drafts on the Internet, but this is not a legal requirement.[314] The president of CAAG said that, in principle, he could ask a court to order the environmental ministry to release a draft, but, in practice, this is not a realistic option, and in any case CAAG's problem is too many requests for comments, not too few.

Second, after receiving the draft, HUMUSZ submits written comments, but there is frequently too little time to respond in depth. These comments are not sent to the press because they are not public documents. Then there is sometimes an invitation-only meeting to review the draft rule with the minister that also includes other interested groups such as business. The revised draft is not routinely made public.

CAAG and the NSC reported similar procedures. CAAG is on the list for drafts dealing with air pollution, but there are so many of them and the comment period is so short that the staff has difficulty keeping up with the flow of paper. Drafts come not just from the environmental ministry but also from others such as the Ministry of Transport and the Ministry of Agriculture for issues dealing with rural and regional development. In one year, CAAG typically comments on 40–50 drafts.

The NSC also routinely reviews drafts from the Ministry of the Environment and the Ministry of Regional Development, and István Farkas, Director of the NSC, worries about tight deadlines of about one week. At the time of my interview in the fall of 2002, the NSC had been told it could participate in the process of designing an environmental development plan needed as part of the EU accession process. This was good news, except that Farkas thought the 30-day comment period was too short for such an important policy-making enterprise. He stated that the Ministries of Economics and of Transport either do not provide drafts or send them too late for responsible reactions. Ratification of the UN's Aarhus

---

[314] Interviews with Lukács and István Somogyvári, Administrative State Secretary, Ministry of Justice, December 12, 2002, Budapest.

Convention has had little impact on these practices. The NSC is working to be sure nonprofit groups will be represented on the new regional
development councils along with business, labor, and local governments.

Bödecs, President of HUMUSZ, and László Jánossy of Birdlife Hungary were frankly critical of the Ministry of the Environment. According
to Bödecs, it has a high level of staff turnover when the government
changes, and each new group has its own ideas and contacts with industry.
Only during two short periods was the minister an expert on the environment. A HUMUSZ publication from 2000 expresses frustration with
the then Minister of the Environment from the Smallholder Party and
complains that he has brought in biased and unqualified staff.[315] Jánossy
thought the ministry was well-intentioned but lacked a clear strategy and
was constrained by the rest of government and previous regulations. He
thought the ministry had been reduced to "fighting fires" and that there
is too much backbiting and conflict. About 30% of the budget goes to
building sewage treatment plants, leaving too little for other issues. Similar sentiments were expressed by the conservation director of WWFH,
who stated that one of the frustrations of his job was the shifting competence and openness of the environmental ministry. The government that
left power in 2002 was, according to him, not open to the participation of
environmental groups, was very political, and did not engage in dialogue.
The new government is better, but in the fall of 2002 it was too early to
know for sure.[316]

Energia Klub, which deals with nuclear power among other issues,
faces a less open regulatory environment. Regulation in this area is still
controlled by laws from before the regime change and is very technocratic
and closed. There is an Atomic Energy Commission with some outside
representation, but it is not independent of government.[317] There are no
formal hearings and no notice, and Energia Klub is not part of the consultation process. It has asked for the group's budget, long-run strategy,
and procedures, but to no avail. The group sees no particular changes for
the better under the government that took power in 2002.[318]

In Hungary's parliamentary system, both statutes and government decrees are drafted inside the government, which then presents draft statutes

---

[315] Bödecs and Jánossy interviews, and *Waste Diver*, 2000, English summary, www.kuka-
buvar.hu.
[316] Interview with Márkus.
[317] Its website is: http://www.haea.gov.hu.
[318] Interview with Ámon.

to parliament. Nevertheless, parliament is not always a rubber stamp, and it usually schedules hearings that can highlight problems with government legislative proposals. Parliament keeps a list of groups that are to receive copies of draft statutes in different areas, and most of the people I interviewed represented groups that had put themselves on such "lobby lists" in their areas of concern. This means that one strategy, in the face of an uncooperative ministry, is to enlist the help of opposition members of parliament at the hearing stage or before.[319] Obviously, this is not a way to make ministry officials happy about consultations with the group, but, like the media strategies described previously, it can be a way of inducing government officials to consult in the future out of political expediency.

Because the Act on the Environment does provide for consultation, if the government denies access or if the decision is opposed to the groups' interests, NGOs can go to the courts either to force greater openness or to challenge decisions after they are made. In general, this is not a fruitful strategy in other policy areas when government laws and norms are at stake. However, in the environmental area, legal actions are sometimes worthwhile. The Hungarian Environmental Management and Law Association (EMLA), founded in 1994, has brought more than 350 cases and has assisted on many others. In one 18-month period EMLA initiated 42 new cases and provided advice on 200 smaller cases. In its 2000–2001 annual report, EMLA outlines its victories and defeats as well as major outstanding cases. The cases are mainly challenges to particular development projects or pollution from particular sources (EMLA 2002: 5). Broad challenges to government rule-making processes are seldom possible.

Legal actions that focus on violations of consultation processes are unlikely to succeed. The alternative is to contest the legality of a decision made by the government, but here too success is unlikely although, as EMLA reports, not impossible. Furthermore, judicial processes are often very costly and slow, with injunctions uncommon.[320] Lukács of CAAG gave an example of a challenged shopping mall that was built during the litigation. An appeal to the Constitutional Court was ineffective because that court is under no time constraints and in this case waited up to 3 years to resolve some issues. EMLA reports one case that was decided after 5 years with damages just covering legal fees (EMLA 2002). In the ordinary courts, environmental disputes are a new type of case for judges who are not prepared to deal with them competently.

---

[319] Interview with Lukács.
[320] Interviews with Droppa, Lukács, and I. Farkas.

Both Lukács and André Farkas of REFLEX suggested that courts have played a useful role in forcing local governments to reveal information under the Freedom of Information Act (FOIA) and to carry out environmental impact assessments. FOIA cases jump the queue in court, and some early lawsuits convinced officials that it was better to supply information than to challenge a request. EMLA has worked on 15 FOIA cases and in 13 it obtained access to the information sought by its clients. It did not need to go to court. One of the cases EMLA won in 2000–2001 was based on the FOIA as a way to get air-quality data from a particular site. Beyond the FOIA, my interview subjects generally were wary of using the courts even though some of them had initiated lawsuits. Thus, in 2001 Energia Klub challenged the constitutionality of one aspect of the Nuclear Act and lost because the Constitutional Court said it had no competence to review the claim.[321] HUMUSZ has sued the government several times to force it to enforce the law against firms that illegally dispose of waste or engage in other illegal activity, but it has seldom been successful.

Conclusions

The environmental sector in Hungary has some relatively well-established nonprofits, including some with a history going back to before the change in regime. Because environmental issues were neglected under the previous regime, some types of pollution and waste disposal problems are particularly obvious to all. Other more subtle harms to humans and to wildlife are not widely known. Environmentalism is associated with opposition to the previous regime and gained public support as a result. However, the economic strains of the transition have made strong environmental protection seem a luxury and have worked against costly policies. Furthermore, sensible environmental policy requires participants in the debate to be informed about scientific and technical issues. Hungary is a country where expertise is respected (Table 1.1). Although this seems to be a positive attitude, it can stand in the way of effective public participation if ordinary people think environmental policy ought to be left to experts who are seen as privy to esoteric knowledge. The environmental groups are trying to break through this attitude, both by being technically competent themselves and by involving ordinary people in protests and educational events. These groups have been only partly successful, but

---

[321] Interview with Ámon.

that is hardly surprising given the difficulties of finding funding, motivating ordinary citizens, educating their own staff, and getting effective access to government processes that are themselves in flux. They use various strategies to work within the existing system of organized advisory committees and elite consultation and to mobilize public support and media coverage.

These groups may face a funding crisis in the near term as external sources of funds shrink and domestic charitable giving fails to take up the slack. As a consequence, they may become relatively more dependent on public funds from the government and the parliament. This can be a threat to their role as independent voices in the formulation of policy unless the procedure for disbursing funds is clearly separated from their policy positions. To survive, they need to tap domestic sources of funding either by improving their fund-raising from individuals and firms or by finding new ways to sell goods and services consistent with their mission.

Assuming these groups can survive and that new groups are created, their prospects as advocacy organizations depend on the openness of the government and the legislature to their interventions. At present, participation occurs either through the formal route of the National Environmental Council or through informal consultations. Sometimes public hearings are held for local issues, but they do not appear to be a major factor. Existing routes have the difficulties discussed above. Hungarian policy makers and NGO leaders need to rethink the relationship between outside advocacy groups and the policy-making process to ensure more publicly accountable policy-making processes.

TEN

Student and Youth Organizations in Poland

Student and youth organizations in Poland present a complementary case with a range of contrasting organizational types. The research includes both "jurisdictional" organizations in the form of university self-governments and civil organization. Some existing groups have also considered becoming "interest groups" analogous to labor unions and professional chambers.

One student group, the Association of Polish Students (ZSP), is the reincarnation of the official student organization under communism. A second important group, the Independent Students' Association (NZS), was formed in the 1980s to contest the authority of ZSP and to protest regime policies. It collaborated with Solidarity and helped coordinate mass protests at the end of the communist regime. Some of its leaders were included in the early roundtable discussions over the future of the country, and some have gone into politics. Other groups have no history of protest or collaboration and are oriented to professional development, often in alliance with the corresponding professional chambers.

These associations interact with the official student self-governments whose university-level leaders are elected and who claim to speak for the entire student community. The National Students' Parliament includes representatives from the university parliaments. Several student groups are trying to create an alternative nationwide structure modeled after the original Roundtables.

All the student organizations face tensions over funding similar to those the Hungarian environmental organizations face. Government provides programmatic funds, and the self-governments distribute public scholarship funds and run dormitories and cafeterias under agreement with the university. The self-governments are deeply entwined with the state and university administration, a fact that may blunt their ability to act as an independent voice. The groups with political party allegiances, ZSP and NSZ, obtain government financial support, at least when their supporters are in power. All groups rely on donations from private firms and foundations and on the sale of services. Within the constraints of financing, student interest, and politics, they are trying to find a niche in which to thrive and gain membership and support.

In interviews, leaders and former leaders struggled with the issue of how to reinvent their organizations, further their own careers, and interact with other types of organizations both inside and outside of government and politics. Should one characterize their organizations as democratic bodies, labor unions for students, lobbyists, service providing organizations, or participants in government?

I begin by summarizing interviews with the two major groups, followed by interviews with two smaller professionally oriented groups, and I end with the student self-governments and the challenge to their role coming from the 2003 Roundtable organized by the leader of ZSP and his attempts to institutionalize the group as the Polish Youth Council.[322]

Association of Polish Students

ZSP dates from the 1950s but claims descent from a collection of older, university-level student "brotherhoods" that provided financial help and ran dormitories and cafeterias. During the socialist period, ZSP was the only official student organization.[323] In the Hungarian environmental movement, the closest analogy is with Birdlife Hungary, founded in the 1970s with official approval to organize birdwatchers. However, ZSP is a much more important organization in the life of the country. Waldemar Zbytek, the chairman in 2003–2004,[324] characterized ZSP in the early

---

[322] Unless otherwise noted, the interviews in this chapter were conducted in Warsaw in December 2003 and January 2004 by Maciej Kisilowski, Masters in Law, Yale University, and candidate for a JSD. He translated into English the interviews that were conducted in Polish. More details and his own analysis are available elsewhere (Kisilowski 2004).

[323] The century-old Academic Sports Organization was also active for the whole period but had a narrower mandate.

[324] The material on ZSP is mostly based on an interview with Waldemar Zbytek by Kisilowski on December 29, 2003. Zbytek is a graduate of the University of Mikolaj Kopernik (Toruń), a chairman of ZSP, chairman of the Polish Youth Council in 2003–2004, and a member of the National Executive Committee of Democratic Left Alliance (SLD), the ruling post-communist party.

period as similar to a labor union with a focus on students' material needs. In the 1960s and early 1970s, it concentrated on cultural, social, tourist, and scientific activities but was not directly involved in political or ideological issues. Its flagship operation was a well-known Warsaw students' club called Hybrydy. Membership levels were high, beginning with something over 50% in the 1950s and rising to over 80% in the 1970s, according to Zbytek. The proportion of students who belonged, however, varied widely across departments. Membership numbers were high partly because ZSP's travel and cultural programs were open only to members and because of the group's operation of student clubs. Furthermore, although it did not control much scholarship aid directly, its leaders actively participated in university committees that distributed aid and allocated other benefits.[325]

In 1973 ZSP added "Socialist" to its title, becoming SZSP and merging with two hard-line communist groups, the Association of Rural Youth and the Association of Socialist Youth. Although Zbytek does not stress this point, other sources claim that the merger and name change gave the group a much more ideological profile.[326] The leaders of the democratic opposition claim that some members of the group actively sought to break up opposition meetings and attacked participants.[327]

During the socialist period, SZSP advocated with the government for higher levels of financial aid for students. It was particularly active during the 1970s both in influencing government policy and in seeking to persuade young people to attend and graduate from university in line with state policy. It advocated for both better conditions for students and higher financial rewards for educated workers. SZSP was quite closely associated with the regime in power. Zbytek observed that the influence of the government on SZSP was high but noted that all organizations had to have some arrangements with the state in order to exist. During part of this period, the Communist Party promoted certain candidates for leadership positions in the organization. The very breadth of the student membership combined with leadership elections based on a secret ballot of the members, however, meant that it was not under tight ideological control.

---

[325] Wielka Encyklopedia Powszechna PWN (1969: 751).

[326] Skuza and Ulicki (2002: 26).

[327] See Kuroń (1991: 76–78), a leading dissident and Minister of Labor in the early 1990s. He reported how in the late 1970s SZSP members attacked his apartment, where underground lectures took place. They seriously beat up another well-known opposition figure and attacked Kuroń's son.

The group existed under martial law between 1981 and 1985, but its magazine was closed, and it faced other restrictions. Tensions emerged and came to a head when the group changed its name in 1982 to eliminate the word "Socialist" returning to its original name, Association of Polish Students (ZSP). The government opposed the change, but as Zbytek reports, in spite of strong political pressures, the leadership "knew it had to happen." He reports the story of how the student leaders, frightened of informing the authorities directly, managed to avoid active government opposition by announcing the name change to a Hungarian student leader in an arranged meeting in a Budapest train station. She told the Hungarian authorities, who told the Polish embassy, who passed the information on to Warsaw. This ploy effectively undermined government attempts to prevent the outcome. The success of this maneuver indicates that the state was unwilling to force a showdown.

In spite of this attempt at independence, the group did not break with the state, which was providing it with funds. Zbytek explained that the group's position was influenced by the fact that it employed several thousand people to run its programs and did not want to jeopardize its funding. As a result of continuing to work with the regime, the group suffered a decline in membership, with many people joining the newly established NZS. By the end of the 1980s, only about 10% of students were members.[328]

After the change in regime, ZSP experienced a crisis. In addition to a steep decline in membership, its activities sharply contracted as a result of a decline in financial support and organizational capacity. At the end of the 1990s, many chapters of ZSP folded, and the group seemed near collapse. However, beginning in 2000 ZSP began to revive, and it has reestablished chapters in some higher education institutions where it had ceased to exist. The group had to adjust to the new system if it wanted to survive. It had managed to persist despite the vagaries of the socialist system, and it needed to figure out how to do the same thing in the new democratic reality.

The first step was to change ZSP's governing charter to require that those who run for office in the organization must be 30 years old or under and to specify that officers can be reelected only once. At the time of the reform, some leaders of the group were over 40 years old. Because

---

[328] Zbytek reported that there were 40,000 members at that time out of a total student population in higher education of 400,000 (Poland, Główny Urząd Statystyczny [Central Statistical Office], 2003:251)

officers of the organization earn salaries, some people had been using their positions in ZSP as a "career." This discouraged students from joining the group, which, in any case, had never required that members be students. The age limit means the leadership can do a better job of representing student interests and that younger students can join ZSP with the hope of being elected leaders. Zbytek claims that ZSP's association with the former socialist regime is of decreasing importance among today's apolitical students, who judge ZSP by its actions. Nevertheless, Zbytek admits that in the past he has been reproached for being associated with ZSP.

Zbytek provided no exact membership figures, but he estimated membership at about 10,000, down from 40,000 in the late 1980s. Thus, current membership is under 1% of university students. Anyone who pays dues of about $1.50 a year can be a member so the group does not make strong personal commitment to the group a condition of membership. Zbytek downplayed the importance of membership numbers, arguing that ZSP could increase membership dramatically by giving members discounts on beer purchases at ZSP-run clubs. Recall that this is the type of tactic employed by SZSP in the 1970s, but Zbytek views it as pointless in the current environment.

The budget of ZSP is 2 to 3 million dollars per year. This makes it the third largest student organization behind the self-governments and the Academic Sport Association (AZS). However, it is much smaller than at the time of the regime change. In 1989, according to Zbytek, 120 people worked in the Warsaw headquarters. Today there are 30 employees in all of Poland. The universities usually provide in-kind support in the form of rent-free offices and free telephones. The national officers receive low stipends and often must interrupt their studies to be based in Warsaw during their 3-year terms.

Only 4%–5% of ZSP's budget takes the form of government grants, although counting the universities' in-kind donations would raise the total significantly. About 10% is earnings on assets, including three student clubs and a palace in Wrocław that was given to the group in the 1960s.[329] Zbytek reports that European Union (EU) grants help cover basic expenses, but domestic donations, totaling about 40% of the budget, are

---

[329] Zbytek was quite unclear about the value of these assets. He guessed they have retained only 3%–4% of assets from the past and that they contribute 10%–15% to income. However, he believes the Wrocław palace is a cash drain because of needed repairs. The group rents its traditional Warsaw headquarters from the city. Zbytek complains that it is too elaborate and costly but too steeped in tradition to abandon.

mostly sponsorships of particular activities. ZSP's main sponsored activities are an annual musical event and a project for freshmen. ZSP also makes money by running exam preparation courses and selling travel services.

The leadership is interested in once again becoming a force among students. Zbytek describes how members of other groups treated ZSP members "coldly, with reserve," especially representatives of groups that seek to be apolitical, such as the European Law Students Association (ELSA). ZSP is clearly associated with national politics and this discourages some groups from cooperating with it. Nevertheless, in early 2003 ZSP organized a national roundtable of student groups in its Warsaw office that included six national groups. This effort, part of ZSP's efforts to reinvent itself, is discussed below.

Independent Students' Association

The other group with political roots is NZS, which began as a mass movement among students in September 1980 just after the strikes in Gdańsk. It was legalized in February 1981 after some strikes by students.[330] According to Witold Repetowicz, a leader in the 1990s, some of the original leaders of NZS were also low-level members of ZSP. NZS grew out of earlier free student associations, some connected with Solidarity. For example, in Kraków there was a Student Committee of Solidarity in the second half of the 1970s, and in 1979 a national group existed called the Movement of Young Poland (Ruch Młodej Polski). In the fall of 1980, students lined up to join the organization; at that time, it was a true mass movement that supported the ideals of Solidarity without a formal association. Nevertheless, Repetowicz points out that even at that early time it struggled over whether to be a students' labor union or a more broadly political organization.

Under martial law NZS, which was identified with Solidarity, was officially disbanded and its property confiscated. The chairman and vice chairman were interned. Some groups operated underground until the mid-1980s when it was reorganized and participated in the early student

---

[330] The material on NZS is mostly based on a December 30, 2003, interview by Kisilowski with Witold Reptowicz. Reptowicz is a graduate of the Faculty of Law, Jagiellonian University, Kraków. He joined NZS in 1992, was vice chairman of the national board in 1993–1994, chairman of the national board in 1994–1995, chairman of the Jagiellonian University committee from 1995–1998, and vice-chairman of the national board in 1998.

self-governments. NZS was not a legal entity in that period, but student self-governments became officially recognized bodies in 1986, and NZS members operated through some of them, often with the tacit support of university administrators.[331] It was deeply involved in the demonstrations inside and outside the universities that eventually contributed to the fall of the regime. NZS was legalized nationally in 1990 amid a debate about its future. One founding member, then a member of the Sejm, argued for the dissolution of NZS on the grounds that its role as a mass movement was in the past. In 1990, others argued that NZS should transform itself into a political party along the lines of FIDESZ in Hungary, which grew out of a group of young opponents of the socialist regime. NZS was allied with the Liberal Democratic Party (KLD) and some members ran on its party list.[332] The "fideszization" of NZS did not occur, however, and the moment was lost when in 1993 the Right suffered a major defeat at the polls and the leaders of NZS split over the proper direction of national policy. Thus, like ZSP, NZS had to remake itself to survive.

Repetowicz became a leader of the organization at that time, joining the national board in 1993 and heading it in 1994–1995. With the change in government in 1993, the group lost most government funding. It also lost foundation financing as it went through a series of leadership disputes, suffered a robbery in its national offices in which all its computers were stolen, and uncovered major financial irregularities caused by the director of finances. Many chapters disbanded. Although 20 chapters had some kind of nominal existence, only 6 were active, and membership was low.[333] Repetowicz described the situation at several universities as "a big disaster." The decentralized organizational structure made it difficult for the national committee to exert control over the university branches.

Partly as a result of Repetowicz's efforts to centralize and reorganize the organization, it began to revive after 1993 both in chapters and in membership. It also improved its financial position with support from the government and Solidarity and from outside foundations. A key supporter in the Sejm, Adam Bielan, assisted NZS in obtaining public funds. Nevertheless, the group continues to struggle financially. NZS has tried to obtain company sponsorship for activities but appears to have been

---

[331] Reptowicz reports that NZS never completely disbanded at Jagiellonian University and in about 1988 was legally recognized by the university as a student group.

[332] KLD ceased to exist in 1993.

[333] There were active chapters at Jagiellonian University in Kraków, Warsaw University, Warsaw University of Technology, Warsaw School of Economics, and the Mining Academies in Kraków and Katowice.

less successful than some other groups. Individual chapters, such as the branch at Jagiellonian University in Kraków receive funding from their universities.

NZS still faces the fundamental question of what type of organization it should be. In the 1990s, part of the dispute was over the extent of political involvement of NZS after the demise of KLD. This was essentially a debate about how closely to associate with the political party Solidarity Electoral Action (AWS), which grew out of the Solidarity movement. NZS was involved in some political contests at the national level even though some university chapters, which are separate legally registered bodies, opposed that policy. Repetowicz also claimed that some university chapters were taken over by small groups with a variety of political agendas. Relations with university self-governments varied, with NZS running lists in the self-government elections in some universities.

NZS continues to struggle to redefine itself in the new environment. The current national board has decertified some university chapters, and competing groups claim to represent NZS in at least one university. Should it seek to influence the self-governments of universities becoming, in effect, a political force but only within the university setting? Should it act more like a "union" of students that seeks to organize to push for national or regional policies favorable to higher education? Should it ally itself more closely with a national political party? Should it be an independent, voluntary student organization, separate from the self-governments, that organizes events of interest to students and seeks to solve students' problems on an individual basis? At present, it fills all these roles with different levels of emphasis in different universities and at the national board. The group's perceived affiliation with the political parties on the right/liberal side in the 1990s meant its fortunes rose and fell with the government in power. The ongoing controversy over the group's political affiliation and purpose has led to conflict. NZS is not now a mass movement of the type that organized student strikes against the authorities in its early days. Its ups and downs point to the general problem of creating independent groups capable of participating in national political debates. The group seems to face a choice between partisan involvement in national politics, on the one hand, and an apolitical stance with a focus on university-level problems and service provision, on the other.

Individual members have used NZS as a platform to advance their own careers in national politics. This can undermine the role of the organization as a representative of student interests as its leaders seek a national stage. Repetowicz does not think the national parties have tried to capture NZS. Rather individual student leaders "serve NZS on a plate" to further their own personal and political interests. He concludes rather sadly that students should not get too involved in politics but should finish their studies. He points to many friends who got so involved in NZS that they failed to complete their university degrees.

Initiative of the Young

The Initiative of the Young (SIM) was established by 15 university students who had been leaders of a federation of self-governments of high school students.[334] According to Dominik Sypniewski, one of the founders, when they began their university studies at Warsaw University in 1999, the university self-governments were dominated by the established student movements described previously. Instead of competing in the self-government elections, these students established their own association to organize educational projects for students. In that way, they avoided the political influences that dominated the self-governments and kept their own group intact. Within 6 months SIM expanded beyond Warsaw to other Polish university cities, but it remained a centralized organization with branches.[335] At that time, the national group had about 200 full members with 1,000 or so students who are either members of the 56 local chapters or were candidates for membership. In 2002, Sypniewski left SIM, turning it over to a group of younger students. He reports that it was his decision "to give them the name of our association, the name which was recognizable among the private firms." Thus, in 2002 SIM was essentially under the personal control of the founders without an independent structure linked to the membership. SIM has never been a mass membership organization.

According to Sypniewski, about 15% of the annual budget of about $200,000 comes from public funds, mostly earmarked project grants. The rest comes from a mixture of donations and contract work. The group

---

[334] Maciej Kisilowski interviewed Dominik Sypniewski on December 22, 2003. He is a student in the Faculty of Law and Administration, Warsaw University, and of the Warsaw School of Economics. In 1996, he cofounded the Federation of Mazovian High School Students' Self-Governments. In 1999–2002, he cofounded and was vice-president of SIM. In 2002–2003, he was a member of the board of the Center for Youth Entrepreneurship Support; he has been president of the center since 2003.

[335] In this it differed from NZS, which is organized in a structure of local organizations with little central control or nationwide projects.

has no membership fees. SIM supplies advertising venues for businesses such as banks and cellular telephone companies in connection with their educational projects. SIM also receives in-kind support in the form of low-rent or free office space either from local governments (for example, the head office in Warsaw) or from university authorities. Until recently, it published a monthly magazine for students, *Observations*, produced with no public funding and distributed free. The newspaper included articles that criticized the self-government system for poorly representing student interests during some major controversies.[336]

Links with the university self-governments vary from cooperative to competitive. Sometimes the leaders of the self-governments saw SIM as "the enemy." In at least one case, at the University of Wrocław, the leader of SIM was also the elected head of the self-government. Sypniewski, however, believes the group has been most successful when it operates independently and avoids the difficulties of cooperating with the self-governments.

SIM has maintained a stance that is independent of the political parties. In the early years, it was heavily involved in policy issues tied to student well-being. In fact, its very independence gave it political influence and attracted government and private sector support for some of its activities. Between 1999 and 2002, many of SIM's activities were associated with the promotion of entrepreneurship and the free market. This led to direct and indirect business support. In addition, the leaders have been quite entrepreneurial in designing fund-raising strategies. For example, one early project was a panel discussion at Warsaw University concerning a proposed law to limit advertising targeted to young people, a category that includes university students. SIM initiated the panel as a way to give the group visibility, and it was then supported by Pro-Marka, a business association that included large companies such as Coca Cola. Pro-Marka helped with know-how and contacts, not cash, but it did finance later projects. Lacking the clear political affiliations of the major groups, it has been able to attract funding from businesses wary of too close an association with either major party. Sypniewski also argued that this nonpartisan stance gives it some influence with politicians as well. Citing the example of a workshop that was supported by the prime minister's office, he claimed that SIM's independence was valuable to the

---

[336] Correspondence from Maciej Kisilowski, July 18, 2004.

government as a source of unbiased advice and opinion that it could not get from groups with clear political affiliations. His claim is essentially that SIM's nonpartisan stance gives it more bargaining power and influence over policy making than the more obviously partisan groups. However, since the change in leadership in 2002, the group has become less involved in policy debates with a consequent loss of funding.

The current leadership emphasizes links with the business community, especially entrepreneurs. It no longer maintains a nationwide structure of groups or publishes a students' magazine. Rather, a small core of members organizes conferences and student events, such as rock concerts. Revenue for day-to-day operations comes from the overhead charges on event sponsorships. The organizational work is done by student volunteers. As an example of their current projects, Artur Turemka, a member of the board, interviewed on July 14, 2004, described a conference on entrepreneurship that he organized in April 2004 at the Warsaw University, School of Management. The conference was sponsored by a number of businesses, and one of the guest speakers was a wealthy Polish businessman. Symbolic of SIM's links to business is its new headquarters in a prestigious Warsaw skyscraper. SIM cooperates closely with the Business Center Club, an elitist business association, and since January 2004 it has collaborated with the Club on a project to promote entrepreneurship. It appears to be evolving into a small elite organization based in Warsaw that is dominated by students who seek a career in business. Turemka expressed little interest in student or university politics.

European Law Students' Association

ELSA is part of a federation of European law student groups. It is similar to other international or European federations for students of economics and business, engineering and related technical fields, and medicine. ELSA has an international focus and emphasizes cultural exchanges and educational projects. Inside Poland, ELSA organizes contests for students as well as training programs and conferences. The President of the Constitutional Tribunal has given his moral support to ELSA and one of its competitions.[337]

---

[337] In Polish, the President of the Court is described as being the "patron" of the contest. This means someone who gives symbolic support, not financial aid, to the event. Public officials frequently play this role for events or organizations of which they approve. It can provide leverage to obtain funding elsewhere. The ex-SIM's official also described

According to Florian Wierzchowski, a board member of ELSA,[338] the group receives very little government money – only about 2% of its budget. It gets financial support and free advice from law firms and the bar associations and sponsorships from private business. Most of the funds are for particular projects, but some can be put toward overhead. The most extensive cooperation is with the American accounting firm Ernst & Young. Wierzchowski believes one reason law firms support ELSA is that they are restricted from advertising. Acting as a sponsor for an ELSA project is one way for a firm to put its name before the public as part of the publicity for the project. ELSA seems to have been quite proactive in contacting law firms and has about 50 sponsors at the national level.[339]

Student Self-Governments and the Polish Youth Council

All universities have elected student self-governments. These are statutory bodies that are part of the university governance structure. Every student is automatically a member of his or her university self-government in the same way all residents of a particular geographic area are citizens of the municipality with jurisdiction over that area.[340] However, the

the Prime Minister as being the patron of a workshop that SIM organized. Once again, this did not imply financial aid, only approval.

[338] Interview by Kisilowski with Florian Wierzchowski on December 22, 2003. He is a student of the Faculty of Law, Silesia University (Katowice). In 2002–2003, he was a member of the national board of ELSA and treasurer. In 2003–2004, he was a member of the national board focusing on marketing.

[339] ELSA obtains free space from the universities where it operates and has no paid staff. The organization also rents an apartment in Warsaw that serves as an office and place to live for ELSA board members when they are in the city. Wierzchowski, although a student at the University of Silesia, appears to spend considerable time in Warsaw. Because of the difficulty of balancing his work for ELSA with his academic commitments, he was on a leave of absence at the time of the interview.

[340] This section is based on three interviews: a December 30, 2003, interview by Kisilowski with Michał Hryciuk, student, Faculty of Electronics and Information Technology and College of Social Sciences and Administration, Warsaw University of Technology, member of the Board of Senators, and chairman of the Social Committee of University Self-Governments, 2002–time of interview; a January 22, 2004, interview by Anna Osińska (Center for Youth Entrepreneurship Support) with Andrzej Szejna, graduate of the Warsaw School of Economics and Faculty of Law and Administration, Warsaw University; chairman of the Students' Parliament of the Republic of Poland (PSRP), 1997–1999; chairman of the Council of the PSRP Foundation, 1999; former president of the Civil Movement: Youth for Poland; Undersecretary of State, Ministry of Economy, Labor, and Social Policy, 2003; Deputy President of Polish Information and Foreign Investment Agency, 2004, and elected to the European Parliament in June 2004; and e-mail interview by Kisilowski on January 26, 2004, with Przemysław Kowalski, student, Faculty

legitimacy of self-governments as representatives of student interests is cast in some doubt by low turnout in elections, which can vary widely across university departments and dormitories, each of which has elected councils. Andrzej Szejna, chairman of the Students' Parliament of the Republic of Poland in 1997–1999, estimates that at the Warsaw School of Economics turnout falls as students go through their studies, falling from over 50% for first-year students to about 25% for fifth-year students. According to Michal Hryciuk, a student government leader at the Warsaw University of Technology, turnout at his university varies from 16% to 25%, although some departments and dormitories with well-organized self-governing bodies have very high participation. Part-time students seldom participate. Zbytek of ZSP, a critic of the self-governments, argues that turnout is sometimes in the single digits, with the self-government leaders discouraging turnout so their own candidates can win.

University Self-Governments

The organization of the university self-governments varies depending on the size of the university. Hryciuk described its organization and role at the Warsaw University of Technology, one of Poland's largest universities. Each department has its own elected student representatives forming a department Council of Self-Government. The council gives opinions on issues such as exam schedules and curriculum and tries to resolve conflicts between students and professors. The student dormitories also have elected Occupants' Councils that represent the one-sixth of the student body that lives in dormitories. These councils send representatives to the Student Parliament – two from each department (the chairman of the council, who is ex officio, and a delegate) and one from each dormitory. Eight seats are reserved for representatives of student groups (formally organized associations or informal groups of students), down from 16 before 2003. These eight seats are the only positions that are voted on by the student body as a whole, and their election is by proportional representation with groups running slates of candidates. Most other universities do not reserve any seats for student groups (Kisilowski 2004). The parliament has 59 members. Thus, the student associations' members account for less than 15% of the total. However, association members also might

of Economics and Agriculture, Warsaw Agriculture University, chairman of Students Union of Agricultural Schools, 2000–2001, chairman of the Social-Economic Committee of PSRP, 2000–2001, chairman of the Foreign Affairs Committee of PSRP 2001–2002, and chairman of the Students' Parliament of the Republic of Poland, 2002–time of interview.

be selected through the department and dormitory elections. Many of the student associations do not participate in the elections either at the university or the department level. Hryciuk reports that at the Warsaw University of Technology NZS and BEST, an association of business and economics students, do try to exert some influence in areas of interest, such as sports, tourism, and culture, and seek representation in the parliament. However, most groups do not run slates but instead concentrate on their own independent activities.[341]

The Chairmanship of the Students' Self-Government is a powerful position, and the selection process often involves a good deal of political maneuvering as rival candidates seek support among departments, dormitories, and student groups. The chairmanships of key committees, such as the one charged with organizing the scholarship award program, are also frequently hotly contested. However, candidates who are too obviously using posts in student self-governments as stepping stones to national political office may lose support for that reason. Hryciuk reports that students are suspicious of overtly political appeals and that there is an unwritten rule that candidates should not belong to a political party.

The parliament has responsibilities in the area of student life including teaching, culture, sports, tourism, international contacts, and dormitories. To outsiders in other student organizations, operation of the self-governments can seem opaque. Hence, Zbytek of ZSP argues for a statute that mandates more open processes that parallel those of local governments and give registered student organizations, such as ZSP, the right to attend meetings and give opinions.

From a financial point of view, the major responsibility of the university self-governments is the dispensation of scholarship funds from the national budget.[342] At the Warsaw University of Technology, money

---

[341] The details vary across universities. For example, the Warsaw School of Economics, a much smaller institution, has no departmental committees. Students directly elect all the members of the university student self-government rather than working through departments and dormitories. This has the potential to permit large student associations to run slates of candidates.

[342] A statute provides that the scholarships are granted by a dean, unless the students' self-government passes a motion asking for the appointment of a students' scholarship committee. In the latter situation, a dean must appoint the committee, and a rector must appoint an appellate committee. See Ustawa z dnia 7 września 1990 roku o szkolnictwie wyższym [Statute of September 7, 1990 on higher education], Dz. U. 1990, No. 65, Item 385 with amendments, article 152a–152h. The committees include students delegated by the organs of departmental and university self-government (respectively) as well as the university staff; students, however, have a majority guaranteed by the law. Statute on higher education, article 152a, section 5, and 152b, section 5.

for scholarships totals $11–12 million annually from the public budget and dormitory fees. At that university, the Student Parliament leaves the actual award of scholarships to department committees and simply sets guidelines (for example, it sets the grade point average cutoff for merit scholarships) and provides training. The department committees determine the students' needs and academic merit and can carry out their own investigations to determine student need.

The rest of the budget, from $300,000 to $400,000, comes mostly from various parts of the national budget. No more than 15% comes from private sponsorships of events. In some other universities, the self-governments run student clubs that earn a profit and contribute substantial sums. In other cases, independent foundations operate clubs, dormitories, or cafeterias with a board selected by the self-government or by the rector. Frequently, this gives the managers of these foundations a degree of control over the self-governments. In some cases, according to Maciej Kisilowski, the managers of the foundations are former student activists, now in their 30s, who through patronage and other favors control the self-governments and maintain their positions. The parliament determines the level of financial support for the dormitories and sets the rates for foundation-run dormitory rooms. All these actions are done in consultation with university authorities, but, in practice, both the Student Parliament and the departmental committees have wide discretion.[343]

The statute on higher education requires that representatives from the student self-government comprise at least 10% of each university's senate, the main governing body of a Polish university. The large state-owned universities guarantee much higher representation. At the Warsaw University of Technology, students hold 12 seats or one-sixth of the total. Hryciuk reports that, because their attendance is relatively good, students typically account for one-fifth to one-quarter of the votes. At the Warsaw University of Economics, Szejna reports that students hold 20% of the seats. The University Senate is an essential part of the university governance structure; it decides on the major issues facing the university including some faculty appointments.[344] The statute also guarantees

---

[343] Hryciuk reports that a student can appeal a low scholarship award to the Deputy Rector, but, in fact, the rector's decision is based on material prepared by a committee of the Student Parliament.

[344] Professorial positions represent employment at a particular university. The award of the national title of Professor, however, is the president's responsibility and is not tied to employment at a particular university. The University Senate plays no role in the

student participation in the electoral bodies for rectors and deans.[345] In practice, the chairman of the student self-government has considerable power in the University Senate if he or she can deliver the student votes in a bloc. As Hryciuk points out, the rector often seeks an accommodation with the students because "professors have their own conflicts, and the interests of different departments vary." The professoriate is deeply divided in many universities between those who were professors under the old regime and those who were politically suspect at that time and could not advance until the change in regime.

Hryciuk and Szejna described how the students exercise power in the selection of the rector at two different universities. Hryciuk offered some details. Student members pledge to vote as a bloc and interview the candidates to determine their views on issues of special concern to students. After vetting the candidates, the students hold their own internal poll to select a single candidate to support. As Hryciuk reports: "It is a very comfortable situation; it enables [the electors] to maintain quite a strong position during the negotiations with the candidates." Of course, the students do not always win, but they have had several successes, including the selection of the last several rectors of the Warsaw University of Technology.

Students' Parliament of the Republic of Poland
At the top of the national self-governing structure there is a statutory body called the Students' Parliament of the Republic of Poland (PSRP) that consists of representatives of the university student self-governments. PSRP is an official body established in 1996 to replace a voluntary federation of university self-governments. It has certain consultation rights with the government and also consults with the Sejm, the senate, and the president about issues affecting students and university life. Three members serve on the government's Council of Higher Education and make up one-tenth of the council membership. These members tend to be the most committed student activists; they are active participants in the council's work, according to Przemysław Kowalski, the chairman of PSRP in 2002–2004 and one of the student members of the council. PSRP

---

awarding of degrees; that is the responsibility of the department research councils, which do not include students.

[345] Higher Education Act article 59, section 1, point 1. The statute does not mandate a fixed percentage, but, in practice, the articles of the large state universities set a share similar to the student share of seats in the University Senate.

also expresses opinions on draft regulations of the Ministry of National Education and Sport and participates in various advisory bodies of that ministry. Its members are on various task forces on issues relating to higher education, and, since 2004, they send a representative to the Economic and Social Committee of the European Union.[346]

As an example of the influence of PSRP, Andrzej Szejna, chairman of PSRP in 1997–1999, mentions an act on credits and student loans that benefited more than 200,000 students with loans that averaged several hundred złotys per month ($100–150). This policy began when he was chairman of PSRP, and he cites it as a major achievement. To him it is an exercise in local democracy that puts the decision-making authority in the hands of students who understand the situation in their own universities and departments.

Szejna argues that PSRP has an impact because of its nonpartisan stance. The Minister of Education could not simply dismiss his arguments by claiming that the group was politically motivated. "That's why he could treat me as a social partner." Yet, he admitted that inside PSRP partisan debates raged and claimed that his own centrist position and lack of party affiliation made him an obvious leader.

Universities with more than 1,000 students have from one to seven representatives depending on size – a formula that produces an unwieldy group. Three hundred and fifty students attended the November 2003 meeting. This group selects a chairman, an executive council, a council of students, and a supervisory board, which do the real work of the group along with numerous committees.[347] According to Kowalski, the structure works fairly well, although he supports a reform to lengthen terms beyond one year.

2003 Roundtable and the Polish Youth Council
In early 2003, Zbytek and the leadership of ZSP organized a roundtable of national youth groups that met in the offices of ZSP in Warsaw. In addition to ZSP, the groups that attended were the Polish Scouting and Guiding Association (ZHP),[348] the Association of Rural Youth, ELSA

---

[346] The website of the Economic and Social Committee is: http://www.esc.eu.int. (last visited November 4, 2004).

[347] Interview with Kowalski.

[348] This is the largest scouting association in Poland and, like ZSP, is the reformed successor to the official group under socialism. There is also a much smaller group called the Union of Scouting of Rzeczpospolita (ZHR) that broke away from ZHP during the

Poland, AIESEC Poland (an association of business students), AEGEE in Poland (a European students association), AZS, and NZS. SIM was not invited because it is no longer a national group, but the leadership of SIM seems unconcerned. Artur Turemka of SIM doubted the value of a national group to represent student interests, pointing to its lack of expertise on educational policy.

Zbytek organized the roundtable in reaction to criticisms of the university self-governments and PSRP, the national parliament. The group proposed creation of the Polish Youth Council (PYC) to provide input to the government and the Sejm on youth issues of national concern as well as opinions on other national policy initiatives. The PYC would be a consortium of student and youth groups rather than part of the national self-government structure. Zbytek sees PYC as "a totally grassroots movement." He wants to give the proposed PYC a voice at the national level that is recognized by the Ministry of Education and operates under a statutory mandate. He sees himself as a leader of the council that would debate and take positions on longer-term policy issues such as the budget deficit and employment and pension policy and that would present policy ideas to the Sejm in the form of draft bills.

According to Zbytek, the PYC "will be able to represent an authentic voice of young people, the voice of the ordinary, average young person." It would be analogous to the Tripartite Commission in the area of labor-business relations. Under one vision of the PYC expressed by Zbytek, the government would have a seat at the PYC table, and the council would be a place to discuss issues facing students and higher education. He recognizes, however, that creation of a new body entirely independent of the self-government structure is not realistic, but in January 2004 he was working with representatives of 12 student groups to propose amendments to the statute on higher education with the hope of moving his project forward.

Even though Zbytek argues that the Roundtable and the PYC are not meant to confront or compete with the self-government structure, they are clearly an alternative route for student and youth influence. He claims that the organizers of the Roundtable asked the leaders of PSRP to participate and that they refused, and he believes PSRP tried unsuccessfully to foment conflicts between the Roundtable participants.

period of martial law and was a locus for some anti-regime activities. At present, both are officially recognized organizations. This information is from Anna Horolets (e-mail July 14, 2004).

The PYC aims to be a consortium of student associations. Thus, it would not be representative in the sense of the self-governments because it is not based on a broad-based electoral process. Furthermore, some member groups have political party affiliations. Nevertheless, even Hryciuk, an active participant in university self-government, recognizes that such an organization might be more effective politically than the self-governments because there are no annual elections and board members can serve for several years. Furthermore, the leaders of the 2003 Roundtable argue that the self-governments, in spite of their nominally broad electoral base, are not truly representative organizations. As Zbytek states, "it is not important that the Parliament formally represents 1.6 million students. That is only a purely statutory, theoretical conclusion.... The number of students who are actually represented by the Parliament is much lower than the number of members of active students' organizations."

Evaluations of Self-Governments
The relationships between associations, self-governments, and the state are in a state of flux and controversy as various organizations and individuals jockey for power. The student leaders had sharply differing views of the self-government structures. Naturally, the three people who were involved in university and national self-governments have a favorable view of these organizations. Kowalski, the chairman in 2002–2004, sees the self-governments as representing the interests of all the students in front of public and university authorities. The national Student Parliament should facilitate the activities of other organizations, but the parliament's responsibilities are broader than those of any other group because it must represent all students, including those not associated with other organizations. The structure is and should remain apolitical in the sense of avoiding affiliation with political parties. However, Kowalski recognizes that participation in self-government elections and committees can be good training for a career in national politics, and he believes many Polish politicians are proud of their experience in student self-government.

One example of this is Szejna, chairman of PSRP in 1997–1999, who in 2004 at age 31 was elected a Member of the European Parliament. Before that he was the Deputy President of the Polish Information and Foreign Investment Agency and the Undersecretary of State in the Ministry of Economy, Labor, and Social Policy. He attributes his success as a leader in the national student self-government and in government to his centrist politics and to the support of some powerful political actors.[349] He sees PSRP as a democratic microcosm that combines students of different political views in a body that works "to create the best solutions for students in Poland, especially in the area of social protection." Like Kowalski, he sees the student self-government as providing a counterweight to ZSP and NZS, one that can focus on representing the interests of all students in Poland. However, he recognizes the obvious tension in moving from the ostensibly nonpartisan PSRP into direct involvement in national politics. The solution crafted by him and his friends was to create their own organization, Civic Movement – Youth for Poland, as a stepping stone.

Hryciuk sees the university self-governments as overseeing the "students' movement" in areas such as research circles and artistic endeavors. Independent associations that are outside the jurisdiction of both student self-governments and the university "cause many problems," but the only thing the university can do is prevent groups from using university facilities. It might, for example, terminate a contract with a group that had been using university office space. At the national level he finds the Roundtable, with its proposal for a PYC, "a strange idea." He recognizes the value of organizations in the spheres of sport, tourism, and culture but believes they should not be involved in the distribution of financial aid to students. This should be the continued responsibility of the more broadly representative and less partisan student self-governments. He seems to view the self-government structure as a way to counter the influence of ZSP and NZS, the two nationwide student organizations that are loosely allied with different national political parties. Szejna argues that the most important student organizations, such as ZSP and NZS, should enter into electoral politics at the university level if they want to have influence and not create a parallel structure.

The interview with Repetowicz of NZS indicates that this sometimes does happen. At the Warsaw University of Technology and the Warsaw School of Economics, NZS participated in the electoral process. At Jagiellonian University in Kraków in the late 1990s "self-government was involved in NZS." In other words, both NZS and the self-government were controlled by the same group. Various factions then tried to take over NZS. "NZS became something more than an organization." This

---

[349] He mentions Leszek Balcerowicz, a well-known liberal economist/politician, former minister, and president of the Polish National Bank, and Aleksander Kwaśniewski, the President of the Republic.

was a time when NZS was weak nationally but remained a major force at Jagiellonian University.

At the opposite extreme, Wierzchowski of ELSA, a member of the Roundtable, criticizes the university and national self-governments. He claims that students criticize their own university self-governments as ineffective and self-serving, and he argues that the scholarships under their control are not given out fairly. ELSA does not run lists of candidates in the self-government elections, although it sometimes cooperates with them in individual cases. He is, however, at a loss to explain why members of his group do not try to run for office and improve the situation at individual universities. He, at least, has no time for university-level politics. At the national level, ELSA's disengagement from the national Student Parliament is clear. It was part of the 2003 Roundtable and supports the establishment of a Polish Council of Youth.

Sypniewski of SIM believes university self-governments serve a useful function, but he is very critical of the Parliament of Students of the Republic of Poland. He believes it serves merely as a stepping stone for young people to get into national politics and does not actually benefit the community of students. A recent disputed election in 2002 confirmed his viewpoint. The parliament had an election for officers, but after the vote, each group declared victory. The resulting impasse made the group look ineffectual, and Sypniewski believes most members of the parliament are more interested in a political career than in doing what is best for students. Its official responses to government requests for opinions are usually "only empty words." Because the parliament depends on the Ministry of Finance for funding, it may hesitate to criticize government policy. According to him, it would be better for the government to bypass the parliament when it seeks an opinion on issues affecting students. Instead, it should consult with student associations such as his own group. To him, these groups are more directly concerned with the interests of students.

Zbytek of ZSP reports that the self-government structure arose as a result of the political changes in Poland, and he mentions that the ZSP members of self-governments at first met with hostility. ZSP has had only a few representatives in the national parliament. Zbytek argues that, far from being nonpartisan, some local university bodies were used as political platforms for particular points of view. He is an alumnus of the University of Mikołaj Kopernik (Toruń). When the rector of that university asked him why ZSP did not run candidates for office, he pointed to a situation in which elections were canceled by the organizers with no reaction from the university. He states that "it is a waste of time and energy to concentrate our activity on election campaigns." ZSP wants to concentrate on "culture, sport, education, tourism, comic books" – things that concern students.

In his more speculative moments Zbytek hopes his own plan for a youth council might be the first step toward establishing a council that "would create a plan for Poland, a plan which would not relate to the very current situation" but would focus on the future in, say 2015, including general policy issues such as the budget deficit, economic development, and pension reform. To him, the Students' Parliament is too political, "not because some political party has control of it, but because it functions like a political system, a political body, in which the coalition and elections have a basic importance." He worries that the student self-governments control large amounts of money with little or no oversight. According to him, "where there is big money and no regulations, pathological situations must start to occur."

As an example, he points to the major national conflict, mentioned by Sypniewski, that developed in 2002 when two people claimed to be the president of PSRP and fistfights took place. "Blood was flowing; windows were broken." He thinks PSRP has created its own isolated political structure under which the incumbents promote their own successors.

This view of the illegitimacy of the student self-governments motivated the leaders of ZSP and some other organizations to organize the 2003 Roundtable outside the self-government structure because "only a fool would confront the self-government." Zbytek believes "the numerous local university organizations, groups, research circles, etc." are the ones "who create the students' movement, not the self-governments." He claims the Student Parliament has played little role in a proposed amendment of the statute on higher education because of its legitimacy crisis. On the other side of the debate, self-government participants point to the limited role of ZSP in many universities where it went out of existence for some period of time before reviving in recent years.

Conclusions

These interviews with student and youth leaders, past and present, illustrate the complex nature of politics, policy, and interest group activity in Poland. Leaders in both the self-governments and the Roundtable claim to be representing Polish students as a whole. The self-governments face the problem of low voter turnout and student apathy. The national associations must confront sharply diminished membership numbers and the same indifference to collective action that threatens the legitimacy of the self-governments. Neither ZSP nor NSZ can any longer claim to be a mass organization. The smaller, more professionally oriented groups make no such claims and, in fact, seem to be proud of their exclusive nature.

Except for purely recreational and educational activities, all these organizations are politically active in the broad sense of that term. They try to influence government policy on issues of interest to students. Some leaders, such as Zbytek of ZSP, aspire to have student and youth groups take positions on broad issues of national policy. Others see their role as more narrowly focused on helping students, especially with respect to the level and distribution of financial aid. One interviewee spoke of his group acting as a "labor union" for students to negotiate for better conditions. Only ZSP and NSZ have well-identified connections with national political parties, although the leaders of other organizations appear also to have political connections with public officials and important figures in and out of government.

At various times in their history the groups have played a range of different roles: official state-supported association, independent mass movement organizing street protests, "labor union" analogue negotiating for scholarship aid, political party adjunct grooming the next generation of leaders, democratic self-government governing on the basis of an electoral mandate, and independent association advocating for students and youth and providing services. No group can do all these things at once, and, when one group settles into a particular niche, this may create conflicts with others that have overlapping mandates. The case of student and youth groups in Poland is a particularly good example of the tendency of the state in Central Europe to gravitate toward formal, official bodies as the exclusive route for group influence. It illustrates the weaknesses of that strategy when the official organization lacks democratic legitimacy and becomes a source of conflict.

Thus, in a different country and in a very different policy area, we see some of the same puzzles and problems that face Hungarian environmental groups. How much should groups cooperate with official bodies such as the National Environmental Council in Hungary or the university self-governments in Poland? Is it acceptable to use leadership in these nongovernmental organizations as a stepping stone to national political office or does that undermine the independence and effectiveness of these organizations? What are the costs and advantages of close affiliation or identification with particular political parties? How can funding levels be maintained through a mixture of public funding, private gifts and sponsorships, and business activities? How do the sources of funding limit a group's ability to establish an independent voice? How should leaders balance the need for expertise against claims of broad popular support? If a group's leaders have privileged inside access to policy makers and politicians, will they be a strong voice for more open and inclusive procedures?

The main difference between the two cases is the presence of an official self-government structure in Poland that plays an important role in universities throughout the country and is in some tension with the civil society organizations. Hungarian environmental nongovernmental organizations also have a national organization, but it lacks the status of a self-government. Nevertheless, in both cases individuals and groups have to decide whether to be part of the national organization or to rely on their own contacts, expertise, and organizing and fund-raising ability. An administrative process that is more open-ended, would encourage the development of groups that are not part of existing hierarchies and that are excluded from formal advisory councils, such as the National Environmental Council in Hungary and the Council of Higher Education in Poland. This would put a greater burden on the government bureaucracy to manage public participation in government policy making, but on the positive side, it would avoid solidifying closed loops of consultation between government and certain organized groups. There is no clear-cut blueprint for how governments can achieve greater openness, but I argue in the concluding chapter that the experience of the United States can provide some guidance both as a model and, in some cases, as a cautionary tale.

ELEVEN

Democratic Consolidation and Policy-Making Accountability

Both Poland and Hungary need to create more open and accountable policy-making processes. Political parties and contested elections are central to the democratic structures of both states, but widespread popular distrust of political parties suggests they cannot carry the entire burden of responsible government. Over half the population is dissatisfied with democracy and lacks confidence in parliament. Delegation to professional bureaucrats is not a sufficient response. Even though people have faith in experts, many lack confidence in the civil service and view them as biased and corrupt.[350] Civil service reform can help, but it is mainly a route to performance accountability, not policy-making accountability. It needs to be integrated with reforms designed to improve the policy-making processes of government.

Monitoring and Participation

I have outlined the strengths and weaknesses of five types of monitoring and participation that can enhance policy-making accountability. Four of the five have inherent limits that imply the need to strengthen the fifth type – open-ended participation by citizens and organized groups in government-led processes. The first four are external accountability, accountability inside the central government, decentralized political accountability, and corporatist social dialogue.

The first requires the state to defer to external constraints imposed by international bodies such as the European Union (EU). Although this

---

[350] See Tables 1.1 and 3.1 and the survey data of Mishler and Rose (1998) and Miller et al. (2001: 61–91).

can provide an effective push toward reform in particular cases, it can provoke a backlash by citizens if extended too far. Citizens may resent being dictated to by outsiders and resist reforms simply because they appear to be imposed. Furthermore, in the special case of the EU, its own push for devolution to member states and even to regions within these states blunts its role as an external guarantor.

The second includes a collection of public institutions that provide oversight. These can enhance performance accountability, but they cannot play a central role in policy making. As an embattled former Hungarian ombudsman stated: "We must bring serious skepticism to...[the evaluation] of *independent* institutions reporting to the government.... The political forces [that are in power]...tend to regard the entirety of the administration as their sole possession...." (Majtényi 2001b: 338–339). These institutions may find it difficult to maintain their strength and independence in a parliamentary system whose unitary legislative/executive structure discourages strong oversight. Their method of appointment opens them up to the criticism that they have partisan agendas.

The third is delegation to lower-level governments with local citizens providing the checks on executive power. Although this option can work for truly local problems, it risks a descent into parochialism that leaves national interests behind. Under conditions that prevail in Central Europe, local power brokers often can operate undemocratically and with less scrutiny and more impunity than national politicians.

The fourth option is social dialogue among organized groups and government officials to reach consensus. This neocorporatist option does represent participation, but it goes too far in elevating the power of certain organized groups over other interests. Advocates of social dialogue denigrate the political accountability of bureaucrats by calling their actions "managerial" in contrast to "pluralist" or "popular." They stress the value of participation not just to influence policy but also to build civic capacity. The aim is a consensual decision based on shared values that can be revealed by dialogue and debate (Beierle and Cayford 2002: 3–4).

In fact, bureaucrat-led processes are more democratic than their critics recognize because of their ultimate accountability to the legislature and the government. In contrast, one should not idealize social dialogue. Corporatist processes are often full of conflict, and, if they are not, it may be because the process excludes key interests.[351] In Hungary and Poland, the representative character of included groups is often poor, and, even

---

[351] See Beierle and Cayford (2002), who find that this is true of some of their cases.

so, consensus is often impossible, in which case the government ministry steps in to impose a solution.

Although all four of these oversight mechanisms can serve useful functions, they are insufficient to constrain government policy making. Government- or bureaucrat-led policy making is an essential aspect of modern government, but it needs to incorporate pluralist values to avoid both the dominance of experts and the risks of politically motivated decisions that overlook interests not well-represented in the law-making process. In a parliamentary system, the governing coalition supports broad statutory mandates that it then implements through the bureaucracy. Statutory language almost never solves all the policy issues raised by the issues incorporated into statutes. Thus, the government must be able to issue decrees with the force of law, but, if it is to do this competently and responsibly, it needs to listen to organized groups and citizens who are informed about and concerned with the policy at issue. They may have scientific and technical expertise, or they may simply be a voice for ordinary citizens concerned about the policy. The participants need to be able to seek court review of any alleged irregularities in the process. Because they may not be representative of broader social interests, however, they should not have ultimate decision-making authority. The only exception would be narrow areas where a social dialogue can occur among a well-specified set of groups that do truly represent the relevant interests.

Some claim that the focus should be on strengthening political parties, not overcoming the existing problems with public participation. However, political parties, even the multiple parties produced by a proportional representation system, are not a good substitute for organizations from business associations and labor unions, on the one hand, to civil-society groups (or even individuals) concerned with issues such as the environment, social welfare, or gender, on the other. Parties represent a conglomeration of interests and are focused on winning elections, not mastering the details of policy. Although there may be some tradeoffs between the development of strong parties and the establishment of well-institutionalized nonparty groups, Hungary and Poland, like other middle-income democracies, appear to have room for both. Too strong a move to incorporate independent groups under political party labels could produce a system of rotating elected cartels that can govern for limited periods of time without considering the interests of those who are currently associated with opposition parties. At present, in Central and Eastern Europe (CEE) there seems to be a tendency for civil society groups to have de facto links to political parties, but that may be, at least in part, due to the absence of other routes to influence.

The United States Experience

The balance between bureaucratic authority and public participation is most well articulated in the United States.[352] Thus, in developing my argument, I examine how these processes operate there and ask whether that experience has any lessons for emerging democracies. The United States places little emphasis on social dialogue of the neocorporatist sort and has no national ombudsman to handle individual complaints. However, policy making inside the executive branch uses an administrative rule-making process that requires notice, hearings, and reason giving followed by judicial review. In recommending more open and participatory policy-making processes in Hungary and Poland, I am drawing on the United States model.

Of course, a major caveat may be the limited transferability of that experience. In interpreting U.S. practice as a guide to reform in the postsocialist countries, one must recognize the differences in political structure and in the organization of society. Furthermore, partial reforms may not have the expected consequences. For example, the introduction of greater rights to participate without effective judicial review can lead to policy distortions.[353] Nevertheless, because I believe the differences are ones of degree, not of kind, the U.S. evidence provides useful background.

Rule Making Under the Administrative Procedure Act
The U.S. Administrative Procedure Act (APA), as amended through the Freedom of Information Act, the Government in the Sunshine Act, the Regulatory Negotiation Act, and the Federal Advisory Committee Act, has struck the balance in a way that is worth consideration by emerging democracies.[354] Rule making is under the control of the executive but must be open to outside influences exerted through APA procedures supplemented by requirements to provide information and keep most processes open. Judicial review is available to ensure that the procedures

---

[352] Research on the operation of American participatory processes used in this chapter was carried out by Lisa Marshall.

[353] For example, Canada introduced greater public participation rights in the environmental area that followed the U.S. model but did not couple them with enhanced judicial review. The result, according to Green (1997), risks underregulation when public interest is low and overregulation when it is high. See also Green (1999) for further analysis of public participation in Canada.

[354] These acts are located at 5 U.S.C. §§ 551–559, 701–706 (Administrative Procedure Act), 552 (Freedom of Information Act), 552b (Government in the Sunshine Act), 561–570 (Negotiated Rulemaking Act), Appendix 2 (Federal Advisory Committee Act).

are followed and that the resulting rules accord with statutory mandates and the constitution. De novo court review is almost never available. There are many practical problems in the American rule-making process but, in principle, it tries to cope with the problem of balancing expertise and bureaucratic rationality against popular concerns for openness and accountability.[355]

The U.S. administrative process, however, has many critics, and reformers in Central Europe need to understand the actual operation of the system if they are to learn from the U.S. experience. Some relevant evidence, collected at both the federal and state levels, permits a guarded optimism about well-designed administrative procedures that include public participation.

As I have made clear, my focus is accountable policy making through legally binding rules, what are often called normative acts or decrees in Europe (*Rechtsverordnungen* in German). I am not concerned with implementation of the law in particular cases (what I call performance accountability). My main concern is with the exercise of delegated power in situations in which the statute leaves considerable policy-making discretion to government ministries.

Much of the American case study research concerns implementation. However, implementation and policy making sometimes overlap, especially if the resolution of a particular case is important to many people and interests – such as the location of a new airport or the designation of a nuclear waste disposal site. Thus, some of these experiences are relevant. My emphasis is on the role of outsiders in policy making, not on their role in monitoring. Monitoring and oversight are important roles for civil society groups and the media, especially when corruption and conflicts of interest need to be controlled (Rose-Ackerman 1999: 162–174; McMillan and Zoido 2004). However, they are not the object of this study.

In the United States, legally binding rules generally are promulgated under the notice and comment rule-making process required by the APA combined with the provisions for judicial review.[356] The APA, passed in 1946, sets up the bare bones of a publicly accountable process by requiring that the preparation of rules with the force of law be noticed in the *Federal*

---

[355] Lindseth (2003: 24) holds a similar view in arguing for the essentially constitutional status of the APA. He argues that the APA "is born of a specifically *constitutional* obligation on the part of the legislature to structure technocratic governance, public and private, to ensure that there will be democratically-legitimate oversight and control – what I call 'mediated legitimacy' – of all agents who exercise delegated normative power."

[356] 5 U.S.C. §§ 553, 701–706.

Register and include a hearing open to "interested persons." Final rules must be accompanied by a "concise general statement of their basis and purpose."[357] Although some types of rules are excluded, in practice, the reach of the APA is broad, and some agencies not subject to its provisions

---

[357] The text of the § 553 dealing with rule making is as follows:

(a) This section applies, according to the provisions thereof, except to the extent that there is involved –
  (1) a military or foreign affairs function of the United States; or
  (2) a matter relating to agency management or personnel or to public property, loans grants, benefits, or contracts.

(b) General notice of proposed rule making shall be published in the Federal Register. . . . The notice shall include –
  (1) a statement of the time, place, and nature of public rule making proceedings;
  (2) reference to the legal authority under which the rule is proposed; and
  (3) either the terms or substance of the proposed rule or a description of the subjects and issues involved. Except where notice or hearing is required by statute, this subsection does not apply –
    (A) to interpretative rules, general statements of policy, or rules of agency organization, procedure, or practice; or
    (B) when the agency for good cause finds (and incorporates the finding and a brief statement of reasons therefore in the rules issued) that notice and public procedure thereon are impracticable, unnecessary, or contrary to the public interest.

(c) After notice required by this section, the agency shall give interested persons an opportunity to participate in the rule making through submission of written data, views, or arguments with or without opportunity for oral presentation. After consideration of the relevant matter presented, the agency shall incorporate in the rules adopted a concise general statement of their basis and purpose. When rules are required by statute to be made on the record after opportunity for an agency hearing [formal rule making], sections §§ 556 and 557 of this title apply instead of this subsection.

(d) The required publication . . . of a substantive rule shall be made not less than 30 days before its effective date, except –
  (1) a substantive rule which grants or recognizes an exemption or relieves a restriction;
  (2) interpretative rules and statements of policy; or
  (3) as otherwise provided by the agency for good cause found and published with the rule.

(e) Each agency shall give an interested person the right to petition for the issuance, amendment, or repeal of a rule.

The term "agency" is defined in §551 (1) as "each authority of the Government of the United States, whether or not it is subject to review by another agency, but does not include (A) the Congress; (B) the courts of the United States; . . . (E) agencies composed of representatives of the parties or of representatives of organizations of the parties to disputes determined by them; (F) courts martial and military commissions; (G) military authority exercised in the field in time of war or in occupied territory; . . ." A "rule" is defined in § 551 (4) as "the whole or a part of an agency statement of general or particular applicability and future effect designed to implement, interpret, or prescribe law or policy or describing the organization, procedure, or practice requirements of an agency . . ." A "rule making" is simply the "agency process for formulating, amending, or repealing a rule" [§ 551 (5)].

voluntarily comply.[358] A rule, whether or not promulgated under APA procedures, can be reviewed in court for conformity with the authorizing statute and the constitution and for conformity with APA procedures.[359] A rule can be struck down for being "arbitrary and capricious" or in some cases for being "unsupported by substantial evidence." I focus on "informal rule making," in which an agency gathers information free of the strictures of a judicialized process.[360] Some statutes require additional procedures; for example, they mandate an oral hearing instead of permitting the agency to satisfy the hearing requirement through submission of documentary evidence alone.[361]

In the almost 60 years since passage of the APA other, more directly participatory, processes have come into favor. In particular, regulatory negotiation is now permitted under the Negotiated Rulemaking Act so long as certain procedures are followed. Under the act, the agency determines membership in the negotiating committee to ensure that it includes all the major interests. The government agency that will promulgate the rule also has a seat at the table and provides staff help and expertise. A facilitator helps to manage the negotiation process, which may take weeks or go on for years. The group aims to come to a consensus on a proposed rule, which is then published in the *Federal Register* as a preliminary to the notice and comment procedures still required by the APA. If the process breaks down without agreement, the agency issues its own proposed rule and proceeds with notice and comment.[362]

Much American scholarship concerning executive branch policy-making processes takes notice and comment rule making as given and discusses alternatives that can supplement it or remove some of the

---

[358] The Department of Health and Human Services and the Department of Housing and Urban Development use notice and comment rule making for rules that otherwise would be exempt. 24 C.F. R. Pt. 10 (HUD).

[359] Exceptions are listed in §701.

[360] Provisions for formal rule making exist in the act at §§ 556–557, and they include more court-like provisions such as cross-examination. Agencies seldom adopt these more formal procedures unless required by law. The courts sometimes have attempted to move agencies toward the more judicialized procedures that are familiar to them, but this move has been resisted because of the Supreme Court decision in Vermont Yankee Nuclear Power Corp. v. Natural Resources Defense Council 435 U.S. 519 (1978).

[361] See, for example, Seacoast Anti-Pollution League v. Costle 572 F. 2d 872, cert. denied, 439 U.S. 824 (1978), holding that the Clean Water Act's provision for a "public hearing" required an oral hearing in an initial licensing procedure also carried out under APA §§ 554, 556–557. The Occupational Safety and Health Act requires that the APA informal rule-making process in §§ 553 be supplemented with informal legislative-type hearings. 29 U.S.C. §§ 652.

[362] 5 U.S.C. §§ 561–570. See also Coglianese (1997, 2001) and Rose-Ackerman (1994).

extra requirements imposed by the courts or by the language of individual statutes. This background needs to be kept in mind if one seeks to draw lessons from American practice for Central Europe, where administrative law does not currently require notice and comment procedures when the government promulgates decrees and guidelines.

Evaluations of Rule Making

In spite of recent interest in regulatory negotiation, notice and comment rule making remains the bedrock of the American regulatory process.[363] Organized groups representing business, labor, public interest causes, and nonfederal governments view participation as an important part of their strategy to influence public policy making.[364] Participation can involve the submission of written comments and participation in oral hearings under APA procedures but also includes informal contacts before proposed rules are published (Furlong and Kerwin 2005).

The rule-making process can be costly and time-consuming both for agencies and for interest groups. In the United States, a major rule making at the Environmental Protection Agency (EPA) averages almost 3 years and requires many hours of input from both bureaucrats and outside interests from industry and the environmental community (Coglianese 1997: 1283–84). Many rules are challenged in court before they go into

---

[363] Between 1992 and 2001, the number of final rules issued each year ranged from 4,132 in 2001 to 4,937 in 1996. The number of newly proposed rules ranged from 2,512 in 2001 to 3,372 in 1994 with more than 4,400 in the pipeline each year. Of the 4,509 rules in the pipeline in October 2001, 149 were major rules, defined as rules with at least a $100 million economic cost (Crews Jr. 2002: 11–16).

[364] According to Kerwin (2003), most of the Washington-based organizations in his surveys participate in rule-making processes. Schlozman and Tierney (1986) also focused on the Washington, DC, component of those who seek to influence agencies and find that it is heavily weighted toward business in both numbers of groups and financial resources. Two-thirds of the groups studied reported that executive agencies were a very important focus of their work and more than three-quarters participate in APA procedures. Golden (1998) studied 11 rule-making dockets at the Environmental Protection Agency (EPA), the National Highway Traffic Safety Administration (NHTSA), and the Department Housing and Urban Development (HUD) and found that, for EPA and NHTSA, the comments were predominantly submitted by business interests. Coglianese's study (1994, appendix C: 228–232) of the Resource Conservation and Recovery Act (RCRA) also documented the dominance of comments from business in RCRA rule makings. In contrast, Golden found that, in HUD rule makings, there was minimal business participation; most comments were from government agencies, public interest groups, and citizen advocacy groups. In all three agencies, many comments originated outside Washington, DC, so the focus of Kerwin and Schlozman and Tierney on Washington-based groups provides a skewed view of actual participation.

effect, introducing further delay. For example, 26% of all published EPA rules are challenged, including 57% of all major rules under the Clean Air Act and the Resource Conservation and Recovery Act (Coglianese 1997: 1316). However, some rule makings attract the interest of only a few groups that submit comments. Marissa Martino Golden's (1998) review of 11 rule-making dockets covered rules that attracted from 1 to 268 comments. Examination of a random sample of 42 rule makings found that the median number of comments was about 30 (West 2004). However, if a rule making generates public concern, the number of comments can be very large. For example, when the Forest Service was considering a rule on roadless areas in national forests, it received more than 1 million comments (Mendelson 2003: 623). However, in such cases most comments are form letters and can be processed quite easily. Nevertheless, both career bureaucrats and political officials may resist increased participation and transparency on the grounds that they threaten to delay action and to distort choices. Furthermore, the very time and trouble introduced by participation requirements may discourage advocates and citizens with little time and money and weak organizational capacities (Schuck 1977).

However, long time delays have no simple link to the volume of comments. One study of 150 EPA rules completed between 1986 and 1989 asked if the elapsed time between the start of the process and the issuance of the final rule was associated with the number of internal participants and the number of comments. Surprisingly, neither had a positive impact, and the number of internal participants even had a small negative impact – the greater the number of such participants, the shorter the elapsed time. The authors suggest that rule making actually is speeded along by procedures that are more inclusive (Kerwin and Furlong 1992: 125–131). The results suggest that delay may be strategic and may depend on whether the agency or the White House wants to hold up resolution of an issue and whether members of Congress try to keep the issue from being decided. To examine this issue, one would need to be able to compare elapsed time with the actual number of hours of staff time spent on particular regulations.

The costs of the rule-making process ought to be balanced against the benefits, but there is little solid research that permits one to assess the net value of open, participatory processes. They are broadly acceptable to those who use the process (Furlong and Kerwin 2005), but only limited evidence exists on their marginal impact. I review what is available, but this is obviously an important area for future research.

The most thorough effort to assess the effect of participation in notice and comment rule making was carried out by Wesley A. Magat, Alan J. Krupnick, and Winston Harrington (1986). They studied EPA rule makings that determined the "best practical technology currently available" for controlling water pollution on an industry-by-industry basis. Because regulated industries submit the most comments, their study sheds some light on the biases introduced by public comment periods that are dominated by regulated entities. The results are optimistic about the ability of EPA officials to resist pressure. Comments that supported weaker standards did not tend to produce weaker standards, and industries with more firms out of compliance with proposed rules did not get weaker standards (Magat et al. 1986: 145–146). However, there is some evidence that well-organized industry groups with a consistent message were able to influence outcomes in their favor (Magat et al. 1986: 147). The latter result suggests the importance of providing some assistance to groups seeking to counter the impact of homogeneous industries with strong trade associations (see also Schuck 1977). If civil society groups do get their message across, they can have an impact. For example, a study of the Forest Service Roadless Areas Rulemaking during the Clinton Administration found that the notice and comment period did produce modifications in the rule that responded to some of the comments from those favoring a strong rule. This was a rule with implications for the amount of logging and mineral exploitation in national forests and hence the level of wilderness protection (Mendelson 2003: 628).

Many proposed rules change very little after the end of the comment period (Golden 1998; Kerwin 2003). As a result, groups seek access to the agency before the proposed rule is published in the *Federal Register*. Peter Strauss (1974) dealt with this issue explicitly in a case study of rule making in the Department of the Interior under the Mining Act. He found that the prenotice procedures were so extensive that agency personnel had little interest in modifying the rule after the public comment period, which was viewed as mostly a formal, public relations requirement (Strauss 1974: 1249–1251). The tendency to ignore public comments was especially pronounced when the agency engaged in prior consultation with advisory bodies that mostly consisted of local and industrial-user interests with little representation from national or conservation interests (Strauss 1974: 1249–1251). Note, however, that if the rule was overtly biased toward the regulated industry, the publicity attendant on the notice and comment process would provide unfavorable public relations for the agency. This concern will feed back to the agency and affect its willingness to buckle under to interest group pressure.

Agencies have sometimes used the rule-making process as a way to put an issue on the public agenda that has been kept out of the public eye by special interest influence on the legislature. The publicity surrounding the agency request for comments and its public hearings can give an issue salience in the eyes of citizens and open the door to policy changes even if no rule results. The Roadless Areas rule making was one such example according to Nina Mendelson (2003: 656). She claims that the value of notice and comment requirements was that policy had to be developed "in a relatively more public, more disciplined, and more transparent way. The agency...[had] to declare its proposed policy publicly, give a public accounting of its reasons..., and to do so in a process providing opportunities for public participation."

As a second example, A. Lee Fritschler (1989) argues that the Federal Trade Commission's (FTC) efforts to require health warnings on cigarette packages raised public consciousness. Public health interests, shunned by Congress, were able to work with the FTC to effect change. The large influx of comments helped raise the salience of the issue. Even though the oral hearings provided little new information, they were part of a generally successful effort to raise the profile of the issue of the health costs of smoking and to generate a settlement with the industry. Thus, notice and comment rule making can be a way to shape the political debate, although obviously not all issues have the resonance of the two issues discussed here.

One problem with strong procedural requirements in rule making stems from agencies' freedom to decide whether to regulate through generic rules or through case-by-case implementation. If the procedural requirements for rule making are too high, agencies may decide to use adjudication instead, perhaps combined with guidelines that have no legal force. This may be costly for regulated entities that would benefit from clearly articulated, legal mandates to guide behavior. There is some evidence that this shift has occurred in the United States when rule-making procedures become too rigid and costly (Asimov 1992; Mashaw and Harfst 1990). However, the continuing importance of rules in the U.S. regulatory state (Crews Jr. 2002) suggests that the problem, to the extent it exists, is not general or acute.

Some statutes limit an agency's discretion to set its own agenda. This is the result not of notice and comment procedures per se but of additional requirements in substantive laws that force an agency to decide certain issues if it receives a petition or if a court decision requires action on a particular issue.[365] These action-forcing requirements can disrupt an agency's efforts to set priorities across the issues that fall under its statutory mandate. Jim Rossi (1997: 181–182) points, in particular, to the Consumer Product Safety Commission, which, among other requirements, must respond to citizen petitions seeking a rule making. Some environmental statutes, such as the Clean Water Act, also include ways for outsiders to influence agency agenda setting (Rossi 1997: 219). Rossi is not in favor of eliminating notice and comment rule making, but he does highlight the costs of externalizing agenda-setting decisions that he believes should be made by agency insiders who are politically accountable.

Finally, those who hope to use procedural guarantees to obtain greater input from the public and from public interest groups need to recognize that these requirements can be explicitly designed to accomplish exactly the reverse result. All process is not alike. For example, the U.S. Toxic Substances Control Act imposes requirements on the EPA that limit its ability to regulate. Procedural requirements imposed by judicial interpretations of the act have further constrained EPA regulatory activity (Haemer 1999).

Project-Level Participation

Additional research concentrates either on implementation in individual cases or on regulatory negotiation, although sometimes comparisons are possible with notice and comment rule making. In a comprehensive review of the case study literature, two researchers evaluated public participation in more than 200 environmental decisions covering federal, state, local, and regional processes over a 30 year period (Beierle and Cayford 2002). Their data include only 13 regulation and standard setting cases, mostly regulatory negotiations. The others are "policy development cases," most with a limited geographic focus; resource planning and management cases dealing with particular geographical areas; and facility siting, hazardous waste disposal, and permitting/operating cases – all dealing with implementation in individual cases. Thus, their study is not much concerned with federal rule-making procedures. Nevertheless, it provides some insights.

The authors conclude that involving the public "not only frequently produces decisions that are responsive to public values and substantially

---

[365] Section § 553 (e) requires agencies to give "interested persons" the right to petition for a rule making but does not say that the agency must act on the petition.

robust, but it also helps to resolve conflict, build trust, and educate and inform the public about the environment" (Beierle and Cayford 2002: 74). The statistical work showed that cases ranked highly by the participants in terms of the process used also scored highly on measures of success, holding other factors constant. The process measure included the capacity and motivation of participants, the extent of participant control over the process, and the responsiveness of the lead agency. Success is an aggregation of variables measuring the substantive quality of decisions, increased trust in government, educating and informing the public, incorporating public values, and resolving conflicts (Beierle and Cayford 2002: 89–94). An inevitable selection bias limits these results because the researchers had to study processes that actually took place rather than a random sample of those that could have taken place. One cannot conclude that public participation will work in all situations but only that in some cases it can be effective. No notice and comment rule makings are included for comparison purposes, and even the strongest defenders of regulatory negotiation do not recommend it for all administrative agency tasks. In fact, one-third of the cases that counted as successes turned out on further examination to have worked either because some particularly divisive issues were kept off the table or because controversial potential participants were excluded (Beierle and Cayford 2002: 29, 60–61).

More nuance concerning the pitfalls and advantages of public participation comes from examining case studies of early efforts by the Army Corps of Engineers, the Forest Service, and the Bureau of Land Management (Culhane 1981; Friesema and Culhane 1976; Hendee 1977; Mazmanian and Nienaber 1979). These studies, although more than 2 decades old, may be particularly valuable to those in Central Europe seeking to design workable participation procedures. They make clear that simply announcing a commitment to more open procedures in statutory language or agency guidelines will not mean much by itself. The process must be internalized and accepted by those inside government agencies. Nevertheless, the findings are optimistic in that they provide examples of bureaucracies that quite rapidly shifted to more open decision-making methods. Culhane (1981: 232–262) studied the Bureau of Land Management and the Forest Service in 1972–1973 soon after administrative and legal changes mandated more public participation.[366] These

---

[366] The National Environmental Policy Act (NEPA) passed in 1969 required that agencies prepare an Environmental Impact Statement (EIS) for all public programs with environmental impacts, a category that includes almost everything the Bureau of Land Management and the Forest Service do. Friesema and Culhane (1976) show how the

agencies manage grazing rights on public land and timber sales in national forests and seek to balance these economic interests with environmental, wildlife, and recreation interests. Advisory committees with a fixed membership that was dominated by economic interests had been the norm until the change in policy. Culhane located three patterns of public participation: undeveloped participation, polarized participation, and well-developed participation.

In one case, nothing changed. There were few public meetings, and those that occurred were poorly attended and designed for the agency to "sell" its positions. This result stemmed partly from the lack of interest and experience of the administrators and partly from the lack of an active environmental movement. Of course, the two can feed on each other. With little real opportunity to participate, potential leaders of civil society advocacy groups have little incentive to take the time and trouble to get organized.

In one Forest Service case, participation occurred but was extremely polarized. This was partly because the forest rangers were critical of the process and did not manage meetings well and partly because the participants were much divided. The public meetings seemed to push the groups farther apart. This is a case in which a poorly handled process exacerbated conflicts instead of resolving them. Mazmanian and Nienaber's study (1979) of public participation in connection with the Army Corps of Engineers water management and flood control projects in 1972–1974 is another case in which technocrats ended up unhappy with an open planning method. Most were critical of public involvement, especially when those who participated opposed the Corps' favored outcome. As a result, some projects were not built (Mazmanian and Nienaber 1979: 166–167). However, the outside participants were enthusiastic, especially those groups that had been excluded in the past. In Central Europe, these negative cases need to be analyzed, given officials' lack of experience with public participation and a citizenry that combines a lack of engagement with civil society groups with sharp political divisions. Thus, the U.S. experience counsels reformers to gain the support of the relevant public officials and to design procedures with care.

The third category suggests that positive results are possible. The Forest Service in one region and the Bureau of Land Management in another had successful experiences with increased public participation at least in

implementation of NEPA gave increased access to environmental and community groups in Forest Service procedures. They criticize the EIS process, however, and argue that it should be better integrated into the overall decision-making processes of the Forest Service.

the view of the participants.[367] Culhane observed a real change in the way officials dealt with interested groups and individuals. Rather than simply using meetings to present and defend a plan, they sought public input before reaching a final decision. This shift is all the more remarkable because, in the case of the Forest Service, a forest ranger stated: "Relating to people was not a Forest Service long suit; we related much better to trees" (Culhane 1981: 242). One reason for the success of the participatory program was that it emphasized informal one-on-one meetings as well as formal public hearings. Of course, administrators had met informally with ranchers and timber industry managers in the past. What was new was consultation with a broader range of interests, including environmental activists. In the successful cases, the operation of a productive public participation process became an element of professional pride for career officials.

Hendee's study (1977) of the Forest Service's roadless-area review in 1971–1973 reaches a complementary result. This was a national review of the nation's forests to determine which should be given a wilderness classification. It required regional foresters to get public input before making recommendations, a new experience for most of them. Hendee's team carried out extensive interviews in 27 national forests and in 10 regional offices. He concluded that public involvement did substantially affect the outcome and that experience with public involvement among foresters developed and reinforced a commitment to it. Participation was not representative in a demographic sense, but Hendee argued that such representativeness is not its goal. Rather the aim must be to involve all the groups affected by the decision, with the ultimate decision left to the Forest Service, which can weigh the interests of nonparticipants as well (Hendee 1977: 100).

Regulatory Negotiation
Another group of studies asked participants both in regulatory negotiation and in notice and comments procedures if they were satisfied with their experiences. The most comprehensive study is by Laura Langbein and Cornelius Kerwin (2000), who interviewed participants in eight negotiated rule makings and six conventional rule makings, all involving

---

[367] Unfortunately, the case studies do not provide a clear measure of the impact of the procedures on substantive policy. The mandate for increased public participation occurred at the same time as policy changes that required these agencies to include environmental and recreational values more fully into their policy making.

the EPA. Although some complained about the costs of participation, 78% of participants believed the benefits of participation outweighed the costs (Langbein and Kerwin 2000: 620). In general, those who participated in regulatory negotiations were more satisfied than those who submitted comments in conventional rule makings. Their higher level of satisfaction was due to their higher satisfaction with the rule that resulted as well as with other aspects of the process (Langbein and Kerwin 2000: 625). They also reported learning more from the process than those engaged in conventional rule making. Greater learning, however, was not associated with greater satisfaction (Langbein and Kerwin 2000: 606–608). However, both groups thought participation affected the outcome.[368] However, using the participants' feelings is obviously a limited measure of success or failure. Those left out of the process by design or through their own lack of organization and resources were not questioned, and the data provide no evidence on the quality of the decisions that resulted compared with processes that are less participatory (Coglianese 2003).

In the negotiated rule-making sample 11% were EPA officials, and 25% were from state and local governments. In contrast, those who submitted comments in the conventional rule makings included only three state and local government representatives or 6% (Langbein and Kerwin 2000). This difference in sample composition may have skewed the results (Coglianese 2001: 430–432). For my purposes, however, it is interesting to discover that officials from federal, state, and local governments, whose counterparts are often among the opponents of greater public involvement in Central Europe, generally expressed satisfaction with a participatory process that goes far beyond the minimal requirement of holding an open-ended comment period. It suggests that public participation can be managed so that career bureaucrats and political actors, such as local government officials, find the process valuable rather than a nuisance. For a number of reasons, I am skeptical that regulatory negotiation ought to be the preferred method of public participation (Rose-Ackerman 1994). But the kinds of participation I am advocating will need to be grafted onto existing bureaucratic and intergovernmental relationships in Central Europe, and the Langbein and Kerwin study suggests that this can be done in ways that are acceptable to officials.

---

[368] However, as Coglianese (2001) points out, the differences may not be as great as Langbein and Kerwin suggest, because one of the negotiated rules had yet to produce a final rule at the time of the survey.

Implications

The research, although inconclusive, provides guidance for the design of workable participation strategies. The American experience suggests that the most important problems with participation in rule making are delay, bias, irrelevance, displacement to other methods, and curbs on agency implementation. The case studies provide examples of all these problems, but they appear mostly to be the result of poorly designed and biased procedures, not participation per se.

Some delay is the inevitable counterpart of expanded participation. Agencies must take the time and trouble to consult. However, the extremely long time between proposed and final rules in the U.S. seems to be driven more by strategic considerations than by the cost of the process per se. The deadlines in Hungary and Poland seem too short, but the U.S. process surely could be streamlined. Furthermore, advances in communication and information technology can speed up the comment process. Most U.S. agencies have developed comprehensive and user-friendly web sites, and many permit comments on draft rules to be submitted via e-mail. Of course, the agencies still need to be able to process comments in an effective manner, but information technology can make the processing of comments more cost-effective.

The case studies suggest that critics have overstated claims of bias and irrelevance, although these problems do obviously sometimes arise. Agencies do issue nonbinding guidelines and implement some laws through the adjudication of individual cases. However, neither displacement strategy seems to be a general problem given the large number of rules that U.S. agencies continue to issue. In any case, the problem of displacement can be overcome if the legislature includes rule-making requirements in statutes and if the courts resist adding incremental requirements. The proponents of participatory processes need to consider the actual workings of the procedural innovations. Rigid, cumbersome, and biased processes are obviously not an improvement.

In the well-functioning cases, the benefits are of several kinds. The most important benefit, although one that can only be inferred from the evidence, is that officials draft proposed rules in light of the forthcoming public participation processes. Even if they consult with a biased selection of interest groups before the public hearing process, officials must consider how their proposals will be greeted by the public and the media when they are publicly posted in the *Federal Register* and later, when they are subject to judicial review. Thus, evidence showing that some rules are little changed between the time the agency published the proposed rule in the *Federal Register* and the time when it issued the final rule does not imply that notice and comment rule-making is irrelevant. Agency officials anticipate that their proposed rule will face public and interest group scrutiny and try to anticipate objections ex ante. The possibility of subsequent judicial challenges by interested groups on all sides also feeds back to the drafting of the initial proposal.[369]

Public hearing processes can raise the salience of an issue with the public and increase public knowledge about a regulatory issue. Furthermore, if the hearing process does lead to modifications in the proposed rule, the case studies suggest that U.S. bureaucrats are not the captives of well-funded groups. Successful efforts at public involvement can lead to choices that better reflect public values and are substantively strong, although, of course, fair and open procedures cannot entirely overcome partisan biases. There is some suggestion in the research that permanent advisory committees and participation in hearings are substitutes. In at least one case, the limited membership of an advisory committee skewed the range of views provided.

Open procedures cost time and money, so poorer countries, such as those in Central Europe, will need to make some compromises to avoid gridlock and to ensure that processes are not just window dressing. Few of the harshest critics of the current U.S. procedures actually support repeal of the notice and comment provisions of the APA. However, it is clear that the practical implementation of more open participatory procedures requires a realistic understanding of the tradeoffs involved.

Recommendations

My argument for deeper and more effective public participation in government policy-making processes is based on a broad view of the democratic project. It is an effort to strike a balance between the obligation of the government to make technically competent policy choices under statutory delegations and its obligation to respond to the concerns of

---

[369] West makes both of these points based on interviews with regulatory officials. He found that a common reason for delay was agency or departmental lawyers seeking to withstand court challenges (West 2004: 72). In one rule that was substantially changed after notice and comment, he quoted an agency official who claimed that the agency staff had "failed to do their homework on this one" by neglecting to consider the interests of some of the producers affected by the rule. In other words, a competent official, knowing that an open comment period is part of the process, will try to anticipate comments and deal with them ex ante.

citizens and organized groups. In a world with cross-cutting cleavages that do not map neatly onto party labels and with statutes that do not specify in detail how to deal with complex modern problems, consultation procedures and judicial oversight are one route to policy-making accountability. They are, to me, a necessary route, given the weaknesses of the alternatives.

My basic claim is twofold. First, legislative texts cannot resolve all the policy issues of interest to private individuals and groups. Thus, the task of putting laws into effect is not just a technical, expert enterprise but is itself deeply political. By "political" I do not mean political party involvement. Instead, I wish to signal that in most policy areas the participants have policy preferences and personal goals that they seek to further in strategic interaction with other actors. Second, given the first claim, modern governments cannot make policy under democratic principles unless the law requires decision makers to consult broadly. A government that tries to channel public input into permanent advisory committees with fixed membership risks freezing out new groups, concerned individuals, and emerging interests. More open-ended procedures do require more time and trouble from public officials, but the benefit is the greater democratic accountability of the resulting public policies.

Given the U.S. experience with public participation in the administrative policy-making process, what direction might law reform take in Central Europe? In Central Europe, and indeed in much of Europe as a whole, support for public participation and consensual procedures coexists with a rule-making process that is essentially bureaucrat-led. Except for some workplace issues, the government does not rely on popular, participatory procedures for the issuance of government decrees. The consultation that does occur concentrates on groups with economic or professional links, such as business associations, labor unions, official associations (such as the chambers for medicine and law), and statutory self-governments – both those with a geographic basis, such as municipalities, and those with an organizational basis, such as university bodies. Reformers are only beginning to think constructively about how to incorporate pluralist elements into high-level government policy making outside the legislative process. The mechanical extension of existing tripartite labor/business/government structures is not sufficient.

Although Poland and Hungary have few formal requirements for open-ended civil society participation in government policy making, there seems no reason, in principle, why they could not move in that direction. However, at present, the lack of participation opportunities within the government and the bureaucracy complements the lack of organizational strength in the private nonprofit sector. There is a tendency for groups with policy agendas to affiliate with political parties, thus losing the benefit of a nonpartisan stance even as they gain some support from their political allies.

To improve policy-making accountability, my analysis suggests that a two-pronged strategy is needed in Central Europe – both a move to a more open and accountable policy-making process inside government and efforts to support the creation and consolidation of independent nongovernmental organizations.

The first prong of a reform agenda includes the public posting of draft rules, open-ended requests for comments, and reason giving. The government or the relevant ministry is ultimately responsible for the legal norms that it issues, but it must be willing to hear alternative viewpoints and to explain why it has selected a particular policy. Interested persons should be able to challenge a rule in court on the grounds that the process was not sufficiently open and inclusive or that the rule is inconsistent with the authorizing statute or the constitution. Existing advisory committees help to channel and organize discussion, but they risk limiting participation to particular channels. Thus, the government should be open to comments from a broader range of interests and individuals. Managing these processes will require some creativity on the part of agencies, although the U.S. evidence suggests that most rule making does not create unmanageable outpourings of comments. Time and page limits are appropriate, but time limits need to be extended beyond those currently in force, which seem much too short. New information technology makes broad participation feasible in middle-income countries like Hungary and Poland. Drafts can be posted on the Internet, as is already being done on a limited basis in Hungary. Comments can also be accepted by e-mail, and agencies can facilitate public participation by developing web sites that are informative and easy to negotiate. Nevertheless, one cost of increased participation must be accepted – the time needed both to allow the outsiders to review drafts and to permit public officials to incorporate this feedback into the final rule.

Formal legal and administrative reforms and technocratic fixes are not sufficient. Careful studies of successful regulatory reforms indicate that the bureaucracy must change as well. Culhane's case studies (1981) of the Forest Service and the Bureau of Land Management show how this can happen and point to the risks and pitfalls. Robert T. Nakamura and Thomas Church (2003: 76–90) provide an instructive case study of

a largely successful reform involving a major U.S. environmental program.[370] They divide their explanation for the reform's success into three
categories: leadership, management, and incentives. The top of the agency
must be solidly behind the reform and provide stable consistent leadership. These officials need to get involved enough in the details to play a
"fixer" role and must be willing to share credit and encourage broad staff
participation in the reformed system. The program should be managed to
build on what the agency is already doing well, make incremental changes,
and respond with flexibility in implementation. The reform needs to be
politically acceptable and hence needs to be well vetted with affected
groups. The agency needs some way to measure and reward success and
to provide disincentives for shirking.

Reforms inside the government need to be complemented with more
effective judicial review. At present, underlying statutes and constitutions provide little basis for the review of government regulations and
norms in CEE. However, even if new statutes specified grounds for review, this might not happen unless the courts are reorganized. Hungary
needs judges with more background in public law and might consider
following the Polish lead and creating an administrative court, as the
Czech Republic did in January 2003.[371] To avoid interference by judges
in the operation of bureaucracies, statutes need to specify the grounds
for review, and these should be limited to procedural violations and clear
inconsistencies between rules and statutes or the constitution.

The second prong requires both a strong legal framework for the creation and maintenance of civil society organizations and the careful design
of public subsidies. An important issue is the strength of groups that operate independently of political parties and concentrate on a small set of
policy issues – be they feminist causes, environmental harms, working conditions, student concerns, or burdensome business regulation. Advocacy
groups exist in both Poland and Hungary, but many are small and poorly
funded and lack professional staff. The evidence suggests wide imbalances
among groups reorganized out of old official groups, new groups with
public or foreign foundation support, and a large fringe of small, poorly
institutionalized groups with few financial resources. In some cases, such
as student and youth groups in Poland, there is tension between official

---

[370] They studied Superfund, a program designed to clean up hazardous waste sites and
apportion the costs.
[371] The *Prague Business Journal* reported on July 28, 2003, that the new Czech Supreme
Administrative Court was off to a good start and was confounding critics. The article is
available to subscribers at http://www.pbj.cz/user/article.asp?ArticleID = 182801.

self-governments and independent associations. Furthermore, even organizations with ample funding may not be effective advocates if much of their funding comes from the state and if they administer government programs. In areas where both official and unofficial organizations exist, the state needs to attend to the views of both and then make its own decision under the law.

The registration of nonprofit advocacy groups should be a simple and inexpensive process that concentrates on avoiding the fraudulent use of the nonprofit form for personal financial gain. In addition, governments may need to provide assistance to poorly organized and funded interests to help level the playing field in the administrative process. However, if governments subsidize nonprofit advocacy groups, support needs to be provided in a way that does not undermine the groups' independence. Matching funds based on membership numbers or private gifts are one option, and tax checkoffs are another. The situation in Hungary, where only one-half of the taxpayers take advantage of a law that permits them to earmark 1% of their taxes for charity, suggests that simply lowering the costs of giving is insufficient. Another option is direct support for participation through grants to cover the marginal costs of informed participation. These funds would have to be disbursed without making judgments on any group's substantive positions. Hungary's program of government grants in the environmental area using a committee with strong nongovernmental organization representation is one option.

The EU expects the candidate governments to cooperate with nonprofits in a number of specific areas by creating partnership groups. However, this mandate has proved difficult to implement. In Poland, the process has not worked effectively because the groups either have not been created or are not representative. The problem is twofold. The government has little incentive to strengthen the sector, and the sector is full of small organizations without any coordinating mechanisms. However, recently some nongovernmental organizations have formed umbrella organizations, so the EU process may be having an impact on the efficacy of the sector.[372] In Hungary, some groups have attempted to organize networks of local groups and to set up coordinating organizations (Karatnycky et al. 1997: 180–182). We have seen several examples in the environmental area organized around issues such as conservation, air quality, and waste disposal.

---

[372] Stowarzyszenie na rzecz Forum Inicjatyw Pozarządowych, "Współpracy Organizacji Pozarządowych z Administracją Publiczną w Procesie Integracji Polski z UE" ("Cooperation of NGOs with Public Administration in the Process of Integrating Poland with the EU"), 2000, www.fip.ngo.pl.

The thrust of EU pressure has been toward collaborative processes in which the stakeholders get together to find solutions. I have expressed my skepticism about this model, particularly in the context of Central Europe. Coordinating the sector into hierarchical organizations is not a sufficient response to the weakness of individual groups. Such umbrella groups may be able to negotiate with their counterpart interest groups or self-governing bodies, but the resulting structure can perpetuate historical organizational patterns even when they fail to reflect present realities. Instead, the national government needs to recognize that many diffuse groups will never be as well organized as business associations and labor unions. Putting civil society groups up against business, labor, and professional chambers in a negotiation over policy misunderstands the nature of civil society and the problem of diffuse groups.

But the problem is not just the weakness of some organized groups. In addition, the countries in CEE also need to strengthen the capacities of the civil service. In the rush to create a private market economy, the need to recruit qualified professionals into government service has not been a high priority. Yet, top civil servants and the political appointees to whom they report have a central role in policy making, and this ought to continue. If one accepts my claim that policy making usually should not be turned over to negotiations between outside groups and public officials, then top government officials must play a central role in setting policy. They need to be accountable both to the legislature and to the groups and individuals with a particular interest in the outcome. However, they also need to be technically competent and to have a professional commitment to governing in the public interest. This ought to include a commitment to carrying out the law as expressed in statutes and the constitution, but it also implies professional norms that value the design of workable, fair programs. My main focus in this study has been on the constraints that outside participation imposes on public officials. However, because I argue that civil servants and cabinet ministers should set policy subject to legislative and judicial oversight, their own competence and professional standards play a fundamental role. This is a crucial aspect of the overall transition to democracy. Government officials need to be able to evaluate the arguments presented by private intervenors and make informed judgments about how much weight to give them. One criticism of the current situation is that the debates are narrow and self-serving.[373] Polish

---

[373] János Kornai worries that in the debate over health care in Hungary "there is no fair dialogue between conflicting political approaches, ethical dilemmas, macro-economic

and Hungarian populations have high average levels of education and technical sophistication. However, both countries need to train the new generation in tools of policy analysis and program design and to set favorable civil service employment conditions so as to attract high-quality applicants.

In Central Europe, there is some urgency in creating an environment in which public officials can respond well to open-ended public participation without seeing it as merely a nuisance that they seek to contain and marginalize. Existing permanent advisory committees and tripartite processes are not sufficient. Better administrative processes can give officials information about the costs and benefits of particular programs in both technical and political terms. The goal is to permit them to make more competent and politically acceptable decisions, not to have civil society groups take over that function. My proposals for the consolidation of democracy in Central Europe are a reflection of how far these countries have come in creating electoral systems and reforming the state and the economy in the last decade and a half. The problems that remain are those of countries that have democratic electoral and constitutional structures, secure borders, no organized violence, and a functioning private sector. They are not different in kind from those facing democracies with much longer histories than those in Central Europe. True, the scale of the difficulties is larger for some issues, and the existing institutions in the public and the private sectors are fragile and untested, but no one expects an imminent breakdown of the state. This observation is not meant to breed complacency, but it does mean that Central Europe can learn from experiences elsewhere, both success stories and failures. Its politicians and policy makers can be in a productive dialogue with those in wealthier, more established democracies as the region seeks ways to create more accountable policy-making institutions that can garner popular support.

---

considerations. Instead, under the disguise of civil society narrow-minded interest-groups are fighting for special (hidden) interests.... [There is] very little rational argumentation. Very little moral reasoning" (e-mail correspondence with the author July 13, 2004).

APPENDIX 1

Interviews

Interviewee	Position at Time of Interview and Relevant Past Positions	Place and Date of Interview
Ádám, Antal*	Professor, School of Law, University of Pécs	Pécs, Hungary Oct. 12, 2002
Ámon, Ada	Executive Director of Energia Klub	Budapest, Hungary Dec. 2, 2002
Bércesi, Ferenc*	Head of the Central Government's Administrative Office of Baranya County in southern Hungary	Pécs, Hungary Dec. 3, 2002
Bitsky, Botond	Head, Constitutional and Legal Department, Office of the President of the Republic of Hungary	Budapest, Hungary Nov. 29, 2002
Bödecs, Barnabás	Chairman of HUMUSZ	Budapest, Hungary Jan. 4, 2003
Bulla, Miklós	Secretary General, Hungarian National Environment Council	Budapest, Hungary Dec. 20, 2002
Droppa, György	Member of the Board of Directors of Danube Circle, Co-chairman of the Green Party	Budapest, Hungary Nov. 27, 2002
Farkas, István	Director, National Society of Conservationists	Budapest, Hungary Dec. 18, 2002
Farkas, André	Consultant, REFLEX	Győr, Hungary Jan. 16, 2003 (by telephone)
Fülöp, Sándor	Executive Director, Environmental Management and Law Association	Budapest, Hungary Oct. 29, 2002

(continued)

Interviewee	Position at Time of Interview and Relevant Past Positions	Place and Date of Interview
Göncz, Kinga	Political State Secretary, Ministry of Social, Health and Family Welfare, Government of Hungary	Budapest, Hungary Dec. 28, 2002
Hauser, Roman	President of the Polish Supreme Administrative Court, 1994–2004	Warsaw, Poland Dec. 4, 2002
Herczog, László	Deputy Secretary of State in Charge of Employment Policy, Hungarian Ministry of Economic Affairs	Budapest, Hungary Jan. 9, 2003
Hryciuk, Michał[†]	Student, Warsaw University of Technology; member of the Board of Senators, Chairman of the Social Committee of University of Self-Governments, 2002–time of interview	Warsaw, Poland Dec. 30, 2003
Jánossy, László	Director, MME/BirdLife Hungary	Budapest, Hungary Dec. 9, 2002
Kalas, György	Legal representative/advisor, REFLEX, Environmental Protection Association	Győr, Hungary Jan. 16, 2003 (by telephone)
Kilényi, Géza	D.Sc., Professor Pázmány Péter Catholic University, Budapest, former Justice of the Hungarian Constitutional Court	Budapest, Hungary Dec. 18, 2002
Kolasiński, Jacek	Vice-Director of the President's Office, responsible for international relations, Polish Supreme Chamber of Control	Warsaw, Poland Dec. 5, 2002
Kovács, Árpád	President of the Hungarian State Audit Office	Budapest, Hungary Jan. 9, 2003
Kovács, Ilona*	Professor, Director of the Center for Regional Studies of the Hungarian Academy of Pécs	Pécs, Hungary Oct. 22, 2002
Kowalski, Przemysław[†]	Student, Warsaw Agriculture University; Chairman of the Students' Parliament of the Republic of Poland, 2002–time of interview	Warsaw, Poland (by e-mail) Jan. 26, 2004
Kuti, Éva	Head, Section on the Voluntary Sector, Central Statistical Office, Hungary	Budapest, Hungary Nov. 14, 2002
Lukács, András	President, Clean Air Action Group	Budapest, Hungary Dec. 20, 2002
Majtényi, László	First Hungarian Ombudsman for Data Protection and Freedom of Information, lawyer	Budapest, Hungary Oct. 14, 2002

Interviewee	Position at Time of Interview and Relevant Past Positions	Place and Date of Interview
Márkus, Ferenc	Conservation Director, World Wildlife Fund-Hungary	Budapest, Hungary Nov. 18, 2002
Mészáros, Péter	Professor, Budapest University of Technology and Economics, and President of Green Future	Budapest, Hungary Nov. 28, 2002
Petrétei, József	Professor, Vice Dean and Head of Department, Department of Constitutional Law, Faculty of Law, University of Pécs	Pécs, Hungary Nov. 15, 2002
Repetowicz, Witold[†]	Vice-chairman of the National Board of the Independent Students' Association in 1993–1994, Chairman of the National Board in 1994–1995, Chairman of the Jagiellonian University Committee in 1995–1998, Vice-chairman of the National Board in 1998	Warsaw, Poland Dec. 30, 2003
Sadowski, Andrzej	Director, Adam Smith Research Center	Warsaw, Poland Dec. 3, 2002
Sekuła, Mirosław	President, Supreme Chamber of Control in Poland	Warsaw, Poland Dec. 5, 2002
Somogyvári, István	Administrative State Secretary, Hungarian Ministry of Justice	Budapest, Hungary Dec. 12, 2002
Sypniewski, Dominik[†]	Student, Warsaw University and the Warsaw School of Economics. Co-founder and Vice-president of the Initiative of the Young 1999–2002, member of the Board of the Center for Youth Entrepreneurship Support in 2002–2003, and President of the Center since 2003	Warsaw, Poland Dec. 22, 2003
Szejna, Andrzej[‡]	Chairman of the Students' Parliament of the Republic of Poland, 1997–1999; Undersecretary of State, Ministry of Economy, Labor, and Social Policy in 2003; Deputy President of Polish Information and Foreign Investment Agency in 2004; member of the European Parliament since 2004	Warsaw, Poland Jan. 22, 2004

(*continued*)

Interviewee	Position at Time of Interview and Relevant Past Positions	Place and Date of Interview
Turemka, Artur[†]	Student, Warsaw University, and Board Member of Initiative of the Young with responsibility for public relations, 2002–time of interview	Warsaw, Poland July 15, 2004
Wierzchowski, Florian[†]	Student, Silesian University, and Board Member of European Law Students Association in Poland, 2002–time of interview	Warsaw, Poland Dec. 22, 2003
Wóycicka, Irena	Professor, Institute for Research on the Market Economy, Warsaw, and advisor and then Deputy Minister at the Polish Ministry of Labor, 1989–1994	Warsaw, Poland Dec. 5, 2002
Wyrzykowski, Mirosław	Justice, Polish Constitutional Tribunal	Warsaw, Poland Dec. 5, 2002
Zbytek, Waldemar[†]	Chairman of the Association of Polish Students (ZSP)	Warsaw, Poland Dec. 29, 2003
Zentai, Viola	Project Manager, Open Society Institute/Local Government Initiative	Budapest, Hungary Nov. 14, 2003
Zoll, Andrzej	Polish Commissioner for Civil Rights	Warsaw, Poland Dec. 3, 2002

* Interviewed by Katalin Füzér.
† Interviewed by Maciej Kisilowski.
‡ Interviewed by Anna Osińska.

European Values Study 1999/2000

Description of the Data

The data used in the tables in the text are drawn from the European Values Study (EVS) 1999/2000, a third follow-up of earlier waves in 1981 and 1990. The EVS is a well-established network of social and political scientists, investigating basic values, beliefs, attitudes, priorities, and preferences of the Europeans and exploring the similarities, differences, and changes in these orientations. An important goal of this wave was to examine whether the emerging concept of one common European identity has an empirical basis.

The questionnaire for the first wave was produced after a detailed explorative study with experts and a pilot study in 1980. A new questionnaire for the third wave was designed taking into account past experience and the new findings of various research groups. In this wave, representative national samples (of different sizes) were interviewed with uniformly structured questionnaires in 33 European countries: Austria, Belarus, Belgium, Bulgaria, Croatia, the Czech Republic, Denmark, Estonia, Finland, France, Germany, Great Britain, Greece, Hungary, Iceland, Ireland, Italy, Lithuania, Luxembourg, Latvia, Malta, Northern Ireland, the Netherlands, Poland, Portugal, Romania, Russia, Spain, Sweden, Slovakia, Slovenia, Turkey, and the Ukraine. The earlier waves had fewer countries in the sample.

The EVS data files, 33 of them for the individual countries, and one integrated data set, come in SPSS format, in an exploration utility, the ZA

Codebook Explorer. They report individual answers for each question by country. The sample sizes for each country's survey are as shown in Table A.9.

Computations

The initial round of analysis for each country was from the integrated data set in SPSS. The SPSS command Analyze->Crosstabs-> was used to generate frequencies and percentages for each answer for every question. SPSS reported these frequencies at the country level. Each SPSS output file for each question was then exported to Excel for further calculation.

To aggregate the data to the regional level – that is, to Western Europe, Eastern Europe, and Central Europe – for easy comparison with Hungary and Poland, population weighted averages were computed in Excel. The countries in the EVS were sampled with quite a uniform sample size and not according to their populations, which often vary widely. Any reasonable aggregation of European countries therefore must be population weighted. Thus, for each question, in a different Excel file: first, population weights were given to each country percentage by multiplying the country by its population size according to the World Factbook. Then, given that each question had a different number of countries answering, the population-weighted data were aggregated to the regional level separately for each question by selecting the countries in each region, summing the percentages, and dividing by the population in the region (of the countries included in that question). This was done separately for each question of interest that was asked on the survey. Depending on the question, some answers were then combined to further aggregate the results. Missing countries are listed below each question. Tables A.1 to A.8 summarize the demographic characteristics of the samples for each region and for Hungary and Poland. The regional results are population weighted, as described above.

Respondents' Demographic Characteristics by Region

Table A.1. *Highest Education Level*

Region	Highest Education Level			
	Less than Elementary (%)	Elementary (%)	Secondary (%)	Higher (%)
Eastern Europe	3	11	64	21
Central Europe	8	36	41	16
Poland	5	51	29	14
Hungary	9	50	30	11
Western Europe	8	36	38	18

Note: The categories above have combined some categories asked in the original EVS questions. Specifically, the categories are answers to the following:

Less than elementary education level if the respondent answered "yes" to "inadequately completed elementary education."

Elementary education level if the respondent answered "yes" to "completed (compulsory) elementary education" or to "completed (compulsory) elementary education and basic vocational qualification."

Secondary education level if the respondent answered "yes" to "secondary, intermediate vocational qualification" or to "secondary, intermediate general qualification" or to "full secondary, maturity level certificate."

Higher education level if the respondent answered "yes" to "higher education – lower-level tertiary certificate" or to "higher education – upper-level tertiary certificate."

Source: EVS 1999/2000, question 94.

Table A.2. *Percent Living with Parents*

Region	Percent Living with Parents
Eastern Europe	19
Central Europe	21
Poland	18
Hungary	17
Western Europe	14

Source: EVS 1999/2000, question 95.

Table A.3. *Employment Status*

Region	Employment (%)							
	30 Hours a Week or More	Less than 30 Hours a Week	Self-Employed	Retired/ Pensioned	Housewife	Student	Unemployed	Other
Eastern Europe	45	7	2	28	4	4	10	1
Central Europe	40	4	5	31	6	5	9	2
Poland	38	4	6	35	4	4	8	1
Hungary	41	3	3	35	3	3	7	6
Western Europe	36	9	5	22	12	6	7	2

Source: EVS 1999/2000, question 96.

Table A.4. *Type of Employment*

Region	Type of Employment (%)							
	Employer/ Manager/ Professional Worker	Middle and Junior Level Non-Manual Worker	Foreman and Supervisor/ Skilled Manual	Semi-Skilled Manual/ Unskilled Manual	Farmer: Employer, Manager on Own Account	Agricultural Worker	Member of Armed Forces	Never Had a Job
Eastern Europe	20	22	9	40	0	6	2	0
Central Europe	17	21	33	16	7	2	1	2
Poland	14	17	33	17	11	1	0	6
Hungary	17	19	31	28	1	4	1	0
Western Europe	21	34	20	19	2	2	1	2

Source: EVS 1999/2000, question 103.

Table A.5. *Income Scale*

Region	Income Scale, Counting All Wages, Salaries, Pensions, and Other Incomes, after Taxes and Deductions, as Coded by the Respondent (%)									
	Low	2	3	4	5	6	7	8	9	High
Eastern Europe	13	10	12	11	11	10	9	9	7	8
Central Europe	14	11	16	15	16	9	8	5	4	4
Poland	15	9	19	19	23	8	5	2	0	0
Hungary	9	11	21	21	22	9	5	2	0	0
Western Europe	8	13	15	15	13	11	10	7	4	4

Note: Portugal had different categories (only a scale of 6) for answering this question and thus was not included in the calculation for Western Europe.
Source: EVS 1999/2000, question 110.

Table A.6. *Population of Town Where Interview Was Conducted*

Region	Population of Town Where Interview was Conducted (%)		
	Less than 100,000	100,000–500,000	More than 500,000
Eastern Europe	53	23	24
Central Europe	73	17	11
Poland	71	19	10
Hungary	69	12	19
Western Europe	57	20	22

Source: EVS 1999/2000, question 112.

Table A.7. *Socioeconomic Status*

Region	Socioeconomic Status of Respondent (%)			
	Upper, Upper-Middle Classes	Middle, Nonmanual Workers	Skilled, Semiskilled Manual Workers	Unskilled, Unemployed Manual Workers
Central Europe	5	33	45	17
Poland	2	26	53	20
Hungary	5	38	33	25
Western Europe	16	35	30	18

Note: Portugal, the Netherlands, Denmark, Finland, Iceland, Northern Ireland, Ireland, Estonia, Latvia, Lithuania, Romania, Bulgaria, Greece, Russia, and Luxembourg did not have responses for this question.
Source: EVS 1999/2000, question 110a.

Table A.8. *Sex of Respondent*

Region	Sex of Respondent (% Male)
Eastern Europe	40
Central Europe	46
Poland	45
Hungary	47
Western Europe	46

Source: EVS 1999/2000, question 84.

Table A.9. *European Values Study 1999/2000: Sample Size by Country*

Country	Sample Size
France	1,615
Great Britain	1,000
Germany	2,036
Austria	1,522
Italy	2,000
Spain	1,200
Portugal	1,000
The Netherlands	1,003
Belgium	1,912
Denmark	1,023
Sweden	1,015
Finland	1,038
Iceland	968
Northern Ireland	1,000
Ireland	1,012
Estonia	1,005
Latvia	1,013
Lithuania	1,018
Poland	1,095
Czech Republic	1,908
Slovak Republic	1,331
Hungary	1,000
Romania	1,146
Bulgaria	1,000
Croatia	1,003
Greece	1,142
Russia	2,500
Malta	Omitted in analysis
Luxembourg	1,211
Slovenia	1,006
Ukraine	1,195
Belarus	1,000
Turkey	Omitted in analysis

References

Access Initiative. 2002. *Hungarian Report, Part I and II.* http://www.accessinitiative.org/hungary.html.

Adserá, Alicia, Carles Boix, and Mark Payne. 2003. Are You Being Served? Political Accountability and Quality of Government, *Journal of Law, Economics, and Organization* 19: 445–490.

Arato, Andrew. 1994. Constitution and Continuity in the Eastern European Transitions, in Irena Grudzińska-Gross, ed., Amsterdam: Slovak Committee of the European Cultural Foundation, pp. 155–171.

Arato, Andrew. 2000. *Civil Society, Constitution, and Legitimacy*, Lanham, MD: Rowman & Littlefield.

Arcimowicz, Jolanta. 2001. *Urząd Rzecznika Praw Obywatelskich w Polsce [The Office of the Ombudsman in Poland]*, Warsaw: The College of Social Sciences and Administration of the Warsaw University of Technology.

Armstrong, Kenneth. 2002. Rediscovering Civil Society: The European Union and the White Paper on Governance, *European Law Journal* 8: 102–132.

Asimov, Michael. 1992. California Underground Regulations, *Administrative Law Review* 44:43–77.

Bailey, David, and Lisa de Propris. 2004. A Bridge too Phare? EU Pre-Accession Aid and Capacity Building in the Candidate Countries, *Journal of Common Market Studies* 42: 77–98.

Balázs, István. 1993. The Transformation of Hungarian Public Administration, in Joachim Jens Hesse, ed., *Administrative Transformation in Central and Eastern Europe: Toward Public Sector Reform in Post-Communist Societies*, Oxford: Blackwell, pp. 75–88.

Barnard, Catherine. 2002. The Social Partners and the Governance Agenda, *European Law Journal* 8: 80–101.

Beetham, David, ed. 1994. *Defining and Measuring Democracy*, London: Sage.

Beierle, Thomas C., and Jerry Cayford. 2002. *Democracy in Practice: Public Participation in Environmental Decisions*, Washington, DC: Resources for the Future.

Bercusson, B. 1999. Democratic Legitimacy and European Labor Law, *Industrial Law Journal* 28: 153–170.

Bernard, Nick. 2000. Legitimating EU: Law: Is the Social Dialogue the Way Forward? Some Reflections Around the UEAPME Case, in Jo Shaw, ed., *Social Law and Policy in an Evolving European Union*, Oxford: Hart Publishing, pp. 279–302.

Besley, Timothy, and Andrea Prat. 2004. *Handcuffs for the Grabbing Hand? Media Capture and Government Accountability*, London: London School of Economics. http://econ.lse.ac.uk/staff/prat/papers/media.pdf.

Bignami, Francesca. 2003. The Challenge of Cooperative Regulatory Relations after Enlargement, draft, Durham, NC: Duke University School of Law.

Böröcz, József, and Melinda Kovács, eds. 2001. *Empire's New Clothes: Unveiling EU Enlargement*, Telford, UK: Central European Review. http://www.rci.rutgers.edu/~eu/Empire.pdf.

Boulanger, Christian. 2002. Europeanisation Through Judicial Activism? The Hungarian Constitutional Court, presented at Contours of Legitimacy Conference, European Studies Center, St. Anthony's College, Oxford University, May 24–25.

Bowen, Jeff, and Susan Rose-Ackerman. 2003. Partisan Politics and Executive Accountability: Argentina in Comparative Perspective, *Supreme Court Economic Review* 10: 157–211.

Bozóki, András. ed. 2002. *The Roundtable Talks of 1989. The Genesis of Hungarian Democracy*, Budapest: CEU Press.

Brunner, Georg. 2000. Structure and Proceedings of the Hungarian Constitutional Judiciary, in László Sólyom and Georg Brunner, eds., *Constitutional Judiciary in a New Democracy: The Hungarian Constitutional Court*, Ann Arbor MI: University of Michigan Press, pp. 65–102.

Brunnetti, Aymo, and Beatrice Weder. 2003. A Free Press Is Bad for Corruption, *Journal of Public Economics* 87: 1801–1824.

Brzeziński, Marek, and Lech Garlicki. 1995. Judicial Review in Post-Communist Poland: The Emergence of a *Rechstaat? Journal of International Law* 31/1: 13–59.

Buchowski, Michael. 1996. The Shifting Meaning of Civil and Civic Society in Poland, in Chris Hann and Elizabeth Dunn, eds., *Civil Society: Challenging Western Models*, London: Routledge, pp. 79–98.

Buonanno, Laurie, Sharon Zablotney, and Richard Keefer. 2001. Politics Versus Science in the Making of the New Regulatory Regime for Food in Europe, *European Integration Online Papers* 5(12). http://eiop.or.at/eiop/texts/2001–012a.htm.

Caddy, Joanne. 2000. Implementation of EU Environmental Policy in Central European Applicant States: The Case of EIA, in Christoph Knill and Andrea Lenschow, eds., *Implementing EU Environmental Policy, New Directions and Old Problems*, Manchester: Manchester University Press, pp. 197–221.

Cameron, David. 2002. The Challenges of EU Accession for Post-Communist Europe, presented at the American Political Science Association Annual Meeting, Boston, August.

Carius, Alexander, Ingmar von Homeyer, and Stefani Bär. 2000. The Eastern Enlargement of the European Union and Environmental Policy: Challenges,

Expectations, Multiple Speeds and Flexibility, in Katharina Holzinger and Peter Knoepfel, eds., *Environmental Policy in a European Union of Variable Geometry? The Challenge of the Next Enlargement*, Basel: Helbing & Lichtenhahn, pp. 141–180.

Cirtautas, Arista Maria. 2001. Corruption and the New Ethical Infrastructure of Capitalism, *East European Constitutional Review* 10(2/3): 79–84.

Coglianese, Cary. 1994. *Challenging the Rules: Litigation and Bargaining in the Administrative Process*, Ann Arbor, MI: UMI Dissertation Services.

Coglianese, Cary. 1997. Assessing Consensus: The Promise and Performance of Negotiated Rulemaking, *Duke Law Journal* 46: 1255–1349.

Coglianese, Cary. 2001. Assessing the Advocacy of Negotiated Rulemaking: A Response to Philip Harter, *New York University Environmental Law Journal* 9: 386–447.

Coglianese, Cary. 2003. Is Satisfaction Success? Evaluating Public Participation in Regulatory Policymaking, in Rosemary O'Leary and Lisa B. Bingham, eds., *The Promise and Performance of Environmental Conflict Resolution*, Washington, DC: Resources for the Future Press, pp. 69–86.

Collier, David, and Robert Adcock. 1999. Democracy and Dichotomies: A Pragmatic Approach to Choices about Concepts, *Annual Review of Political Science* 2: 537–565.

Commission of the European Communities. 2001a. *2001 Regular Report on Hungary's Progress Towards Accession*, SEC(2001) 1748, Brussels, Nov. 13. http://europa.eu.int/comm/enlargement/report2001/hu_en.pdf.

Commission of the European Communities. 2001b. *2001 Regular Report on Poland's Progress Toward Accession*, SEC(2001) 1752, Brussels, Nov. 13. http://europa.eu.int/comm/enlargement/report2001/pl_en.pdf.

Commission of the European Communities. 2001c. *White Paper on Governance*, COM(2001) 428 final, Brussels: European Union. http://europa.eu.int/comm/governance/white_paper/index_en.htm.

Commission of the European Communities. 2002a. *2002 Regular Report on Hungary's Progress Towards Accession*, COM(2002) 700 final, SEC(2002) 1404.

Commission of the European Communities. 2002b. *2002 Regular Report on Poland's Progress Towards Accession*, COM(2002) 700 final, SEC(2002) 1408.

Commission of the European Communities. 2003a. *Comprehensive Monitoring Report on Hungary's Preparations for Membership, 2003*. http://europa.eu.int/comm/enlargement/report_2003/index.htm.

Commission of the European Communities. 2003b. *Comprehensive Monitoring Report on Poland's Preparations for Membership, 2003*. http://europa.eu.int/comm/enlargement/report_2003/index.htm.

Constitution Watch: Hungary. 2001a. *East European Constitutional Rev.* 10(1): 20–22.

Constitution Watch: Hungary. 2001b. *East European Constitutional Rev.* 10(2/3): 20–23.

Constitution Watch: Poland. 2000. *East European Constitutional Rev.* 9(1/2): 28–31.

Constitution Watch: Poland. 2001a. *East European Constitutional Rev.* 10(1): 30–32.

Constitution Watch: Poland. 2001b. *East European Constitutional Rev.* 10(2/3): 32–35.

Cook, Linda J., and Mitchell Orenstein. 1999. The Return of the Left and Its Impact on the Welfare State in Russia, Poland and Hungary, in Linda J. Cook, Mitchell A. Orenstein, and Marilyn Rueschemeyer, eds., *Left Parties and Social Policy in Postcommunist Europe*, Boulder, CO: Westview Press, pp. 47–108.

Crews Jr., Clyde Wayne. 2002. *Ten Thousand Commandments: An Annual Snapshot of the Federal Regulatory State*, Washington, DC: The Cato Institute.

Csepeli, Gyögy, Antal Örkény, Mária Székelyi, and Ildikó Barna. 2004. Blindness to Success: Social Psychological Objectives Along the Way to a Market Economy in Eastern Europe, in János Kornai, Bo Rothstein, and Susan Rose-Ackerman, eds., *Creating Social Trust in Post-Socialist Transition*. New York: Palgrave, pp. 213–240.

Culhane, Paul J. 1981. *Public Lands Politics: Interest Group Influence on the Forest Service and the Bureau of Land Management*, Baltimore: Johns Hopkins University Press (for Resources for the Future).

Czeszejko-Sochacki, Zdzisław. 1999. The Procuracy and Its Problems: Poland, *East European Constitutional Review* 8(1/2): 90–95.

Dąbrowska, Justyna, Marta Gumowska, Jakub Wygnański. 2003. *Wolontariat, Filantropia i 1% – Raport z Badania [Volunteerism, Philanthropy and 1% – 2003 Research Results]*, Warsaw: Klon/Jawor Association 2003.

Dąbrowska, Justyna, Marta Gumowska, Jakub Wygnański. 2002. *NGOs in Poland – 2002 Research Results*, Warsaw: Klon/Jawor Association.

Dahl, Robert. 1971. *Polyarchy: Participation and Opposition.* New Haven, CT: Yale University Press.

Dahl, Robert. 1989. *Democracy and Its Critics.* New Haven, CT: Yale University Press.

Dekker, Paul, Peter Ester, and Henk Vinken. 2003. Civil Society, Social Trust and Democratic Involvement, *The Cultural Diversity of European Unity: Findings, Explanations and Reflections from the European Values Study*, Leiden: Brill, pp. 217–253.

Dix, Alexander. 2001. The Influence of Hungarian Freedom of Information Legislation Abroad – The Brandenburg Example and Experience, in László Majtényi, ed., *The Door onto the Other Side: A Report on Information Rights*, Budapest: Adatvédelmi Biztos Irodája, pp. 231–238.

Djankov, Simeon, Caralee McLiesh, Tatiana Nenova, and Andrei Shleifer. 2003. Who Owns the Media? *Journal of Law and Economics* 46: 341–381.

Dorf, Michael C., and Charles Sabel. 1998. A Constitution of Democratic Experimentation, *Columbia Law Review* 98: 267–473.

Dunn, Delmer D. 1999. Mixing Elected and Nonelected Officials in Democratic Policy Making: Fundamentals of Accountability and Responsibility, in Adam Przeworski, Susan C. Stokes, and Bernard Manin, eds., *Democratic Accountability and Representation*, Cambridge, UK: Cambridge University Press, pp. 297–326.

Ekiert, Grzegorz, and Jan Kubik. 1999. *Rebellious Civil Society: Popular Protest and Democratic Consolidation in Poland, 1989–1993*, Ann Arbor: University of Michigan Press.

Elster, Jon. 1997. Afterward: The Making of Postcommunist Presidencies, in Raymond Taras, ed., *Postcommunist Presidencies*, Cambridge: Cambridge University Press, pp. 225–237.

Elster, Jon, Claus Offe, and Ulrich Preuss. 1998. *Institutional Design in Post-Communist Societies: Rebuilding the Ship at Sea*, Cambridge, UK: Cambridge University Press.

Engel, Kirsten, and Susan Rose-Ackerman. 2001. Environmental Federalism in the United States: The Risks of Devolution, in Daniel C. Esty and Damien Geradin, eds., *Regulatory Competition and Economic Integration*, Oxford, UK: Oxford University Press, pp. 135–153.

Environmental Management and Law Association. 2002. *Identified Legal, Institutional, and Practical Barriers to Public Access to Environmental Information to Support Public Involvement in Hungary for Danube Pollution Reduction Goals*, draft, Budapest: EMLA.

Eriksen, Erik Oddvar, and John Erik Fossum, eds. 2000. *Democracy in the European Union: Integration Through Deliberation?* London: Routledge.

European Ombudsman. 2003. *Annual Report 2002*, Strasbourg. http://www.euro-ombudsman.eu.int.

Farkas, István. 2002. Hungarian Situation on Public Participation in Regional Development, in Petr Pelcl, ed., *Public Participation in Regional Development in Central Europe*, Aarhus Convention and Regional Development Project. Regional Environmental Center, Szentendre: Hungary, pp. 57–67.

Føllesdal, Andreas. 2000. Subsidiarity and Democratic Deliberation, in Erik Oddvar Eriksen and John Erik Fossum, eds., *Democracy in the European Union: Integration through Deliberation?* London: Routledge, pp. 85–110.

Friesema, H. Paul, and Paul, J. Culhane. 1976. Social Impacts, Politics, and the Environmental Impact Statement Process, *Natural Resources Journal* 16: 338–356.

Fritschler, A. Lee. 1989. *Smoking and Politics: Policymaking and the Federal Bureaucracy*, 4th ed. Englewood Cliffs, NJ: Prentice Hall.

Frost, Amanda. 2003. Restoring Faith in Government: Transparency Reform in the United States and the European Union, *European Public Law* 9: 87–104.

Furlong, Scott R., and Cornelius, M. Kerwin. 2005. Interest Group Participation in Rulemaking: What Has Changed in Ten Years? *Journal of Public Administration Research and Theory*, in press.

Füzér, Katalin. 2002. Wirtschaftlicher Notstand: Konstitutionalismus und ökonomischer Diskurs im postkommunistischen Ungarn. (translated from English by Jasna Miletic), in Christian Boulanger, ed., *Recht in der Transfomation. Rechts- und Verfassungswandel in Mittel- und Osteuropa*, Berlin: Berliner Debatte Wissenschaftsverlag, pp. 173–195.

Gal, Susan, and Gail Kligman. 2000. *The Politics of Gender after Socialism*, Princeton, NJ: Princeton University Press.

Galligan, Denis J., Richard, H. Langan, and Constance, S. Nicandrou. 1998. *Administrative Justice in the New European Democracies: Case Studies of Administrative Law and Process in Bulgaria, Estonia, Hungary, Poland and Ukraine*, Budapest: Open Society Institute/Constitutional and Legal Policy Institute and Centre for Socio-Legal Studies, University of Oxford.

Galligan, Denis J, and Daniel, M. Smilov. 1999. *Administrative Law in Central and Eastern Europe 1996–1998*, Budapest: Central European University Press.

Garlicki, Leszek. 2002. *Polskie Prawo Konstytucyjne (Polish Constitutional Law)*, Warsaw: Liber.

Gill, Graeme. 2002. *Democracy and Post-Communism*, London: Routledge.

Gilowska, Zyta. 2001. Reforma Finansów Publicznych [Public Finance Reform], in Grzegorz Gorzelak, Bohdan Jałowiecki, Mirosław Stec eds., *Reforma Terytorialnej Administracji Kraju* [*Reform of the National Territorial State Administration*], Warsaw: Wydawnictwo Naukowe "Scholar," pp. 73–102.

Gliński, Piotr. 2001. The Ecological Movement as the Element of the Civil Society, in Helena Flam, ed., *Pink, Purple, Green: Women's, Religious, Environmental and Gay/Lesbian Movements in Central Europe Today*, Boulder, CO: East European Monographs, pp. 112–168.

Gliński, Piotr. 2002. The Shaping of Civil Society in Poland: The Trend and an Outlook, in Hans-Peter Meier-Dallach and Jakob Juchler, eds., *Postsocialist Transformation and Civil Society in a Globalized World*, New York: Nova Science Publications, pp. 57–74.

Golden, Marissa Martino. 1998. Interest Groups in the Rule-making Process: Who Participates? Whose Voices Get Heard? *Journal of Public Administration and Theory* 8: 245–270.

Gorges, Michael J. 1996. *Euro-Corporatism? Interest Intermediation in the European Community*, Lanham, MD: University Press of America.

Gorzelak, Grzegorz, Marek Kozak, and Wojciech Roszkowski. 1998. Regional Development Agencies in Poland, in Henrik Halkier, Mike Danson, and Charlotte Damborg, eds., *Regional Development Agencies in Europe*, London: Jessica Kingsley, pp. 104–124.

Green, Andrew J. 1997. Public Participation and Environmental Policy Outcomes, *Canadian Public Policy* 23: 435–458.

Green, Andrew J. 1999. Public Participation, Federalism and Environmental Law *Buffalo Environmental Law Journal* Spring, 169–213.

Greskovits, Béla. 1998. *The Political Economy of Protest and Patience*, Budapest: Central European University Press.

Grzymała-Busse, Anna. 2002. *Redeeming the Communist Past: The Regeneration of Communist Parties in East Central Europe*, Cambridge, UK: Cambridge University Press.

Grzymała-Busse, Anna. 2003. Political Competition and the Politicization of the State in East Central Europe, *Comparative Political Studies* 20: 126–151.

Grzymała-Busse, Anna, and Pauline Jones Luong. 2002. Reconceptualizing the State: Lessons from Post-Communism, *Politics and Society* 30: 529–554.

Haemer, Robert B. 1999. Reform of the Toxic Substances Control Act: Achieving Balance in the Regulation of Toxic Chemicals, *Environmental Lawyer*, September, 99–134.

Halkier, Henrik, Mike Danson, and Charlotte Damborg, eds. 1998. *Regional Development Agencies in Europe*, London: Jessica Kingsley.

Hańderek, Piotr. 2002. Current Situation of Regional Development in Poland, in Petr Pelcl, ed., *Public Participation in Regional Development in Central Europe*, Aarhus Convention and Regional Development Project. Regional Environmental Center, Szentendre: Hungary, pp. 48–56.

Harper, Krista M. 1999. *From Green Dissidents to Green Skeptics: Environmental Activists and Post-Socialist Political Ecology in Hungary*, dissertation submitted to the Department of Anthropology, University of California, Santa Cruz; Ann Arbor, MI: UMI Dissertation Services.

Heinemann, Friedrich. 2002. The Political Economy of EU Enlargement and the Treaty of Nice, *European Journal of Political Economy* 19: 17–31.

Hendee, John C. 1977. Public Involvement in the U.S. Forest Service Roadless-area Review: Lessons from a Case Study, in W. R. Derrick Sewell and J. T. Coppock, eds., *Public Participation in Planning*, London: John Wiley & Sons, pp. 89–103.

Henne, Thomas. 2003. Book Review: Environmental Policy in Germany and the United States: *Controlling Environmental Policy* by Susan Rose-Ackerman, *American Journal of Comparative Law* 51: 207–228.

Héthy, Lajos. 1994. Tripartism in Eastern Europe, in Richard Hyman and Anthony Ferner, eds., *New Frontiers in European Industrial Relations*, Oxford: Blackwell Business, pp. 312–336.

Héthy, Lajos. 1995. Anatomy of a Tripartite Experiment: Attempted Social and Economic Agreement in Hungary, *International Labor Review* 134: 361–376.

Héthy, Lajos. 2001. *Social Dialogue and the Expanding World: The Decade of Tripartism in Hungary and in Central and Eastern Europe 1988–99*, Report 70, Brussels: European Trade Union Institute.

Hines, Frances. 2000. Co-operation and Shared Responsibility: New Challenges for Environmental Policy in Eastern Europe, in Katharina Holzinger and Peter Knoepfel, eds., *Environmental Policy in a European Union of Variable Geometry? The Challenge of the Next Enlargement*, Basel: Helbing & Lichten-hahn, pp. 287–316.

Howard, Marc Morjé. 2003. *The Weakness of Civil Society in Post-Communist Europe*, Cambridge, UK: Cambridge University Press.

Hungarian National Environmental Council, Secretariat. 2002. *Hungarian National Environmental Council 2000–2001*, Budapest.

Hungary. 1998. *Act XX of 1949 as Amended: Constitution of the Republic of Hungary*. Available in English in László Sólyom and Georg Brunner, eds., *Constitutional Judiciary in a New Democracy: The Hungarian Constitutional Court*, Ann Arbor, MI: University of Michigan Press, pp. 379–406. Current version at http://archiv.meh.hu/nekh/Angol/6-1-1.htm.

Hungary, Központi Statisztikai Hivatal [Central Statistical Office]. 2000. *Környezetvédelmi Célú Nonprofit Szervezetek [Environmental Nonprofit Organizations]* Budapest.

Hungary, Központi Statisztikai Hivatal [Central Statistical Office]. 2002. *Nonprofit Szervezetek Magyarországon 2000*. Budapest. http://www.ksh.hu/pls/ksh/docs/index_eng.html.

Hungary, Miniszterelnöki Hivatal. 2000. *Government and Public Administration in Hungary*, Budapest.

Hungary, State Audit Office. 2002a. *The State Audit Office*, Budapest.

Hungary, State Audit Office. 2002b. *The State Audit Office Strategy*, Budapest.

Hungary, State Audit Office. 2002c. *Control and Fighting against Corruption in a Global World – Considering the Hungarian Experience*, Budapest, June.

Iankova, Elena. 1997. Social Partnership after the Cold War: The Transformative Corporatism of Eastern Europe, in John Brady, ed., *Central and Eastern Europe – Industrial Relations and the Market* Economy, Dublin: Oak Tree Press, pp. 37–78.

Iankova, Elena. 2002. *Eastern European Capitalism in the Making*, Cambridge, UK: Cambridge University Press.

Iankova, Elena, and Lowell Turner. 2004. Building the New Europe: Western and Eastern Roads to Social Partnership, *Industrial Relations Journal* 35: 76–92.

Izdebski, Hubert, and Michal Kulesza. 1999. *Administracja Publiczna: Zagadnienia Ogólne (Public Administration: General Issues)*, Warsaw: Liber.

Jaggers, Keith, and Ted Robert Gurr. 1995. Tracking Democracy's Third Wave and the Polity III Data, *Journal of Peace Research* 32: 469–482.

Jancar-Webster, Barbara. 1998. Environmental Movement and Social Change in the Transition Countries, *Environmental Politics* 7: 69–90.

Jann, Werner. 2003. *Public Administration* 81: 95–118.

Jasiewicz, Krzysztof. 1997. Wałęsa's Legacy to the Presidency, in Ray Tares, ed., *Postcommunist Presidents*, Cambridge, UK: Cambridge University Press, pp. 130–167.

Jenkins, Robert M. 1999. The Role of the Hungarian Nonprofit Sector in Postcommunist Social Policy, in Linda J. Cook, Mitchell A. Orenstein, and Marilyn Rueschemeyer, eds., *Left Parties and Social Policy in Postcommunist Europe*, Boulder, CO: Westview Press, pp. 175–206.

Joerges, Christian. 2001. "Deliberative Supernationalism" – A Defense, *European Integration Online Papers* 5 (8): 1–11. http://eiop.or.at./eiop/texts/2001–008a.htm.

Joerges, Christian, and Renaud Dehousse. 2002. *Good Governance in Europe's Integrated Markets*, Oxford: Oxford University Press.

Joerges, Christian, Yves Mény, and J. H. H. Weiler, eds. 2001. *Mountain or Molehill? A Critical Appraisal of the Commission's White Paper on Governance*, Florence, Italy: Robert Schuman Centre for Advanced Studies, European University Institute.

Joerges, Christian, and Jürgen Neyer. 1997. From Intergovernmental Bargaining to Deliberative Political Processes: The Constitutionalisation of Comitology, *European Law Journal* 3: 273–299.

Joerges, Christian, and Ellen Vos, eds. 1999. *EU Committees: Social Regulation, Law, and Politics*, Oxford: Hart Publishing.

Johnson, Nevil. 1983. *State and Government in the Federal Republic of Germany*, Oxford: Pergamon.

Jovanović, Miroslav N. 2000. Eastern Enlargement of the European Union: Sour Grapes or Sweet Lemon? Draft. Geneva: UN Commission of Europe, Trade Division.

Karatnycky, Adrian, Alexander Motyl, and Boris Shor. 1997. *Nations in Transit – 1997: Civil Society, Democracy and Market in East Central Europe and the Newly Independent States*, New Brunswick, NJ: Transaction Publishers.

Kerekes, Zsuzsa. 2001. Freedom of Information in the Commissioner's Practice in László Majtényi, ed., *The Door onto the Other Side: A Report on Information Rights*, Budapest: Adatvédelmi Biztos Irodája, pp. 287–303.

Kerwin, Cornelius. 2003. *Rulemaking: How Government Agencies Write Law and Make Policy*, 3rd ed., Washington, DC: CQ Press.

Kerwin, Cornelius M., and Scott, R. Furlong. 1992. Time and Rulemaking: An Empirical Test of Theory, *Journal of Public Administration Research and Theory* 2: 113–138.

Kisilowski, Maciej. 2004. The Fig Leaf: How the Concept of Representativeness Deprives Polish Decision-Making of Accountability, Draft, New Haven, CT: Yale Law School, July.

Klich, Agnieszka. 1996. Human Rights in Poland: The Role of the Constitutional Tribunal and the Commissioner for Citizens' Rights, *St. Louis-Warsaw Transatlantic Journal* 1996: 33–63.

Knill, Christoph, and Andrea Lenschow. 2000. Do New Brooms Really Sweep Cleaner? Implementation of New Instruments in EU Environmental Policy, in Christoph Knill and Andrea Lenschow, eds., *Implementing EU Environmental Policy, New Directions and Old Problems*, Manchester: Manchester University Press, pp. 251–286.

Kohler-Koch, Beate. 2001. The Commission White Paper and the Improvement of European Governance, in Christian Joerges, Yves Mény and J. H. H. Weiler, eds., *Mountain or Molehill? A Critical Appraisal of the Commission's White Paper on Governance*, Florence, Italy: Robert Schuman Centre for Advanced Studies, European University Institute. http://www.iue.it/RSCAS/Research/OnlineSymposia/Governance.shtml

Korkut, Umut. 2002. European Union Accession Process in Hungary, Poland, and Romania: Is There a Place for Social Dialogue? *Perspectives on European Politics and Society* 3: 297–324.

Kornai, János. 1992. *The Socialist System: The Political Economy of Communism*. Princeton, NJ: Princeton University Press.

Körösényi, András. 1999. *Government and Politics in Hungary*. Translated by Alan Rewick. Budapest: Central European University Press.

Kosztolányi, Gusztáv. 2001. An Ombudsman to Protest Us, *Central Europe Review*, Vol. 3, Nos. 21–24 (June 11, 18, 25, and Summer Special, 2001). http://www.ce-review.org/01.

Kovács, Árpád, and János Lévai. 2001. *Corruption and the Struggle Against It – Opportunities for Financial Control*, Budapest: State Audit Office, July.

Krastev, Ivan, and Georgy Ganev. 2004. The Missing Incentive: Corruption, Anticorruption, and Reelection, in János Kornai and Susan Rose-Ackerman, eds., *Building a Trustworthy State in Post-Socialist Transition*, New York: Palgrave, pp. 151–172.

Kulesza, Michał. 1993. Options for Administrative Reform in Poland, in Joachim Jens Hesse, ed., *Administrative Transformation in Central and Eastern Europe: Toward Public Sector Reform in Post-Communist Societies*, Oxford: Blackwell, pp. 33–40.

Kunicova, Jana, and Susan Rose-Ackerman. 2005. Electoral Rules and Constitutional Structures as Constraints on Corruption, *British Journal of Political Science*, vol. 35, in press.

Kurczewski, Jacek, and Joanna Kurczewska. 2001. A Self-Governing Society Twenty Years After: Democracy and the Third Sector in Poland, *Social Research* 68: 937–976.

Kuroń, Jacek. 1991. *Gwiezdny Czas 'Winy i Wiary' Ciag Dalszy [Celestial Time: "Guilt and Faith" Continued]*, London: Aneks.

Kuti, Éva. 1993. *Defining the Nonprofit Sector: Hungary*, Working Paper 13, Baltimore: Johns Hopkins Comparative Nonprofit Sector Project.

Kuti, Éva, Miklós Králik, and Miklós Barabás. 2000. *NGO Stock-Taking in Hungary*, NGO Studies No. 1, Budapest: World Bank Regional Office Hungary.

Langbein, Laura I., and Cornelius, M. Kerwin. 2000. Regulatory Negotiation Versus Conventional Rulemaking: Claims, Counterclaims, and Empirical Evidence, *Journal of Public Administration Research and Theory* 10: 599–632.

Leś, Ewa, Sławomir Nałęcz, and Jakub Wygnański. 2000. *Defining the Nonprofit Sector: Poland*, Working Paper No. 36, Baltimore: Johns Hopkins Comparative Nonprofit Sector Project.

Łętowska, Ewa. 1996. The Commissioner for Citizens' Rights in Central and Eastern Europe: The Polish Experience, *St. Louis-Warsaw Transatlantic Law Journal* 1996: 1–14.

Łętowski, Janusz. 1993. Polish Public Administration between Crisis and Renewal, in Joachim Jens Hesse, ed., *Administrative Transformation in Central and Eastern Europe: Toward Public Sector Reform in Post-Communist Societies*, Oxford: Blackwell, pp. 1–11.

Lewin, Leif. 1994. The Rise and Decline of Corporatism: The Case of Sweden, *European Journal of Political Research* 26: 59–79.

Lindseth, Peter L. 2001. "Weak" Constitutionalism? Reflections on Comitology and Transnational Governance in the European Union, *Oxford Journal of Legal Studies* 21: 145–163.

Lindseth, Peter L. 2002. Good Governance in Europe's Integrated Market, in Christian Joerges and Renaud Dehousse, eds., *Good Governance in Europe's Integrated Markets*, Oxford: Oxford University Press, pp. 139–163.

Lindseth, Peter L. 2003. Agents Without Principals?: Delegation in an Age of Diffuse and Fragmented Governance, prepared for Second Workshop on Self-Regulation, European University Institute, Nov. 14–15.

Lorentzen, Anne. 1998. Transition, Institutions and Regional Development in Hungary, BAZ County, in Henrik Halkier, Mike Danson, and Charlotte Damborg, eds., *Regional Development Agencies in Europe*, London: Jessica Kingsley, pp. 141–162.

Ludwikowski, Rett R. 1998. "Mixed" Constitutions – Product of an East-Central European Constitutional Melting Pot, *Boston University International Melting Pot* 16: 1–70.

Magat, Wesley A., Alan J. Krupnick, and Winston Harrington. 1986. *Rules in the Making: A Statistical Analysis of Regulatory Agency Behavior*, Washington, DC: Resources for the Future Press.

Majone, Giandomenico. 2001. Delegation of Regulatory Powers in a Mixed Polity, final draft, Florence, Italy: European University Institute.

Majtényi, László, ed. 2001a. *The Door onto the Other Side: A Report on Information Rights*, Budapest: Adatvédelmi Biztos Irodája.

Majtényi, László. 2001b. The Cause of Data Protection in East Central Europe, in László Majtényi, ed., *The Door onto the Other Side: A Report on Information Rights*, Budapest: Adatvédelmi Biztos Irodája, pp. 319–340.

Marek, Dan, and Michael Baun. 2002. The EU as a Regional Actor: The Case of the Czech Republic, *Journal of Common Market Studies* 40: 895–919.

Marschall, Miklós. 1990. The Nonprofit Sector in a Centrally Planned Economy, in Helmut K. Anheir and Wolfgang Seibel, eds., *The Third Sector: Comparative Studies of Nonprofit Organizations*, Berlin: Walter de Gruyter, pp. 277–291.

Mashaw, Jerry, and David Harfst. 1990. *The Struggle for Auto Safety*, Cambridge, MA: Harvard University Press.

Matey, Maria. 1997. Industrial Relations in Poland During the Transformation Period, in John Brady, ed., *Central and Eastern Europe – Industrial Relations and the Market* Economy, Dublin: Oak Tree Press, pp. 139–150.

Mazmanian, Daniel A., and Jeanne Nienaber. 1979. *Can Organizations Change? Environmental Protection, Citizen Participation, and the Corps of Engineers*, Washington, DC: The Brookings Institution.

McCubbins, Mathew, and Thomas Schwartz. 1984. Congressional Oversight Overlooked: Police Patrols versus Fire Alarms, *American Journal of Political Science* 28: 165–179.

McMenamin, Iain. 2002. Polish Business Associations: Flattened Civil Society or Super Lobbies? *Business and Politics* 4: 301–317.

McMillan, John, and Pablo Zoido. 2004. *How to Subvert Democracy: Montesinos in Peru, Journal of Economic Perspectives* 18: 69–92.

Mendelson, Nina A. 2003. Agency Burrowing: Entrenching Policies and Personnel Before a New President Arrives, *New York University Law Review* 78: 557–666.

Millard, Frances. 1998. Environmental Policy in Poland, *Environmental Politics* 7: 145–161.

Miller, William L., Åse, B. Grødeland, and Tatyana, Y. Koshechkina. 2001. *A Culture of Corruption: Coping with Government in Post-Communist Europe*, Budapest: Central European University.

Mishler, William, and Richard Rose. 1997. Trust, Distrust and Skepticism: Popular Evaluation of Civil and Political Institutions in Post-Communist Societies, *Journal of Politics* 59: 418–451.

Mishler, William, and Richard Rose. 1998. *Trust in Untrustworthy Institutions: Culture and Institutional Performance in Post-Communist Societies*, Studies in Public Policy No. 310, Glasgow, Scotland: Centre for the Study of Public Policy, University of Strathclyde.

Moravcsik, A. 1998. *A Choice for Europe: Social Purpose and State Power from Messina to Maastricht*, Ithaca, NY: Cornell University Press.

Mosher, James S., and David Trubek. 2003. Alternative Approaches to Governance in the EU: EU Social Policy and the European Employment Strategy, *Journal of Common Market Studies* 41: 63–88.

Mueller, John. 1996. Democracy, Capitalism and the End of Transition, in M. Mandelbaum, ed., *Post-Communism: Four Views*, New York: Council on Foreign Relations, pp. 102–167.

Mueller, John. 2004. Attitudes Toward Democracy and Capitalism: A Western Benchmark, in János Kornai and Susan Rose-Ackerman, eds., *Building a Trustworthy State in Post-Socialist Transition*, New York: Palgrave, pp. 198–213.

Munck, Gerardo L., and Jay Verkuilen. 2002. Conceptualizing and Measuring Democracy, and following commentaries *Comparative Political Studies* 35: 5–57.

Nakamura, Robert T., and Thomas W. Church. 2003. *Taming Regulation: Superfund and the Challenge of Regulatory Reform*, Washington, DC: The Brookings Institution.

Nelicki, Aleksander. 2001. Kształtowanie się struktur administracji powiatowej i wojewódzkiej [Shaping the Structures of the Powiat and Voivoidship Administration], in Grzegorz Gorzelak, Bohdan Jałowiecki, Mirosław Stec eds., *Reforma Administracji Terytorialnej Kraju [Reform of the National Territorial Administration]*, Warsaw: Wydawnictwo Naukowe "Scholar," pp. 51–72.

Nemes, Gusztáv. 2003. *Rural Development and Pre-accession Preparation in Hungary: Is There an Alternative Way?* OSI International Policy Fellowship Final Policy Paper, Budapest: OSI. http://www.policy.hu/nemes/OSIfinal.pdf.

Nunberg, Barbara. 1999. Hungary's Head Start on Reform: The Advanced Transition Experience, in Barbara Nunberg with Luca Barbone and Hans-Ulrich Derlien, eds., *The State After Communism: Administrative Transitions in Central and Eastern Europe*, Washington, DC: The World Bank, pp. 97–154.

Nunberg, Barbara, and Luca Barbone. 1999. Breaking Administrative Deadlock in Poland: Internal Obstacles and External Incentives, in Barbara Nunberg with Luca Barbone and Hans-Ulrich Derlien, eds., *The State After Communism: Administrative Transitions in Central and Eastern Europe*, Washington, DC: The World Bank, pp. 7–52.

O'Donnell, Guillermo. 1994. Delegative Democracy, *Journal of Democracy* 5: 55–69.

O'Donnell, Guillermo. 1996. Illusions about Consolidation, *Journal of Democracy* 7: 34–51.

O'Donnell, Guillermo. 1999. Horizontal Accountability in New Democracies, in Andreas Schedler, Larry Diamond, and Marc F. Plattner, eds., *The Self-Restraining State: Power and Accountability in New Democracies*, Boulder, CO: Lynne Rienner.

Okraszewska, Aldona, and Jacek Kwiatkowski. 2002. Country Report – Poland: The State of Democracy in Poland's Gmina, in Gábor Soós, Gábor Tóka, and Glen Wright, eds., *The State of Democracy in Central Europe*, Budapest: Local Government and Public Service Reform Initiative, Open Society Institute, pp. 181–284.

Olsen, Johan P. 1983. *Organized Democracy: Political Institutions in a Welfare State – The Case of Norway*, Bergen, Norway: Universitetsforlaget.

O'Neil, Patrick H. 1997. Hungary: Political Transition and Executive Conflict: The Balance or Fragmentation of Power? in Ray Tares, ed., *Postcommunist Presidents*, Cambridge, UK: Cambridge University Press, pp. 195–224.

Ost, David. 2000. Illusory Corporatism in Eastern Europe: Neoliberal Tripartism and Postcommunist Class Identities, *Politics and Society* 28: 503–530.

O'Toole, Jr., Laurence J., and Kenneth Hanf. 1998. Hungary: Political Transformation and Environmental Challenge, *Environmental Politics* 7: 93–112.

Pevehouse, Jon C. 2002. With a Little Help from My Friends? Regional Organizations and the Consolidation of Democracy, *American Journal of Political Science* 46: 611–626.

Pickvance, Katy. 1998. *Democracy and Environmental Movements in Eastern Europe: A Comparative Study of Hungary and Russia*, Boulder, CO: Westview Press.

Pickvance, Katy, with Luca Gábor. 2001. Green Future – in Hungary, in Helena Flam, ed., *Pink, Purple, Green: Women's, Religious, Environmental and Gay/ Lesbian Movements in Central Europe Today*, Boulder, CO: East European Monographs, pp. 104–111.

Poland. 1997. *Constitution of the Republic of Poland.* http://www.kprm.gov. pl/english/97.htm.

Poland, Commissioner for Civil Rights Protection. 1998. *National Ombudsmen: Collection of Legislation from 27 Countries*, Warsaw, Poland, Constitutional Tribunal. 1999. *A Selection of the Polish Constitutional Tribunal's Jurisprudence from 1986 to 1999*, Warsaw.

Poland, Główny Urząd Statystyczny [Central Statistical Office]. 2003. *Rocznik Statystyczny Rzeczpospolitej Polskiej [Statistical Yearbook of the Republic of Poland]*, Warsaw.

Poland, Ministerstwo Spraw Wewnętrznych i Administracji, Departament Wdrażania i Monitorowania Reformy Administracji Publicznej [Ministry of Internal Affairs and Administration, Department of Implementation and Monitoring of the Reform of Public Administration]. 1999. *Polska Administracja Publiczna po Reformie: Ustrój – Kompetencje – Liczby [The Polish Administration after the Reform: Regime – Competences – Numbers]*, Warsaw.

Poland, Naczelny Sąd Administracyny [Supreme Administrative Court]. 2000. *XX Lat Naczelnego Sądu Administracyjnego [20 years of the Supreme Administrative Court]*, Warsaw.

Poland, Naczelny Sąd Administracyny [Supreme Administrative Court]. 2002. Informacja o Dzialalności Naczelnego Sądu Administracynego w Roku 2001 [Information on Activities of the Supreme Administrative Court in 2001]. Warsaw.

Poland, Najwyższa Izba Kontroli [Supreme Chamber of Control]. 2001a. *Zagrożenie korupcją w świetle badań kontrolnych Najwyższej Izby Kontroli przeprowadzonych w roku 2000 [The Danger of Corruption in Light of Control Activities by the Supreme Chamber of Control in the Year 2000]*, Warsaw.

Poland, Supreme Chamber of Control. 2001b. *NIK: Supreme Chamber of Control Poland*, Warsaw.

Poland. Supreme Chamber of Control. 2002. *Annual Report 2001*, Warsaw.

Pridham, Geoffrey. 2002. EU Enlargement and Consolidating Democracy in Post-Communist States – Formality and Reality, *Journal of Common Market Studies* 40: 953–973.

Przeworski, Adam, Michael E. Alvarez, José Antonio Cheibub, and Fernando Limongi. 2000. *Democracy and Development: Political Institutions and Well-Being in the World, 1950–1990*, Cambridge, UK: Cambridge University Press.

Putnam, Robert. 1988. Diplomacy and Domestic Politics: The Logic of Two-Level Games, *International Organization* 42: 427–460.

Regulski, Jerzy, ed. 2002. *Samorząd i Demokracja Lokalna – Osiągnięcia, Zagrożenia, Dylematy [Self-government and Local Democracy – Achievements,*

Threats, and Dilemmas], Warsaw: Foundation in Support of Local Democracy. www.frdl.org.pl.

Rodden, Jonathan, and Susan Rose-Ackerman. 1997. The Allocation of Government Authority: Does Federalism Preserve Markets? *Virginia Law Review* 83: 1521–1572.

Rose-Ackerman, Susan. 1992. *Rethinking the Progressive Agenda: The Reform of the American Regulatory State*, New York: Free Press.

Rose-Ackerman, Susan. 1994. Consensus Versus Incentives: A Skeptical Look at Regulatory Negotiation, *Duke Law Journal* 43: 1206–1220.

Rose-Ackerman, Susan. 1995. *Controlling Environmental Policy: The Limits of Public Law in Germany and the United States*, New Haven, CT: Yale University Press.

Rose-Ackerman, Susan. 1999. *Corruption and Government: Causes, Consequences and Reform*, Cambridge, UK: Cambridge University Press.

Rose-Ackerman, Susan. 2001a. Trust and Honesty in Post-Socialist Societies, *Kyklos* 54: 415–443.

Rose-Ackerman, Susan. 2001b. Trust, Honesty and Corruption: Reflections on the State-Building Process, *Archives of European Sociology* 42: 526–570.

Rose-Ackerman, Susan, and Achim A. Halpaap. 2002. The Aarhus Convention and the Politics of Process: The Political Economy of Procedural Environmental Rights in Timothy Swanson and Richard Zerbe, eds., *Research in Law and Economics – 2001*, 20: 27–64.

Rossi, Jim. 1997. Participation Run Amok, *Northwestern University Law Review* 92: 173–249.

Rothstein, Bo. 1998. *Just Institutions Matter*, Cambridge, UK: Cambridge University Press.

Rothstein, Bo. 2004. Social Trust and Honesty in Government: A Causal Mechanisms Approach, in János Kornai, Bo Rothstein, and Susan Rose-Ackerman, eds., *Creating Social Trust in Post-Socialist Transition*. New York: Palgrave, pp. 13–30.

Sajó, András. 1996. How the Rule of Law Killed Hungarian Welfare Reform, *East European Constitutional Review* 5/1: 31–56.

Salamon, Lester M., Helmut, K. Anheier, Regina List, Stefan Toepler, S. Wojciech Sokolowski, and Associates. 1999. *Global Civil Society: Dimensions of the Nonprofit Sector*, Baltimore, MD: Johns Hopkins Center of Civil Society Studies.

Salamon, Lester M. S. Wojciech Sokolowski, and Associates. 2004. *Global Civil Society: Dimensions of the Nonprofit Sector*, Volume Two, Bloomfield, CT: Kumarian Press, Inc.

Salzberger, Eli M., and Stefan Voight. 2002. On the Delegation of Powers: With Special Emphasis on Central and Eastern Europe, *Constitutional Political Economy* 13: 25–52.

Sandholtz, Walter, and Alec Stone Sweet, eds. 1998. *European Integration and Supranational Governance*, Oxford: Oxford University Press.

Scheppele, Kim Lane. 1999. The New Hungarian Constitutional Court, *East European Constitutional Review* 8(4): 81–87.

Scheppele, Kim Lane. 2001. Democracy by Judiciary (Or Why Courts Can Sometimes Be More Democratic than Parliaments), paper prepared for a conference on Constitutional Courts, Washington University, St. Louis.

Scheppele, Kim Lane. 2003. Constitutional Negotiations: Political Contexts of Judicial Activism in Post-Soviet Europe? *International Sociology* 18: 219–238.

Schimmelfennig, Frank, Stefan Engert, and Heiko Knobel. 2003. Costs, Commitment and Compliance: The Impact of EU Democratic Conditions on Latvia, Slovakia, and Turkey, *Journal of Common Market Studies* 41: 495–518.

Schlozman, Kay Lehman, and John T. Tierney. 1986. *Organized Interests and American Democracy*, New York: Harper & Row.

Schuck, Peter. 1977. Public Interest Groups and the Policy Process, *Public Administration Review* 37: 132–140.

Schumpeter, Joseph. 1942. *Capitalism, Socialism, and Democracy*, New York: Harper & Brothers.

Schwartz, Herman. 1999. Surprising Success: The New Eastern European Constitutional Courts, in Andreas Schedler, Larry Diamond, and Marc R. Plattner, eds., *The Self-Restraining State: Power and Accountability in new Democracies*, Boulder, CO: Lynne Rienner, pp. 195–214.

Schwartz, Shalom H., Anat Bardi, and Gabriel Bianchi. 2000. Value Adaptation to the Imposition and Collapse of Communist Regimes in East-Central Europe, in Stanley A. Renshon, and John Duckitt, eds., *Political Psychology: Cultural and Crosscultural Foundations*, New York: New York University Press, pp. 217–237.

Skura, Zenon, and Włodzimierz Ulicki, eds. 2002. *Leksykon ludzi ZSP [Lexicon of ZSP people]*, Vol. I, Warsaw: Ogólnopolska Komisja Historyczna Ruchu Studenckiego i Stowarzyszenie Ruchu Studenckego "Ordynacka."

Smulovitz, Catalina, and Enrique Peruzzotti. 2000. Societal Accountability in Latin America, *Journal of Democracy* 11: 147–158.

Sólyom, László. 2000. Introduction to the Decisions of the Constitutional Court of the Republic of Hungary, in László Sólyom and Georg Brunner, eds., *Constitutional Judiciary in a New Democracy: The Hungarian Constitutional Court*, Ann Arbor, MI: University of Michigan Press, pp. 1–64.

Sólyom, László. 2001. The Role of the Ombudsman: Interpreting Fundamental Rights and Controlling Laws, in László Majtényi, ed., *The Door onto the Other Side: A Report on Information Rights*, Budapest: Adatvédelmi Biztos Irodája, pp. 239–262.

Sólyom, László, and Georg Brunner, eds. 2000. *Constitutional Judiciary in a New Democracy: The Hungarian Constitutional Court*, Ann Arbor, MI: University of Michigan Press.

Soós, Gábor, and Judit Kálmán. 2002. Country Report – Hungary: Report on Local Democracies in Hungary, in Gábor Soós, Gábor Tóka, and Glen Wright, eds., *The State of Democracy in Central Europe*, Budapest: Local Government and Public Service Reform Initiative, Open Society Institute, pp. 15–107.

Stark, David, and László Bruszt. 1998. *Postsocialist Pathways: Transforming Politics and Property in East Central Europe*, Cambridge, UK: Cambridge University Press.

Stone Sweet, Alec. 2003. Integration and the Europeanization of the Law, in P. Craig and R. Rawlings, eds., *Law and Administration in Europe*. Oxford, UK: Oxford University Press, pp. 197–224.

Strauss, Peter. 1974. Rules, Adjudications, and Other Sources of Law in an Executive Department: Reflections on the Interior Department's Administration of the Mining Law, *Columbia Law Review* 74: 1231–1275.

Supreme Audit Institutions of the Central and Eastern European Countries, Cyprus, Malta and the European Court of Auditors [cited as Supreme Audit Institutions] 2001. *Relations Between Supreme Audit Institutions and Parliamentary Committees*, Limassol, Nov.

Świątkiewicz, Jerzy. 2001. *Rzecznik Praw Obywatelskich w polskim systemie prawnyn. Stan na 30 czerwca 2001 [The Commissioner for Citizens' Rights in the Polish Legal System, State of Affairs on June 30, 2001]*, Warsaw: Law and Economics Practice Publishing House.

Szabó, Gábor. 1993. Administrative Transition in a Post-Communist Society: The Case of Hungary, in Joachim Jens Hesse, ed., *Administrative Transformation in Central and Eastern Europe: Toward Public Sector Reform in Post-Communist Societies*, Oxford: Blackwell, pp. 89–103.

Szalai, Júlia. 1995–1996. Self-Governance and Representation of Conflicting Interests, in Mihály Laki, Júlia Szalai, and Ágnes Vajda, eds., *Participation and Changes in Property Relations in Post-Communist Societies: The Hungarian Case*, Budapest: Active Society Foundation, pp. 42–76.

Szikinger, István. 1999. The Procuracy and Its Problems: Hungary, *East European Constitutional Review* 8(1/2): 85–95.

Sztompka, Piotr. 1999. *Trust: A Sociological Theory*, Cambridge, UK: Cambridge University Press.

Taras, Ray, ed. 1997. *Postcommunist Presidents*, Cambridge, UK: Cambridge University Press.

Taras, Wojciech. 1993. Changes in Polish Public Administration 1989–1992, in Joachim Jens Hesse, ed., *Administrative Transformation in Central and Eastern Europe*, Oxford: Blackwell.

Tőkés, Rudolf. 1996. *Hungary's Negotiated Revolution: Economic Reform, Social Change, and Political Succession, 1957–1990*. New York: Cambridge University Press.

Uslaner, Eric, and Gabriel Badescu. 2004. Honesty, Trust, and Legal Norms in the Transition to Democracy: Why Bo Rothstein Is Better Able to Explain Sweden Than Romania, János Kornai, Bo Rothstein, and Susan Rose-Ackerman, eds., *Creating Social Trust in Post-Socialist Transition*. New York: Palgrave, pp. 31–52.

Vachudova, Milada Anna. 2000. EU Enlargement: An Overview, *East European Constitutional Review*, 9(4): 64–69.

Vachudova, Milada Anna. 2001a. The Czech Republic: The Unexpected Force of Institutional Constraints, in Jan Zielonka and Alex Pravda, eds., *Democratic Consolidation in Eastern Europe, Volume 2: International and Transnational Factors*, Oxford: Oxford University Press, pp. 325–362.

Vachudova, Milada Anna. 2001b. *The Leverage of International Institutions on Democratizing States: Eastern Europe and the European Union*, EUI Working Paper RSC No. 2001/33, Badia Fiesolana: European University Institute.

Vajda, Ágnes. 1995–1996. Foundations and Associations: Citizen Initiatives, the Denationalization of the Non-Profit-Oriented Sector: General Trends in Hungary, Local Organisation in a Provincial Town, in Mihály Laki, Júlia Szalai, and Ágnes Vajda, eds., *Participation and Changes in Property Relations in Post-Communist Societies: The Hungarian Case*, Budapest: Active Society Foundation, pp. 77–112.

Várfalvi, István. 2001. Az önkormányzati pénzügyi- finanszírozási rendszer átalakítási lehetőségei [The Possibilities of Transforming Local Government Financing] Budapest: Ministry of the Interior. http://web.b-m.hu/web/euik.nsf/6AFEF54BFB243413C1256DCA0049C27D/$FILE/Az%20önkormányzati%20pénzügyi%20-%20Várfalvi%20István.doc.

Verebélyi, Imre. 1993. Options for Administrative Reform in Hungary, in Joachim Jens Hesse, ed., *Administrative Transformation in Central and Eastern Europe: Toward Public Sector Reform in Post-Communist Societies*, Oxford: Blackwell, pp. 105–120.

Vogel, David. 1980–1981. The Public-Interest Movement and the American Reform Tradition, *Political Science Quarterly* 95: 607–627.

Waller, Michael. 1998. Geopolitics and the Environment in Eastern Europe, *Environmental Politics* 7: 29–52.

Weiler, Joseph. 1995. Does Europe Need a Constitution? Reflections on Demos, Telos, and the German Masstricht Decision, *European Law Journal* 1: 1219–1258.

West, William F. 2004. Formal Procedures, Informal Processes, Accountability, and Responsiveness in Bureaucratic Policy Making: An Institutional Analysis, *Public Administration Review* 64: 66–80.

Wielka Encyklopedia Powszechna PWN [The PWN Great Encyclopedia]. 1969. Vol. 12, Warsaw: Państwowe Wydawnictwo Naukowe.

Wierzbowski, Marek, ed. 2003. *Prawo Administracyjne*, 5th ed., Warsaw: Wydawnictwo Prawnicze LexisNexis.

Zieliński, Tadeusz. 1994. Contribution, in European Union, *Proceedings of the 4th Round Table with European Ombudsmen*, EU document H/Omb 94 (21), pp. 40–44, 121–126.

Zoll, Andrzej. 2002. *Information of the Commissioner for Civil Rights Protection, Prof. Andrzej Zoll, for 2001*, Warsaw: Commissioner for Civil Rights Protection.

Żylicz, Tomasz, and Katharina Holzinger. 2000. Environmental Policy in Poland and the Consequences of Approximation to the European Union, in Katharina Holzinger and Peter Knoepfel, eds., *Environmental Policy in a European Union of Variable Geometry? The Challenge of the Next Enlargement*, Basel: Helbing & Lichtenhahn, pp. 215–248.

Index